from **home** *to* HOMELAND

from **home** *to* HOMELAND

What **Adoptive Families** Need to Know before Making a **Return Trip** to **China**

edited by
Debra Jacobs, Iris Chin Ponte, and Leslie Kim Wang

With an introduction by Amy Klatzkin

Yeong & Yeong Book Company
St. Paul, Minnesota

from **home** *to* **HOMELAND**

What Adoptive Families Need to Know before Making a Return Trip to China

Yeong & Yeong Book Company
St. Paul, Minnesota

yeongandyeong.com

Cover photo: Sami Khoury
Cover and book design: Ann Delgehausen, Trio Bookworks

Cataloging-in-Publication data is on file at the Library of Congress, http://catalog.loc.gov/.

ISBN: 978-1-59743-003-6

Printed in Canada
15 14 13 12 11 10 1 2 3 4 5

This book is printed on acid-free paper.

For the Laohu, Hao Pengyou,

and Xingfu Pengyou girls,

and children everywhere

making return trips

Contents

VIII Home Again: Lasting Impact of the Trip

IX Thoughts for Further Inquiry: What the Research Tells Us

Introduction

Amy Klatzkin

The homeland trip has become a rite of passage for families with children from China. While not as commonplace as Lunar New Year parties, red envelopes, and Chinese middle names, "going back" has joined the list of things many parents feel they must do for their children's sake. Catering to adoptive families' needs, a small industry of homeland tour companies has emerged, offering all-inclusive journeys to historic sites, scenic places, and cultural events, together with bounteous shopping opportunities and optional side trips to orphanages.

That was not yet the case when I walked through the gateway of the Changsha No. 1 Social Welfare Institution (SWI) in the fall of 1999. I was there on reconnaissance. My then six-year-old daughter, after two trips to other parts of China, wanted to come back to see her orphanage, and I wanted to make sure she would be welcome. Friends who had recently adopted a baby from Changsha reported that the director discouraged contact; the photo album we'd sent to our daughter's caregiver, they said, never reached her.

No one had yet returned to the SWI just for a visit. If the director did indeed discourage contact, we could be turned away—and that could be devastating to our daughter. For so many adopted children, rejection is where the pain is, and she did not need to experience any more rejection in the land of her birth. If anyone was going to be turned away, I wanted it to be me. Having lived in China in the 1980s, I knew that if I wrote a letter asking to visit, the request would be easy to refuse. But if I just showed up, maybe they wouldn't throw me out.

They didn't. I met with the director, who had a dozen photos of adopted children under the glass on his desk. Good sign. I gave him a small photo album and a modest donation in a red envelope. He told me the orphanage population was increasing faster than he could increase the staff. Staffing was always based on the previous year's population, he explained, and so the baby floor was staffed for 60 infants and toddlers when it now housed 80—more than triple the number in residence when our daughter lived there in the autumn of 1993. The SWI was running out of cribs and clothing. And by the way, what was I doing there? Where was my family?

I told the director they were back in San Francisco but wanted to visit next year. Would that be possible? Smiling broadly, he encouraged us all to come visit any time we were in Changsha. Then I asked, as casually as I could manage, "Would it be possible to see the babies?"

Moments later I was on a creaky elevator rising slowly to the eighth floor of a new building. As I stepped into the hallway, I saw the woman who had handed my daughter to me in January 1994. She had no idea I was coming and stopped in her tracks when she saw me. Then her face lit up, and she said, "I know you! You're Zhou Sheng's mama!" She hugged me, paused a moment to search her memory, and then recited the orphanage names of the three other babies and one toddler who were adopted together that day. She also thanked me for the photos we'd sent—the ones I'd been told she'd never received—and was thrilled to hear that the whole family would be coming the following year.

Before leaving, I stopped by the old courtyard building where our daughter had spent the tenth to twentieth weeks of her life. By the time she returned in December 2000, that courtyard was a hole in the ground awaiting new construction, and there were more than 100 infants and toddlers up on the baby floor. Many of those little ones appear in *Kids Like Me in China,* the book our daughter wanted to write to raise money for school fees for the older children at Changsha No. 1.

When we returned with copies of the book in December 2001, the eighth floor housed around 120 babies. In 2002 the population up there was closer to 180, and by 2004 it had topped 200. Today that whole building is gone, replaced by a new facility for elder care. Hardly any healthy infants arrive anymore, and international adoptions from all over China have dwindled. The great exodus of mostly female children may be winding down after nearly two decades during which tens of thousands of Chinese children joined adoptive families all over the world. Now they are returning by the busload.

All those babies in *Kids Like Me in China,* most of them adopted internationally within a year of the book's publication, are in the upper grades of elementary school now, and their parents may well be considering a trip back to China. For many families, including ours, these trips have transformed children's view of themselves and their origins, leading to greater self-esteem and pride in their Chinese heritage. In the following pages you'll read about several such journeys.

But not every child has a wonderful time in China—and when things don't go well, they can go spectacularly wrong. Therapists who work with adoptive families after difficult homeland trips use the word *trauma* to describe what some children go through. In planning a homeland tour, parents often don't recognize the risk in taking young children back to the site of their abandonment. A room jammed with cribs, each with multiple occupants, can frighten children as they try to imagine *themselves* living like that. Being surrounded by people they look like but can't talk to or understand can be disorienting. Children adopted at an older age may be flooded by memories they've long kept at bay. Young kids may not be nearly as keen as their parents to find foster or birth families; on the contrary, they may secretly fear they'll be left in China with people who are now strangers to them.

The family homeland trip has much in common with the original adoption journey. We parents can become so caught up in our enthusiasm that we miss the cues our children give—rarely in words—that they are ambivalent, confused, worried, or scared. We're also prone to interpreting their experience based on our own, without giving them the chance to define that experience for themselves. I've stood with parents talking about the transformative power of the homeland trip—how their children embraced their heritage, loved their orphanage director, bonded with their foster mother, and fell in love with China—while in another room the kids talked about how much fun they had sitting together in the back of the tour bus and how annoying it was to be herded in and out of an embroidery factory they never wanted to visit in the first place.

If the kids have a good time in China, isn't that enough? So what if the best part was splashing around with the other adopted kids in the hotel pool. Their memory of China will be positive, and they'll have built new connections with kids who share their origins and don't need to ask why they look different from their parents.

But what about the children who don't have fun, who are overwhelmed and frightened by emotions they don't understand? China can never be just another country to a child who was born and abandoned there. While parents relive the joy of the adoption journey, kids may be thinking more about what happened to them before that.

The homeland trip offers a great opportunity to help children develop a coherent narrative that makes sense of their complicated and not altogether joyous beginnings. That can be a powerful project for parent and child to create together; it requires staying attuned to your child's feelings even when they don't match the testimonials on the heritage tour's website. The tour that works for one child may not work for another.

Preparation is key, and that's where this volume begins. Subsequent sections provide advice on choosing how to travel (independently or as part of a tour group), making meaningful connections while there, and visiting orphanages, abandonment sites, and foster families. Yet even with good preparation, there are no guarantees. Midway through the volume you'll find two parents' responses to the emotional challenges of returning to China; a later section also provides insight into how homeland trips affect children after they return. In between, four adoptees share their views of going back, and three parents describe the benefits and challenges of moving their families to China for months or years. The book closes with research findings on how people in China view international adoption and on adoptive parents' and children's views of homeland trips.

I hope this broad array of perspectives, advice, and experiences will help you decide what is right for your family. May it also inspire you to connect with Chinese American people, cultures, and history here at home, for being born in China is only one piece of our children's complex identity. Discovering what it means *to them* to be Chinese in America may, in the long run, be an even more transformative journey.

I

getting READY

Preparing Children and Families for the Trip

Facing Fears and Empowering Children—Before the Trip

1

Debra Jacobs

Reflecting on our return trip to China, I asked my older daughter if she had felt prepared for all we experienced. "Yes," she replied; although the trip wasn't always easy, she had felt ready for it. Helping her to get ready took some work, but proved well worth the effort. We had a fantastic trip, even if some of the experiences my daughter had in China weighed heavily on her emotions. The preparation we had done before leaving helped to lighten the load.

My older daughter had first traveled to China with me when she was five years old, when I adopted her younger sister. That trip offered her a wonderful, if sanitized, introduction to the country of her birth. Our travel group was huge, so big that we took up an entire floor of the hotel, and much of the trip was about getting on and off the bus with a gaggle of Americans. Fortunately, other families brought older siblings as well, so my daughter had an instant group of friends. As on any adoption trip, the focus was on the babies. We hung out at the hotel, visited some tourist attractions, and did a little shopping, but we rarely ventured out on our own.

This return trip would be very different. We would be traveling independently with just one other family. We wanted to be outside the safety of a group, in the hope of having more direct and authentic experiences. We also would be visiting our children's orphanages and finding sites. By now, my daughter was three years older and much more in tune with the losses associated with adoption. The emotional stakes when we adopted her sister had been high; now they were even higher.

Looking at Pictures, Talking It Over

When the trip became something more than a vague, future possibility, we began looking at photo albums from our adoption trips and at picture books of China. At first, we looked at emotionally neutral pictures: the Great Wall and the Forbidden City, bustling cities and quiet countryside, people on bicycles and streets crowded with cars, sidewalk markets and urban parks. These images sparked discussion of what we might see and do on our trip. While my friends and I planned our itinerary, we included our children by asking them what they would most like to do and see in China and giving them decision-making authority whenever possible. This helped them to feel some ownership of the trip.

The photos we looked at together also generated discussion of some of the different and challenging things we might see. We talked about vendors at markets who would often be enthusiastically hawking their wares and cars honking incessantly and seemingly never stopping for pedestrians. There would be many people smoking and spitting, large crowds of people in the cities, and people in poverty or with disabilities begging, which is not so different from urban areas near our home. We talked about and "practiced" using squat toilets. And we warned the children that people may swarm around them, curious about why they were with Caucasian adults. We wanted them (my girls, aged eight and four, and my friends' children, aged eight and five) to have to face as few challenging surprises as possible.

In time, I began to look at more emotionally charged photographs with my daughters. These included images of the hotels where I'd first met them, their orphanages, and the cities where their orphanages were located. Our conversations moved back and forth between excited planning for all of the fun and interesting things we would do in China and heavy discussions of what we would likely see at the orphanages, including children with disabilities and children who might never find a forever family.

I tried to elicit the source of the inarticulate upset that occurred when some of these discussions took place, and realized that we needed to face the fears head-on. Some of the children's fears—and how I responded to them—are described below:

- **What if I don't like the food?** The hotels will have Western breakfasts and we'll bring food you like. (One negative outcome of the trip is one daughter's newfound dislike of peanut butter, which I brought as a source of protein, knowing she would not like most of the food offered in China. She got so sick of it that she won't go near it now).
- **What if people speak to me in Chinese and I don't understand?** Most of the time we'll be with people who can translate for us.
- **What if I get lost?** You won't. I'll be with you every minute. But just in case, every hotel has a card with the name and address written in Chinese characters. You'll take one in your pocket every time we leave the hotel. Show it to a police officer or another person and they'll help you get back to the hotel.
- **What if we never come back?** My daughters never expressed this fear, but I had heard that some children need reassurance that they would indeed be returning home. At Joyce Pavao's suggestion (Joyce is founder of the Center for Family Connections and author of *The Family of Adoption)* I posted a calendar on the refrigerator door. It marked off the days until the trip, the duration of our visit, and, with a big red X, the day we would come back home.

Fears about visiting the orphanage and finding site were more difficult to articulate. I assured my eight-year-old that I would be by her side every minute. I also e-mailed the person arranging our orphanage visit to ask whether we would be able to meet any caregivers who had taken care of and remembered my daughter. I passed on any information I learned to my daughter, even if it was not what she wanted to hear. Dealing with disappointment before the trip was better than going with raised hopes and having them dashed.

My younger daughter, four years old, was excited to visit her orphanage. To her, at a preschool developmental level, the visit did not pack an emotional punch. Still, we talked again and again about the babies, children, and caregivers we might see and planned the gifts we would bring to the orphanage.

My children didn't always want to look at the pictures or talk about the trip, and I stopped whenever they indicated with their body language, if not their words, that they had had enough. I knew we'd revisit these photographs and conversations another time.

Preparing in a Group

My children have been members of a Chinese culture group since each of them was two. In my older daughter's group, several families were planning return trips around the same time, so the girls prepared together. One family who had made a trip the previous year showed a video with highlights of their visit. For some of the girls, the video was both fascinating and difficult to watch, raising issues they would soon be facing when they visited their own orphanages and finding sites.

The group leader spent several sessions role-playing situations the girls had raised as troubling: "What happens if I get sick in China?" Again, "What if I get lost?" "What will I eat?" To the girls' great amusement, their group leader even squatted down and held up the bottom of her pants to demonstrate use of a squat toilet. In the safety of the group, with friends they'd known since they were babies and whose life journeys mirrored theirs, the girls were able to express and work through some of their concerns about the trip.

Class Project

Our two eight-year-olds (my daughter and my friends' daughter) have been close friends for years and were in the same second-grade class at school. Sometimes, when my friend, Meredith, picked the girls up from school, their conversations in the back seat of the car turned to our upcoming trip. Since our travel plans had not worked out during school vacation, we were pulling the girls out of school for almost three weeks, and this meant other children were curious about where they were going and why. Talking it over with Meredith, the girls decided to present the trip to the class in a more formal way instead of simply fielding random questions. With Meredith's help, they came up with the idea of making a map showing our travel route.

Meredith bought a large map of China and the girls spent an afternoon laboriously cutting it out and gluing it to poster board. Then we downloaded and printed wallet-sized photos of each of the places we would visit and the girls glued them to the map. We helped them string yarn from the photos to their corresponding cities. Then we scheduled a time to come into the classroom and speak to the class about the trip.

The girls were very proud of their map and each spoke, a bit, about their upcoming trip, with Meredith and I taking over when they needed us. Their classmates asked questions, including "How long is the plane ride?" and "Will your little sister and brother come too?" The girls promised their classmates that they would stay in touch via a blog that Meredith had set up.

The school project gave our daughters a visual representation of the trip—they could see places we would visit and in what order. They worked hard on their map, and through the project they became more invested in the trip. And it allowed them to share their journey with their teachers and classmates in a very concrete way.

Blogging

Meredith set up a blog for all of us to contribute to so we could share our experiences on the trip with friends and family. (A piece of advice about this: use a well-known site for your blog. We couldn't access ours once we left Beijing and had to e-mail entries to a friend in the United States and ask him to post them on our blog).

Our eight-year-olds had one assignment while traveling: write in the blog each day. This provided a sense of connection with home, as family members, friends, and classmates would be reading and hopefully responding to their entries. It gave them a vehicle for processing some of their experiences, and a certain sense of control: they could write, or *not* write, about anything they wanted. And the blog offered a place for expressing their thoughts and feelings about actually experiencing many of the things for which we had prepared.

Being Ready

Our trip proved to be everything we had hoped for and more, and our children were ready for much about China that is different from the United States. They were adventurous and intrepid travelers, in part because that's how they face life and, in part, because they were prepared. Having good friends with whom to play and share the experience was also crucial for my children. While many moments on the trip were difficult and even painful, the work we had done before leaving empowered our children and paved the way for a deep and positive return trip.

A Homeland Tour Preparation Primer

2

Practical Preparation Tips, Ideas, and Projects

Iris Culp

Why is it important to prepare for your homeland trip with more than a simple packing list and a few items of lightweight travel clothing? A return trip is more than a physical journey. It is also an emotional one, which can help to provide a secure base for our children's identity development and their lives as adults. The following checklist offers ideas for preparation that will help your trip become such a secure launching pad. You can pull items from this general preparation tool kit to match your own family's "personality" and meet the needs of your children at various ages.

Lifebook

If you're looking at taking a trip in a few years, an ideal way to start preparing is to complete a lifebook for, or with, your child. Having regular lifebook conversations that provide a backdrop to the places you will likely visit on a return trip is invaluable. Many adult adoptees talk about the feeling that the story of their life begins at adoption—the equivalent to having a photo of oneself cut off at the knees. Key life pieces are missing. A lifebook can help address this desire for some pre-adoptive context. While we cannot always provide our children with explicit, concrete answers to challenging questions ("What about when I was born? Why couldn't my birthparents keep me?"), a lifebook does provide the context to process the joys and losses inherent in the adoption experience. You can join a Yahoo! group such as "China Lifebooks" or attend a lifebook workshop to get inspiration. (See the resources at the end of this chapter for additional details.)

Cultural Norms

A great tool for understanding China in a deeper way, and preparing for cultural differences you will encounter on a homeland trip, is to discuss how different societies have differing cultural norms. Explore some of these differing norms ahead of time or you may miss a rich experience. What is considered rude in China? What is considered rude in America? You can discuss staring, spitting, dating, public displays of affection and more. While this may sound appropriate for older children, it's also an insightful learning opportunity for the adults in the travel group. What are typical games different ages of children play in China? How do adults and kids socialize together there, and how does that differ from ways in which American kids and parents socialize? How do gender differences play out in both societies? You can also take it deeper and explore ideas about why these two societies developed different norms. This can lead to some great discussions and an examination of what norms your family wants to purposely align with.

Country and Age Comparisons

What are some of the differences in the daily life of a ten-year-old (or however old your child is) in China and a ten-year-old in America? How many hours are spent in school each day? How many hours doing homework? What about extracurricular activities? How many hours helping out the family? What are typical expectations placed on a child in China? How does that compare to expectations placed on American children? This avenue is rich with opportunities for learning. Does your child have a particular sporting or musical interest? You can make it a project to explore how Chinese children her age pursue that interest, whether it's gymnastics, ice-skating, piano, or art. If you would like to delve deeper, your tour provider can arrange opportunities for you to meet with young people who are engaged in the same interests and hobbies that your child enjoys.

Social Issues Exploration

With older children, it may be interesting to look at social issues within the countries for comparison. One option is to explore different social issues once a month during "China night." What are some social problems facing each country? What is considered poverty in America? What is considered poverty in China? How many people are above the poverty line in each country? What government solutions are available? What other solutions are available? What about begging in the two countries? How many elderly people live in each country, and where do they typically live? Compare and contrast what assistance or social programs are available for elderly people in China and in North America. Compare and contrast pension system options. What are the pressing social issues that China is facing in the next decade? How do these compare with the pressing social issues within America? Is there any overlap, and how is your family's life affected by that? How is the typical Chinese family affected by social issues within China?

Fun Trivia Facts

Collect "fun facts" about China, and create your own game show night or personal quiz program. Do you like "Jeopardy" or "Duel?" Create your own version. How many people live in China? How many TV's are there in China? How many cell phones? You can really have fun with this, and Google is a great tool, of course, to help you out. You can even go so far as to create your own game board if you really get into this one. Why should you never give yellow flowers to someone that you're meeting in China, or why would you insult your friend in China if you gave her a clock for her birthday? What does the color red symbolize in China? What color is used at funerals? Name three countries that border China. You get the idea; make it fun facts that your kids enjoy.

City Series

Do a "China city" series. Set aside one evening a month to explore a different city in China. Pick cities in which you are interested or cities that are on your itinerary. Study each city in depth. Get photos of the city, especially of sites you are planning to see. Look for online photos of places you may visit there, such as museums, parks, or historical sites. Find an American city on the same latitude. Compare what is the same about the two cities, and discuss what might be different. "Google Earth" the city and see what you can find.

Pre-Trip Photo Album

Do an "advance" photo album project. Find magazine or online pictures of places you plan to visit. Put these photos on the left side of each spread in the album. Save the right side of each spread for the photos you will take during your visit. When you return home, take your personal photos and put them on the right side of each spread, along with your notes about what you saw while visiting the site. You can also makes notes about how the sites you saw differed from what you expected. This photo journal can be easily shared with friends and family once you return. It can also serve as a reminder of differences between what you expected and what China was actually like, which can open up great discussion topics for your family.

SWI Project

You may already know quite a bit about the orphanage or Social Welfare Institute where your child lived in China, through involvement in a Yahoo! group or from those precious bits of information you received on Adoption Day. Now is a good time to get fresh facts and dig a bit deeper to research the place where your child's life story began. What is the name of the director? Find and show photos, if available. How many babies are usually cared for there? What age ranges of children reside there? Is it a home for people who are elderly or who have disabilities, as well as for orphaned children? How many children with disabilities live there, and what are their special needs? How many nannies work there? What information is available about the SWI? (This will vary widely, of course.)

Discuss what your family might see during the SWI visit. Consider making a scrapbook of photos of your child from his or her adoption to the present, to provide as a gift to the director or the nannies. Do you plan to bring something for the children who reside there, such as school supplies or art supplies? Find out what might be most useful. Research how open this orphanage has been with previous returning visitors. Try to find out what type of welcome your family might expect. If you are bringing two (or more) children back for a visit, think about how you can help prepare them for two possibly very different welcomes.

Check Your Cultural IQ of China

Another great way to have fun while learning is to do a "Between the Cultures" night. Go online and check your cultural "IQ" of China. If your family loved the game show format, do it that way. Have some more fun and compare traditions in America to traditions in China. See if you can find ten traditions that are a perfect match and ten that are total opposites. (Hint: Think which society values elders and which society prizes youthfulness.) You can adapt this activity to fit the age of your children and make it as simple or as elaborate as you like.

Travel Planning Book

Start by listing everything you plan to see. Then make a list of all the essentials you need to bring, such as passports and travel documents, clothing, and camera gear. You can then make a travel "scavenger" list of what you want to find in China. This can include a souvenir from peddlers on the Great Wall; a pebble from your SWI visit; a paper menu from a restaurant; a pearl ring from Guangzhou; a business card from the adoption medical clinic; or other items that catch your imagination. Your planning list can include photos of everyday life in China that you would like to take. These could include photos of a souvenir shop owner; a teenager driving a bicycle; an elderly person doing tai chi in a park; a toddler wearing split pants—you can create your own "slice of life" photo book upon your return. Also for packing purposes, you can check out the typical weather patterns for the locales you plan to visit.

Then find comparable cities in the U.S., so you can mentally gauge how to prepare for the weather in those cities.

Asian Video Night

Have a China video night series, and invite traveling friends or family. Have a sleepover and pop some popcorn, or just do family sleeping bags in the living room. Find some good documentaries about China, as well as entertainment films. Make sure to discuss what you've seen after watching the films. It's essential to allow time for your kids to ask questions. Take time and listen to their questions. See if they have any concerns about traveling. As you discuss your trip plans, make certain to discuss when you will return home to the U.S. Some adopted youngsters develop a fear of traveling to China if you don't reassure them that you will be returning home to the U.S. together.

China Theme Party

Send out Chinese invitations with a simple character stamp on folded paper or send out e-vite invitations with a Chinese theme. Encourage everyone to dress up for the party. Put some joss sticks in a vase and make some paper-cut decorations for walls and windows. Create the ambience for a fun, light-hearted party. Make Chinese food (or order take out). Pot stickers, rice, spring rolls, almond cookies, fresh fruit, and juices make a great light party meal. Dress up in a *cheongsam* (mandarin-collared dress) or in a Chinese jacket and pants, if you have them. Otherwise, wear red, gold, or black.

In Summary

These are a few suggestions for preparing to mentally and culturally engage with China during your trip. The more opportunities you take for preparation, the more you may be able to gain from the experience. Remember, this trip is not just an international vacation; it's much more. Taking the time to delve into some aspects of cultural preparation can provide greater context and meaning for your family's trip. Make the most of it. The following section lists some practical resources you can use to support the activities described in this chapter.

Resources to Support Preparation Activities

Websites

www.askasia.org An educational website for students and teachers covering thirty countries that comprise Asia.

www.fwcc.org Listing of Families with Children from China organizations.

www.chineseculture.com A one-stop resource for learning about different facets of China, including culture, traditions, games, history, language and the Mandarin characters for English names.

www.kepu.net.cn/english The Science Museums of China website (English). Note: Check out the "panda-cam" on this website!

Video/DVD Resources

Culture series by www.pearlriver.tv/documentaries.htm—*New Year in Ping Wei, One Day in Ping Wei, Return to Ping Wei,* and *Land of the Dragon.*

Found in China—A documentary by Tai-Kai Productions following a trip to China.

Books for Parents/Adults

Chang Jung, *Wild Swans: Three Daughters of China*

Beth O'Malley, *LifeBooks: Creating a Treasure for the Adopted Child*

Emily Prager, *Wuhu Diary: On Taking My Adopted Daughter Back to Her Hometown in China*

Cindy Probst, *Adoption Lifebook: A Bridge to Your Child's Beginnings*

Jay W. Rojewski and Jacy L. Rojewski, *International Adoption from China: Examining Cultural Heritage and Other Post-Adoption Issues*

Books for Children

Shelagh Armstrong, *If the World Were a Village: A Book About the World's People*

Sara Dorow and Stephen Wunrow, *When You Were Born in China: A Memory Book for Children Adopted from China*

Sherrie Eldridge, *Forever Fingerprints: An Amazing Discovery for Adopted Children*

Ying Ying Fry and Amy Klatzkin, *Kids Like Me In China*

Doris Landry, *Before I Met You: A Therapeutic Pre-Adoption Narrative Designed for Children Adopted from China*

Multicultural Book Sources

www.shens.com Shen's Bookstore has thousands of books related to multicultural issues for children in grades K–8.

PACT's Multicultural Book Source, by Pact, an Adoption Alliance. An "opinionated" guide rates hundreds of books, including those from specialty adoption publishers, and it highlights hard-to-find resources for a wide range of families.

Preparing Children for a Return Trip

3

Serena Fan

What if I get lost? What if someone talks to me in Chinese? What will I eat? What if I get sick there? I don't want to use the squat toilets!

The above concerns were voiced by children who participate in a Chinese culture playgroup that takes place in a suburb of Boston. The playgroup consists of nine families with children adopted from China. This group meets twice a month and provides a safe space for children to learn about Chinese culture and to discuss difficult issues, such as identity and bullying.

In 2007, several families in the group decided to make return trips to China. At the time, the children were all eight to nine years old. Parents worked on their own to address their children's anxieties about the trip, but felt that some lessons in the group on "what to expect in China" would help ease the children's fears. As the leader of the playgroup that year, and as a Chinese-American woman originally from Hong Kong, I developed some lessons and activities to deal with their concerns. In this chapter, I will provide an overview of the work I did with the children that helped prepare them for their return trips.

Opening Up the Dialogue and Addressing Anxieties

Discussing the experience of returning to China with your child, well before departure, is vital. Some children will claim to have no worries, as the trip may be too far away to seem real. Nevertheless, conversing early with children about possible issues they may face in China can help to ease conscious or subconscious fears and elicit questions that will open up opportunities for further discussion.

In the group, three activities spread over three sessions helped initiate pre-departure conversations. For the first activity, I showed a series of photos I had taken of a local school in Hong Kong. As they watched the slide show on my laptop, the children made observations about the set-up of the classroom (that everyone had to sit in rows and the chairs did not look very comfy!), and about the outside surroundings of the school (that a behavior chart with every child's name was publicly posted on the wall in the hallway). After showing the photographs, I asked the children to compare their own schools to the one in the pictures. Some of the children in the group planned to visit a school in China. While schools in Hong Kong likely differ from those in mainland China, the children began thinking about what they might expect to see on their visit. This activity also helped engage all the children in the process of noticing similarities and differences between the environment of the United States and that of China.

The second activity was a presentation by a mother and two sisters in the group about their return trip to China the previous year. The two girls spoke first, showing pictures of themselves at their orphanages and finding sites, commenting on what they saw and their feelings that day. Then their mother spoke about meeting the family that found and took care of one of her daughters for a night before taking her to the orphanage, and how it felt to be able to say "thank you" to them personally. The presentation generated numerous questions from all the other mothers, but the girls remained mostly silent, needing time to digest all the information. A couple of the girls lay curled in their mothers' laps throughout the slideshow and discussion, which clearly brought up some difficult issues for them. Nevertheless, sharing this powerful experience among trusted friends with similar life histories proved, in some way, reassuring. It allowed the children a glimpse of what it could be like for them when they visited their orphanages and finding sites, and opened pathways for discussions at home about fears and expectations around those visits.

Finally, for the last activity, I asked the parents in the playgroup what their children were most anxious about regarding traveling in China. After compiling a list, I created skits to help children address their worries. Role-playing the scenarios with the use of doll puppets, with one doll as the parent and the other as the child, provided a buffer that decreased children's proximity to the issues. Using puppet characters created a more relaxed setting that allowed us to address possibly sensitive or embarrassing issues that the girls might have felt uncomfortable about voicing to the group as personal concerns. Having the puppets converse in parent-child conversations helped the children to understand that such discussions are valuable and that they should not be afraid to talk about these kinds of issues with their parents. Below are the skits that were created from the children's concerns.

Getting Sick

Both parents and children expressed fears of becoming sick while on the trip. Of course, parents should consult a doctor before leaving to discuss vaccinations, possible illnesses, and which medications to bring. It is important to acknowledge to children that while becoming sick is a very real possibility, parents will bring the necessary medicines and provide children with the best care possible. The skit presented to the children focused on hygiene, including frequent hand washing and using antibacterial gels before eating.

CHILD: Mommy, I can't wait to go to China, but at the same time, I'm a little scared.

Parent: Yeah, me too. Do you want to tell me what you're scared about?

Child: Well, I'm scared that I'll get sick.

Parent: That shouldn't happen, because you have received all the necessary vaccinations. It's unlikely you'll get sick because we're going to be really careful about what we eat and drink, and about using Purell a lot. If you do get sick, we're bringing lots of medicine with us to help you feel better.

Child: Oh. Well, I hope I won't get sick then.

Parent: I hope so too. We'll just have to remember to wash our hands a lot.

Bathrooms

Children were also quite concerned about the conditions of bathrooms in China. Even though China is rapidly improving in this area, there are still numerous places in both rural and urban areas that have traditional squat toilets. In cities, there are usually the options of both squat and Western-style toilets. However, many rural areas have toilets that consist of simply a hole in the ground. Addressing the different conditions of bathrooms that children might encounter on their trip is essential, so as to prevent any surprises and negative reactions. The skit for this issue was lighthearted and garnered the most laughter.

Child: I'm scared of the bathrooms. I've heard I might have to squat over a hole in the ground. Yuck! Is that true?

Parent: Well, the bathrooms in the hotel will be the same as at home, but in public places they are going to be different, so we'll try to use the bathroom before we leave the hotel. But you know, sometimes you will just have to use the public bathrooms. You know what Serena told me? She said that the public bathrooms are getting to be much better now, so they're not as bad.

Child: But what if I have to use one? I don't want to get dirty! And I heard it is really stinky!

Parent: Serena told me that what she does is, she rolls up her pants and makes sure she spreads her legs wide enough. (Move the puppet's leg to demonstrate.) She also holds her nose if she thinks it's going to be stinky. But Serena says it's really not that bad, so we should be okay too.

Using puppets made it easier to demonstrate how to use a squat toilet and also eased embarrassment for everyone. In many ways, this turned out to be the most useful discussion; after returning from China, a parent reported that the children were completely unfazed by the bathrooms, even though some of them were not the most pleasant smelling! Some parents noted that they had their children practice squatting at home in the bathroom before the trip, which also proved useful.

Language

Several children voiced concern that because they look Chinese, strangers in China might speak to them in Mandarin. They worried about what to do in a situation where they would be unable to comprehend the language, much less respond. At playgroup, we discussed polite ways to respond to the speaker, such as, "Sorry, I do not understand. Can you please say it in English?" I also suggested that they ask a tour guide or an adult for help.

Children also worried about their inability to express needs, such as ordering food or asking for directions, but they were most concerned about what to do if they became lost. One child expressed fears that the Chinese government would detain her if she became separated from her parents, and her inability to communicate would cause her to have to stay in China forever. Once again, the use of a short skit followed by an activity that provided them with a tool to communicate helped alleviate their concerns.

The skit emphasized the unlikelihood that the child would become lost in crowded places, because an adult would always be watching and everyone would be holding each other's hand. Nevertheless, after reaffirming this notion, I also gave a safety plan to the children. I explained that at every hotel, they could get a business card with the name, address and phone number of the hotel. Then I explained that if they were ever separated from their parents, they simply had to get into a taxi or find a police officer to hand the card to, and they would know where to take them.

For the follow-up activity, I gave each child a name-tag holder in which to place the business cards. I advised them to wear the holders around their necks, so they were always available. Additionally, the children asked me to write some Chinese phrases they thought they would need often, such as "I don't understand Chinese," "Where is the bathroom?" or "Can you please call this number?" They copied these sentences onto a small card that they placed into their name-tag holder. This name-tag holder was a useful way to address their language-related issues. It became in essence their security blanket, which gave them the confidence to communicate with others and eased their fears of becoming lost.

Keeping an Open Mind

These general concerns may overlap with your child's, or she may have other worries about traveling to China not addressed here. In either case, acknowledging your child's anxiety and discussing it openly, either through skits with puppets or through direct conversations, will help to ease fears and prepare your child for the trip. If you need more support, families who have already made a trip to China may help, or you can consult an expert. Conveying a positive attitude is the most vital preparation for the trip. As a parent, you may have even more worries than your child does, but keeping a positive outlook will help your child feel comfortable. Acknowledge that you also have concerns but are not dwelling on them. Instead, focus on aspects of the trip that you are looking forward to. This will hopefully help to put everyone more at ease for the adventure ahead.

Before You Pack

4

Developmental Considerations in Planning a Heritage Trip

Ellen E. Pinderhughes,* Ph.D., *and
***Richard B. Pinderhughes,* Psy.D.**

Adoption is a lifelong process. So, too, is identity development. There are predictable points in development when we experience a reformulation of our sense of self. However, just when we think we have ourselves figured out, new experiences challenge us in ways that might send us back to the drawing board of self-understanding. The good news is that there is always room for growth from those opportunities that prompt re-examination of our identity. For some children, a return trip to China is one such experience.

Increasingly, accounts of homeland trips (e.g., Prager, 2001; Stanek, 2007; Yngvesson, 2003) highlight that although families often travel together, each family member may experience the trip's events in different ways. These experiences can be quite complex.

For a *child* traveling back to China, the complexities lie in contrasting her trip's experiences with her life in the West. In China, she will be among others who look like her. Emily Prager quotes her five-year old daughter, Lulu, during her first day in China: "Everyone is Chinese. I am Chinese . . . It feels like good" (Prager, 2001, p. 17).

Experiencing that "vast mirror of sorts" can be highly affirming. A child also may find stares and occasional glares when with her non-Chinese adoptive parent. Although the public nature of the adoption is not new, experiencing this reaction in the context of being with others who look like her will be new and may be unsettling.

Parents may experience joy and pride in their awareness that their child sees herself in everyone around her. For perhaps the first time, however, parents themselves must face the reality of being different, and being unable to share the child's experience of connection to other Chinese people. "I look like everyone else. You two don't!" (Brown, 2002, quoted in Volkman, 2003).

Families can find it comforting to be together on this journey. Children watch parents as they navigate their child's birth culture, which can make many children feel proud. Within the "family-ness" of the trip, though, there may be times when each individual feels incredibly alone. Parents may feel alone in the reality that they are so different from their child, in the reality of being a minority in another culture (especially if for the first time) or in the struggle to be as supportive as they had hoped to be for their child. Children may feel alone in intense grief for their birth family as they visit the orphanage, police station, or finding site. Jenna Cook's essay "Returning Home: Step by Step" (in this volume) vividly describes the complex tangle of emotions an adoptee may feel during homeland trips at various ages.

With international adoption posing one of the more complex adoption experiences, parents and children may experience "multiple-layered longings" (Volkman, 2003). There can be a longing to experience a place that is perceived to hold a key to one's wholeness. Desire for pieces to complete the puzzle that is one's adoption story may be the most obvious longing; yearning for a feeling of closure or wholeness about who one is and what one's journey to date has been also exists. Sometimes there is longing for a tangible representation of one's reality—smells, sounds, even soil (Yngvesson, 2003) or a brick from an orphanage long since dismantled (Volkman, 2003).

Exploring and understanding these multiple longings can facilitate better preparation for the journey and can influence how different family members may view, and subsequently experience, the trip. As Ponte, Wang, and Fan show in their essay "Searching for Origins" (in this volume), some parents are very clear about what they hope for themselves and their children, whereas the children often frame their expectations in the words of their parents.

Considerations in Planning the Trip

Typical issues that families consider when making any trip, such as the duration of the visit and what sights and landmarks to include, take on more complexity when planning a heritage trip. Longer visits, if financially possible, may provide the child and family with the chance to experience China in a more casual and relaxed manner than a fully-scheduled shorter visit might offer. In addition, on longer trips parents and children have more time to reflect and process their experiences "in context."

Parents have many considerations to weigh before stepping on the plane. What are the respective needs of each family member, and what might be appropriate goals for the child? Should the family visit any orphanage? Should they visit the child's orphanage? Should they visit her abandonment site? How do the family's typical activities at home inform the development and planning of the trip? At home, what cultural activities related to the child's birth country has the family participated in with their child? What activities has the child participated in alone? How long has the family openly discussed the trip and what conversations have they had?

Depending on the nature of the family's openness with conversation around the issues of adoption in general, conversations about the trip and its details could be experienced differently by all family members. Although each member may be excited, the child's exhilaration may be tempered by the apprehension of returning to a place that holds a sense of loss. In addition, more concrete fears of abandonment may emerge if the child develops thoughts of being "left again" or of being returned to the orphanage. In contrast, parents may anticipate that a trip to the orphanage would provide a sense of closure for the child. Having had open conversations around issues of adoption paves the way for family members to understand and expect that these feelings are normal, helping both child and parent feel supported in this journey.

Key Themes for Children at Different Points in Development

As parents plan for return trips, considering key themes for children at different points in development will help them understand what their child may experience in China and upon returning home. It is critical to keep in mind, however, the wide variation in development among children of the same age.

Early Childhood, Ages 3–6

During the early childhood years, children are pretty literal in their thinking. Children also are particularly aware of physical differences between themselves and their families, so travel to China could be very affirming in helping them to see themselves in others all around them.

Their emotional development, though progressing, has not matured, and they can easily be overwhelmed with intense emotional experiences. Intellectually, these children are "egocentric" thinkers—they view the world as revolving around them and their needs. They also have difficulty holding two conflicting ideas or thoughts at the same time. So, meeting prior caregivers or visiting their orphanage may be quite unsettling. The divisive experience of divided loyalty can be felt quite powerfully. One parent, Mary, who took her five-year-old daughter back to meet her foster mother, noted that her daughter refused to look at the foster mother, instead clinging to Mary. Later, when Mary expressed her upset about her daughter's behavior toward the foster mother, her daughter grabbed Mary by the shirt and said, "I only wanted one Mommy, anyway!"

On the other hand, some children don't tune in at all to these intense experiences, instead connecting at a more basic or superficial level. At this age, children's anxieties show up in their behaviors, whether shy and retreating or "hyped-up." As they look ahead to and experience a heritage trip, children need reassurance from parents that their reaction is understandable and normal. Parents might encourage children to draw their fantasy of what they might see so that they can compare it to what they actually experience. This experience can be expressive and cathartic, and provides the child with a frame of reference for some of the actual experiences on the trip. Parents of children this age might find *Wuhu Diary* (Prager, 2002) helpful.

Middle Childhood, Ages 7–10

These children are beginning to think more abstractly and can better understand that there must have been a reason they were adopted. Children at this age often perceive, through this understanding, that they had been placed or abandoned in order to have found a family. Their capacity to handle intense emotions has matured a bit, so while they may be more susceptible than younger children to feeling the loss of abandonment, they may also be more able to talk about the complex feelings they experience. Thus, it is much easier for children this age to contemplate their life as it might have been for them in China.

For some children, having these thoughts while in China, at an orphanage or a finding site, can be overwhelming. Whether they choose not to discuss their thoughts at the time (Fry, 2001) or talk openly, they will be comforted when they know that parents have made themselves available to talk and support them. Preparation for a heritage trip with children of this age should focus on helping children anticipate the mixed feelings they may have. As with younger children, encouraging them to draw pictures of their expectations and fantasies can help pre-trip discussions, as well as processing during and after the trip. Children this age would find *Kids like Me in China* (Fry, 2001) helpful.

Pre-Teen Years, Ages 11–13

Some adoption professionals describe these years as the last chance to take a first heritage trip before the difficult teen years (Stanek, 2007). However, children at this age vary widely in their emotional maturation. Thus, parents must decide what is best for their children. If parents are uncertain, consulting an adoption professional about their unique family situation may help. This is an age when children find a clearer voice for their evolving sense of self, and their greater emotional maturity can help them to manage and express their different feelings about the trip. Being available—and yet giving children this age some emotional space to reflect on their experiences—is an important parental support. Parents and children may find viewing *Found in China* (Stanek, 2007) together quite helpful, as it documents the experiences and thoughts of children and parents during and after a heritage trip.

Young Adolescent Years, Ages 13–15

Young teenagers typically struggle with their identity, often feeling uncomfortable about the ways in which they are different from others. Early adolescence also is a time when children seek to distinguish themselves from their parents and from what they perceive their parents want for them. With increasingly evolving abstract thinking skills, they may find themselves challenging parents (or wanting to) in ways that may be unnerving to parents.

Trips to China taken during this period, particularly first-time trips, may pose a further risk to teens' sense of self and their task of feeling comfortable with their uniqueness. Visits to finding sites or orphanages can highlight a sense of loneliness within one's family, especially if the adoptee is the only family member who experienced the pre-adoption reality that is invoked in the visit. For some teens, this experience can destabilize them upon returning home, requiring support from professionals (B. J. Lifton, personal communication, February 21, 2007).

Preparation for a heritage trip with young adolescents should focus on discussions that help them anticipate that they may experience confusion and loneliness. During the trip, parents should be prepared to help normalize the adoptee's feelings and experiences. This can be a confusing and painful time for parents, as children may push parents away or withdraw. Parents will want to sort out their own issues separately so that they can find ways to be available and supportive of their children.

Each Family Is Different

There are many issues to weigh when considering taking a heritage trip, including the child's age and level of development, as well as how the family has been framing and incorporating into daily life their reality as an international adoptive family. Parents must consider their child's and family's unique needs, as there is great diversity among children, and they will want to decide with their children when the family is really ready to take a heritage trip. For some children, a trip at an age as young as five or six may make sense, whereas for others, waiting until they are more emotionally mature may be best. Preparation is essential and can include many discussions about goals, uncertainties, fantasies, fears, and hopes.

During the trip, family members will have many opportunities to discuss and process their experiences. Parents should be sure to build in time for these discussions.

Finally, after families return home, they will find that each member will continue to unpack their experiences for years after they have unpacked their suitcases. Anticipating this, family members can support each other through this important opportunity for individual and family growth.

References

Fry, Ying Ying. 2001. *Kids Like Me in China*. St. Paul: Yeong & Yeong.

Prager, Emily. 2001. *Wuhu Diary: On Taking My Adopted Daughter Back to Her Hometown in China*. New York: Anchor Books.

Stanek, Carolyn. 2007. *Found in China*. Tai-Kai Productions.

Volkman, Toby Alice. 2003. "Embodying Chinese Culture: Transnational Adoption in North America." *Social Text 74*, 21 (1): 29–55.

Yngvesson, Barbara. 2003. "Going 'Home:' Adoption, Loss of Bearings, and the Mythology of Roots." *Social Text 74*, 21 (1): 7–27.

5 | The Art of Chinese Gift Giving

Iris Chin Ponte, Ph.D.

It was my sixth birthday. My family and friends were all singing "Happy Birthday" to me. I blew out the candles and everyone clapped. My Chinese grandmother came over to me and handed me a *hongbao* (red envelope). I said, "Thank you Grandma," and began to open the envelope. All of my Chinese relatives gasped. I looked up to see everyone staring at me in disapproval. My mother moved me from the table and explained, "Never open a red envelope in front of people. It is very rude." I was horrified.

My Chinese family members taught me the important role that gift giving and receiving play in maintaining *guanxi*, or social connections, in Chinese communities. The lessons I learned about how to give and receive gifts were sometimes painful, but they don't have to be for you. By following some basic guidelines in both personal and business situations, you will show proper respect to your Chinese hosts, friends, and associates, who will appreciate your efforts.

Chinese customs dictate that whenever you visit a friend or acquaintance, you should never show up empty-handed. For this reason, gift purchasing and planning is important when preparing for your trip to China. At the same time, don't worry too much about whether you're following Chinese gift-giving practices to the letter; Chinese people are generally forgiving of foreigners and their limited exposure to Chinese culture.

Chinese Gift-Giving Etiquette

In China, as in other countries, there is a cultural script to follow when giving or receiving a gift. If you are in the role of the giver, hold the gift or envelope with both hands. Be sure to downplay the act of giving. For example, you can say, "My family would like to give a token of appreciation," or "We wanted to give something in thanks." Words like these minimize the gift and demonstrate modesty (even if the gift is large).

If you are in the role of receiver, it is important to act as if you are not worthy of the gift. For example, before you receive the gift (with both hands) you can say, "Oh my, you didn't need to do that," or "This is too much trouble." You cannot refuse a gift because you will be perceived as unappreciative. Once you receive the gift, do not open it right away (especially envelopes). Instead, wait until you are in a private space. This demonstrates that the gesture is more important than the gift. If the giver requests that you open it immediately, then do so and make sure to express enthusiasm over the contents.

Giving to the Orphanage

In my work with many families that have made return trips, and in my own visits to several orphanages in China, I have learned some guidelines for giving gifts to orphanages and orphanage staff.

Some families might be prepared to give large gifts to their child's orphanage, such as a new water heater, a washing machine or new beds. If you plan to give a large item, contact the orphanage in advance to find out what they need. In order to avoid misunderstandings or hurt feelings, do not assume on your own that they are in need of a particular item. Instead, ask for a list of items of varying costs that would be helpful to both the children and the staff.

Prior to departure, some families decide to hold a fundraiser that enables them to purchase larger items. One family explained to me, "We really didn't have the funds independently to buy the orphanage a new water heater. However, we set up a small fundraiser at our daughter's school, with family and friends, and it ended up being enough to buy the water heater and a new washing machine. When we arrived at the orphanage, the machines had already arrived and everyone was so happy!"

The thought is more important than the gift, so it doesn't matter if you give something big or small. Even small amounts of money can go a long way. For example, one family explained to me that they wanted to give the orphanage some practical items (including shampoo, lotion, and detergent). As part of your orphanage visit, ask if it is possible to visit a local store to buy needed items together with the director or a staff member. This ensures that your money is spent on the items the children need. If this is not possible, a donation to the orphanage can be given through a trusted third party or a nonprofit agency.

Some children also choose to put together a photo album that includes pictures from their life at home that they present to the orphanage staff. Children can write notes in English and Chinese about their life in America.

Giving to the *Ayi*

If you know that you will see your child's primary caregiver, you may want to prepare a special gift for her. Many families like to give photographs of their child as a baby that they pair with current photographs. This is a very thoughtful gift. Items that you can only obtain in America also make very popular gifts, such as candies and cookies. Your child's *ayi* will also certainly appreciate receiving a red envelope with money inside, which is considered to be entirely appropriate. Most women who work as *ayi* make very minimal wages, so a monetary gift will help their families greatly. When giving a monetary gift to the *ayi*, give it in private or wrapped in another gift. Do not give a monetary gift in front of other *ayi* or the director.

Make sure not to give out items such as soap, lotion, make-up or brushes. Giving these types of hygiene items can be misinterpreted and accidentally cause offense. The following is an example of a gift gone wrong:

> Thank goodness we had a Chinese translator. I had purchased beautiful French soaps to distribute to the caregivers in Sara's orphanage. I thought that the little soaps would be very popular. As I started to meet people, I smiled and handed them out. After a little while, I realized that people were looking at me a little funny. Our translator turned to me and said, "I think you should stop giving those out—the women are not dirty." In that moment I realized that a gift that was appropriate back at home was not acceptable here. I asked the translator to explain to the women that these were special soaps meant as gifts and that I was very sorry to offend them. Thank goodness the translator said something or I could have really hurt people's feelings.

Ask your child to participate in the *ayi's* gift by making a card or a drawing. This can be a wonderful project to help prepare your child for the trip and can serve as a way to connect her to the people your family will be meeting.

Giving to the Children at the Orphanage

When you visit your child's orphanage, you will likely meet children of all ages and in a variety of physical conditions. This can be a difficult experience for all involved. While some orphanages make requests for new shoes, clothing, or school items, others are not as specific. Giving children's clothing and other items to the director is acceptable. Do not hand out clothing to individual children; because children in orphanages rarely have the opportunity to keep specific items for themselves, this might lead to confusion and crying. They might be delighted to receive something of their own, only to have it taken away by another child or by orphanage staff members who assume the gift is for sharing. Therefore, I recommend bringing many small gifts such as pencils, markers, erasers, and stickers for older children and a few toys to give to the babies and younger children.

Some adoptees enjoy handing out the gifts themselves while others prefer that their parents help them. Talk with your child and see what she or he would like to bring. Many people enjoy bringing candy to the children. However, orphanage directors have recently begun to request that candy not be given to the children because it contributes to tooth decay. If you would like to give food, bring fruit or crackers instead.

Taking the Orphanage Staff to a Restaurant

As part of the visit to the orphanage, some directors and staff plan a meal together with returning families at a local restaurant. When making arrangements for your visit to the orphanage, you can let the staff know that you would like to take them out for lunch. Although they might plan the location and take charge of ordering the food, there is still the underlying expectation that you will host the meal, unless this meal is included in the fee some provinces are now charging for returning families to visit the orphanage.

At the end of the meal, in order to be polite, they might refuse to let you pay when the bill comes. "Fighting over the bill" in a loud and playful manner is a Chinese custom that allows participants to save face (or *mianzi*) through a public demonstration of mutual generosity. However, no matter how strongly they insist on paying the bill, stand firm and say, "It would make me and my family very happy to treat all of you." People who live in certain very traditional areas of China sometimes stick to the "rule of three." This means that they will refuse your gift or gesture three times before they accept.

Extra Gifts

One of the most important pieces of advice I ever received from a Chinese friend is to always carry extra gifts. During your trip you are going to meet many helpful and wonderful people, from local guides to drivers. Pack your suitcase with American T-shirts (many Chinese friends requested Harvard and Red Sox shirts), magnets of local places, postcards of your home city, hats, and boxed candies.

Gift Wrap

Do not wrap gifts and pack them in your luggage because customs officials at the airport might require you to open them. Instead, it's a good idea to pack wrapping supplies so that you can wrap them when you arrive in China. But keep in mind that it is not a requirement to wrap gifts; this decision is a matter of preference. If you do choose to wrap your gifts, select bright colors of wrapping paper (red, orange, and yellow are considered auspicious colors). Never wrap gifts in black or white, as these colors are considered unlucky.

Enjoy the Gift Giving

As you plan for your trip, keep these suggestions in mind. Start planning your gifts in advance so that it is a fun activity, rather than a stressful one. If you follow these simple guidelines, you and your family will be sure to generate appropriate *guanxi* and make a positive, lasting impression on all of the people you meet in China.

6 | Travel Medicine

Preparing for Homeland Trips

Laurie Miller, M.D.

Homeland trips are becoming increasingly popular with adoptive families. These trips are filled with excitement, poignancy, and a range of other emotions. Parents usually make considerable effort to prepare themselves and their children for the emotional and psychological aspects of these trips; this important preparation is discussed in detail elsewhere in this volume. This chapter discusses health issues for traveling children and parents, and gives recommended resources for additional information.

Families must plan well in advance so that all travelers remain healthy during this emotionally and physically demanding time. Good health is necessary in order for everyone to enjoy the trip and be able to participate fully in all planned activities. Although some of the health risks may seem daunting, good preparation and sensible precautions will

Disclaimer: *This chapter is not meant to substitute for personal medical advice. It is recommended that all travelers consult their personal physician and/or an expert in travel medicine to obtain up-to-date information on this important topic.*

allow parents and children to stay healthy and enjoy the wonderful experiences of a homeland trip.

Adult Travelers

If you have already made one or more visits to China to complete the adoption of your children, you probably feel like a "veteran." However, your adoption trips may have taken place years earlier, and travel recommendations may have changed. Some adult travelers will be going to new destinations with unfamiliar health risks. All adult travelers should consider visiting a specialized "Travel Medicine" clinic (see resources) in order to review routine travel precautions, discuss current destination-specific concerns, and update needed vaccines.

If you have a chronic medical condition, consult your physician about health precautions during travel. Make sure you take adequate supplies of all prescription medicines in your carry-on luggage. Planning for needed prescription medications ahead of time is important, as many insurance companies do not authorize advance refills.

You may consider purchasing emergency evacuation insurance if you have chronic health problems or anticipate a prolonged trip. (Companies offering this kind of insurance include: International SOS: www.internationalsos.com, International Association for Medical Assistance to Travelers: www.iamat.org, or MEDEX: www.medexassist.com.)

Due to concerns about illegal transport of children across international borders, be sure to carry copies of your children's adoption papers and any other pertinent legal documents with you.

Basic Hygiene

Infrequent or inexperienced travelers should review basic travel hygiene (food, water, sanitation) and safety precautions (see Table 1). Use waterless/soapless hand cleansers frequently throughout the day (after toilet, before meals) if other sanitary facilities are unavailable. China is considered to be a high-risk destination for travelers' diarrhea, an illness characterized by the abrupt onset of loose, watery stools associated with

Table 1
Food and Water Hygiene

Possible Infections Acquired from Contaminated Food or Water

Bacterial *Escherichia coli*, shigellosis (bacillary dysentery), typhoid fever and other salmonelloses, cholera

Viral noroviruses, rotavirus, and hepatitis A

Parasitic giardiasis, cryptosporidiosis, protozoa, helminths

Risks

Drinking water, uncooked fruits or vegetables (if unpeeled) or other raw foods, cooked food in unhygienic conditions (power outages interfering with refrigeration, or previously cooked food kept at room temperature for several hours—hotel buffet meals may be suspect). In addition, inadvertent ingestion of water during swimming (lakes, rivers, oceans, or inadequately cleaned swimming pools) can also transmit disease.

Avoid

Salads, uncooked vegetables, and unpasteurized milk and milk products such as fresh cheese, undercooked and raw meat, fish, and shellfish, most food from street vendors, undercooked eggs, ice, fruit juice made with tap water.

Safe to Drink

Beverages such as tea and coffee made with boiled water, canned or unopened bottled beverages, including mineral water, soft drinks, beer, and wine.

abdominal cramps and urgency, sometimes preceded by nausea, bloating, fever, and vomiting. The Centers for Disease Control estimates that about thirty to fifty percent of travelers to high-risk areas develop travelers' diarrhea during a visit lasting a week or two; however, you can greatly decrease this risk by taking appropriate precautions.

Even without treatment, travelers' diarrhea usually resolves within three or four days. Treatment with ciprofloxacin or levofloxacin may reduce the duration and severity of symptoms, but not all organisms causing travelers' diarrhea are susceptible to these antibiotics. Symptomatic relief may be obtained from the use of bismuth subsalicylate (BSS or Pepto-Bismol, one ounce of liquid or two chewable tablets every thirty minutes for eight doses), or from antimotility agents such as loperamide (Imodium) and diphenoxylate (Lomotil or Lonox).

Because of the risks associated with salicylates, BSS (including Pepto-Bismol, Kaopectate and others) should *not* be given to children with viral infections. The antimotility drugs (Imodium, Lomotil, Lonox and others) should *not* be given to children under the age of twelve.

Seek medical attention if you experience diarrhea accompanied by a high fever or bloody stools. Rehydration with ORS (oral rehydration solution) can also provide symptomatic relief. Packet contents should be dissolved in sterile (boiled) water.

Malaria

Malaria prophylactic medication is recommended for travelers to some rural areas of China, but not for those only visiting cities. A travel medicine clinic should supply specific recommendations tailored to your proposed itinerary; plan ahead, as some of these medications need to be started a week or two prior to departure.

The CDC lists the rural areas of the following Chinese provinces as risk areas for malaria: Hainan, Yunnan, Fuijan, Guangdong, Guangxi, Guizhou, Sichuan, Tibet (in the Zangbo River valley only), Anhui, Hubei, Hunan, Jiangsu, Jiangxi, and Shandong. Malaria risk relates to altitude and season: At altitudes below 1,500 meters, there is a risk only during warm weather. North of latitude 33°N, the risky season is July–November; between latitude 25°N and 33°N, there is a risk from May–December; south of latitude 25°N, transmission may occur year-round).

Wearing long-sleeved garments and using bed nets and insect repellent (DEET-containing) are basic ways to prevent mosquito bites that can spread malaria and other diseases. Malaria symptoms include fever, chills, headache, muscle aches, and fatigue; these symptoms may appear up to a year after travel.

Vaccinations for Adult Travelers

Travel medicine experts can also best advise you on needed vaccines. You should be up-to-date on routine vaccines including diphtheria-tetanus, poliovirus, measles-mumps-rubella, and varicella. Hepatitis A and Hepatitis B vaccines are also generally recommended for international travelers. If your itinerary includes East Asia, typhoid vaccine is strongly recommended, and if you plan to visit rural areas you should receive a vaccine for Japanese encephalitis. Also consider getting a rabies vaccine. Many of these vaccines should be updated every five to ten years.

Travelers to more than one country may need additional vaccines. It is best to consult a travel medicine clinic several months before departure in order to allow adequate time to administer needed vaccines.

Other Health Risks

Although most travelers are concerned about the risks of infectious diseases, accidents and injuries are the most common cause of serious problems among travelers. Use seat belts and helmets when possible. Take precautions regarding altitude, sun exposure, and swimming to ensure safety for all travelers. Air pollution is a problem in many cities; this may exacerbate respiratory conditions in susceptible individuals.

Table 2

Specific Health Risks in Some Parts of China

Dengue
Filariasis
Japenese encephalitis
Leishmaniasis
Plague
Tickborne encephalitis
Measles
Schistosomiasis (especially Yangtze River basin)
Leptospirosis
Rabies
Avian influenza (H5N1) Avoid contact with birds, including domestic poultry and wild birds (bird markets, poultry farms). Monitor health for ten days after return home: Report difficulties breathing, fever with cough or sore throat. Additional information: World Health Organization: Avian Influenza or CDC: Avian Influenza websites.

Specific Health Risks for China

Every country has specific health risks (see Table 2 for risks in certain parts of China). These local risks can change rapidly. Prior to departure, seek up-to-date information about any possible health warnings or epidemics from reputable sources such as the CDC or WHO websites. In addition to these specific risks, viral hepatitis (especially A, B, and E) and tuberculosis are widespread.

General Travel Preparation

Make sure you check your individual health insurance prior to departure, to ascertain coverage and protocols for obtaining needed medical services and emergency care while abroad. You may need specific claim forms or other documents if you seek care while traveling. Most care providers (physicians, hospitals) require payment in cash.

So-called "international clinics" are available in many destinations. While the quality of care in these clinics varies, usually the staff speaks English, facilitating communication. The local U.S. consulate or embassy may provide advice about recommended locations to seek medical care. A list of accredited international health-care facilities is available at the International Association for Medical Assistance to Travelers website: www.iamat.org.

Bringing a medical kit in your carry-on luggage makes sense (see Table 3). Having this kit at hand will reduce your anxiety, as most minor illnesses can be prevented or managed. The list should be adjusted for individual needs.

Child Travelers

Many of the above recommendations and precautions also apply to children, including adopted children returning to their birth country, siblings adopted from other countries, siblings who have previously traveled, and siblings who have never traveled outside of the U.S. Child health recommendations must be age-appropriate, recognizing that young children need extremely vigilant supervision regarding food, water, and safety. Consultation with your child's physician well in advance of the planned departure date will allow adequate time for preparation. A pediatric health kit for travel is also suggested (see Table 4).

Basic Hygiene

General principles outlined above regarding food and water safety apply equally to children: Supervise them very closely to reduce the risk of problems. Putting a sock over a hotel water tap can remind children not to drink the water or use it for tooth brushing. Carrying hand sanitizers and a variety of safe foods and drinks during outings will help children avoid travelers' diarrhea, which can be much more serious in children

Table 3
Recommended Medical Kit for Travelers

Medications

Personal prescription medications in their original containers (Copies of all prescriptions should also be carried, including the generic names for medications, and a note from the prescribing physician on letterhead stationery for controlled substances and injectable medications.)

Antimalarial medications, if applicable

Over-the-counter antidiarrheal medication (e.g., bismuth subsalicylate, loperamide)

Antibiotic for self-treatment of moderate to severe diarrhea

Antihistamine

Decongestant, alone or in combination with antihistamine

Anti-motion sickness medication

Acetaminophen, aspirin, ibuprofen, or other medication for pain or fever

Mild laxative

Cough suppressant/expectorant

Throat lozenges

Antacid

Antifungal and antibacterial ointments or creams

1% hydrocortisone cream

Epinephrine auto-injector (e.g., EpiPen), especially if history of severe allergic reaction. Also available in smaller-dose package for children.

Other Items

Insect repellent containing DEET (up to 50%)

Sunscreen (preferably SPF 15 or greater)

Digital thermometer

Oral rehydration solution packets

Basic first-aid items (adhesive bandages, alcohol wipes, gauze, ace wrap, antiseptic, tweezers, scissors, cotton-tipped applicators)

Antibacterial hand wipes or alcohol-based hand sanitizer containing at least 60% alcohol

Moleskin for blisters

Lubricating eye drops

First aid quick reference card

Address and phone numbers of area hospitals or clinics

* *Adapted from the CDC website*

Table 4

Pediatric Travel Health Kit

Supplemental Items for Children: Adjust for Age of Child*

Acetaminophen (child formulation)

Antibacterial wipes

Antibiotic ointment

Antihistamine (child formulation)

Azithromycin (child formulation)

Cold/cough preparation (child formulation)

Diaper rash cream

Dosage syringe

Ibuprofen (child formulation)

Insect repellent

Medications, all regularly taken by the child

ORS packets (oral rehydration solution)

Permethrin (Elimite) for scabies

Safe snacks

Safe water

Sodium sulamyd optic drops

Sunscreen

Thermometer

Vaseline

* *These items are in addition to adult kit items in Table 3.*

than in adults. Children may quickly become dehydrated; you must be ready to manage this (if mild) with oral rehydration solution or to seek medical attention if the diarrhea is persistent or severe. Infants and very young children with diarrhea may require medical attention, especially in the presence of fever greater than 101.5° F, bloody diarrhea, or persistent vomiting.

Children with diarrhea who weigh 10 kg (22 lbs) or more should receive 120–240 mL ORS for each diarrheal stool or vomiting episode. There are limited choices of safe and effective antibiotics for treatment of travelers' diarrhea in children: Azithromycin is considered the first choice (as a single dose or at 10 mg/kg for 3–5 days), since fluoroquinolones such as ciprofloxacin are not approved except under unusual circumstances. Azithromycin flavored suspension does not require refrigeration; however, it should be used within ten days of mixing. Anti-motility agents (loperamide and diphenoxylate) are not approved for children under the age of twelve, and bismuth subsalicylate (BSS or Pepto-Bismol) should be used with caution (salicylate use has been associated with Reye's Syndrome, a serious liver problem, in children with fevers).

Children may also need assistance using unfamiliar styles of toilets, such as the "squat" toilets found in most regions of China.

Malaria and Tuberculosis

Discuss malaria prophylaxis with your child's doctor if you plan to travel to an endemic area. You can find up-to-date recommendations for pediatric malaria prophylaxis at the CDC Travelers Health website. Parents must weigh the risks of treatment against those of exposure.

If your trip is prolonged and your children have lengthy exposure to local citizens (for example, via attendance at a local school), have them tested for tuberculosis exposure before departure and after returning from China.

Accidents and Other Dangers

Accidents are the most common cause of serious problems for traveling children. Carefully supervise motor vehicle rides and street crossings, and closely inspect hotel rooms for child safety (balconies, security of windows and screens, electrical outlets, pesticides). Swimming areas should be carefully scrutinized. Chlorinated, well-maintained pools are best; swimming in natural areas may be hazardous.

Children accustomed to friendly neighborhood dogs must be cautioned about animal contact, as rabies is a very real risk in China and other countries. Consider any animal bite an extreme medical emergency.

In addition, altitude sickness, motion sickness, and sunburn are all risks which disproportionately affect child travelers. Traveling children may become cranky for many reasons (change in schedule, jet lag, etc.), but irritability may also be a sign of serious illness, so monitor your child's mood closely. Discuss potential health risks with sexually active adolescent travelers, including personal safety and sexually transmitted diseases.

Vaccinations for Child Travelers

Vaccinations for children should be up-to-date prior to travel; an accelerated schedule may be given to infants, if needed. Children 3–18 months should receive three immunizations with DTaP and polio vaccines. All children 12 months old or older should receive the varicella vaccine, unless there is a reliable history of chickenpox. Measles-mumps-rubella (MMR) should be given as age appropriate. Typhoid vaccine is recommended for all children older than 24 months traveling to endemic areas. Hepatitis A vaccine should be given to children over 24 months; although children rarely have severe symptoms, those infected efficiently transmit the infection to other children and to adults.

Vaccination against meningococcal meningitis and Japanese encephalitis may be needed (although the latter vaccine is controversial because of side effects), depending on your exact destination.

Conclusion

Although the list of potential health concerns may seem overwhelming, it is important to remember that children can and do travel safely and in good health every day. Careful preparation before departure, followed by sensible precautions during travel, will ensure the likelihood of a safe and healthy trip for the entire family.

Useful Resources

www.aap.org American Academy of Pediatrics
www.cdc.gov/travel Centers for Disease Control and Prevention
www.iamat.org International Association for Medical Assistance to Travelers
www.istm.org International Society of Travel Medicine
www.who.int/ith/en/ World Health Organization

Back to Where It All Began | 7

A Consultation and Therapeutic Model for Family and Country Connections Post-Adoption

***Joyce Maguire Pavao,* Ed.D., L.C.S.W., L.M.F.T**

As a therapist and CEO and founder of Center For Family Connections (CFFC), I have over thirty years of experience working with adoptive families, including thousands of internationally adopted children and their parents (both birth and adoptive). As an adult adopted person myself, I also have a lifetime of experience. Part of the work we do at CFFC—an educational and clinical resource center specializing in the developmental, structural, and systemic issues related to adoption, foster care, kinship and guardianship, as well as the people with whom they are connected—is to help families prepare for homeland visits, and later to "unpack" their experiences on those trips and back at home. In this chapter, I use what we've learned at CFFC with children adopted from China and other countries to help families gain an understanding of the children's perspective and to prepare for traveling and, most of all, for returning home again.

Note: While the majority of adopted children from China are girls, many families have also adopted boys. To acknowledge the boys, who often get short shrift in the China adoption literature, I switch from section to section in this chapter between masculine and feminine pronouns.

Beginning to Open What Was Closed

Think about a return to your child's homeland as the beginning of the opening of a closed adoption. It is also a part of the ongoing process of search that is woven into the lives of all adopted people.

Your child may have been fairly young when you brought him home. He probably spoke no English, or perhaps had formed no language yet at all. His only memories about his country of origin are those that you, his parent, have given him with the photos you took and the memories *you* have of the visit to his country or his orphanage. The child eventually needs to gather and store his own memories and images.

It is wonderful that most countries today with an international adoption program require parents to visit the country of the child when an adoption takes place. It gives them a feel for the reality of their child's beginnings, for the culture, and for the country. Perhaps it also gives them a feel for the orphanage or foster home that their child spent time in before coming to his forever family.

This is a huge change from the practice of 'escorts' carrying babies across the world on an airplane, to meet their adoptive parents at an international airport. And we wonder about attachment issues of children in adoption! Whose attachment problems are they? Not the child's alone. The agencies, the countries, and the families have colluded in the past in not making the transition a smooth one, nor the attachment a careful one that takes into account the losses, trauma, and fear that a child experiences by moving from place to place.

We now know how important it is for children to connect and attach slowly and carefully to their forever family. We know how important transitions are, and how important the people involved in the transitions are to the end result.

Professionals have learned over the years to recommend that families leave the child in the clothing he is wearing for the first day they meet him, with the smells on and around him that are familiar from his past. We encourage parents to let the infant or child get used to their smell, and the feel of different fabrics, before taking away the sensory items that are all that he has known. Many transitions are now done slowly so that children can adapt and attach in a careful and gradual manner. These are things that people did not think about in the past, but that we now know add to the enhancement of connection and attachment.

Even with parents now usually being required to travel to adopt their children, and with what we have learned about helping the child transition to his new family and home, we must still take the child's experiences into account. Imagine if you were taken from your familiar surroundings, flown across the world and plunked down with strangers who looked totally different and did not speak a familiar tongue. Imagine if everything familiar disappeared, just like that! Imagine the shock, the fear, and the feeling of loss that might accompany such a journey.

Often we forget to put ourselves in the shoes of the children, and to realize how very intense the whole process of adoption is. We forget how little is explained to them in the process, how much we assume that they comprehend what is happening, and how often we find out years later that they had no idea what was happening to them or where they were going. A large number of children feel that they were kidnapped since they were taken by strangers very far away from everything they knew. We are often unsure of what exactly is said to them by translators and people that we may not understand.

We do not do the best job of helping the new parents to understand the psychological impact of this experience either. We do not give them the insight that they need about the losses that came before the most recent one. Neither do we inform them about the trauma and neglect that might have been suffered by their child *in utero*, or in the orphanage.

But children are resilient.

They do adapt, they do learn, they do become a part of the lives of the family they are with forever. Inside, though, a part of them longs for something missing. Inside they wonder, 'Who do I look like? What happened to cause me to become disconnected from my past?' Inside, they wonder why they are so different from their forever family.

Children are resilient, but they also deserve some understanding—some help in making sense of their past and their present.

Return trips are one way we can enable children to gain some of the missing puzzle pieces of their lives.

Considerations for the First Trip Back

If a family can afford to, we recommend at least two trips back to the country of birth. The first trip might be just to familiarize the child with the place and to give her the opportunity to store some of her own memories and pictures—a chance to see what it is like in her country of origin, and what the children in her orphanage do every day. This trip gives the child a chance to see the city or town where she came from, a chance to eat the food, walk the paths, smell the smells, and look at faces that may seem familiar.

One important decision to make on this first trip is choosing a translator. Will that translator be someone who understands the importance of this visit, and of every word that is spoken? Does that translator—who will be a crucial gatekeeper to your child's experience of her birth country, and to yours—have the empathy and the understanding to take care of both the birth country people and the visiting family, while watching and responding to the reactions of the child?

Remember, no matter how old your child is for this first return, she will be very anxious about getting there and will possibly fear that she might be staying there. After all, she feels she was once "taken" from there and may wonder if she will now be "returned." It can be both a hope and a fear: Will she now have to stay in her country of origin and lose another set of parents?

When making plans for the trip, be sure to show a calendar and talk about everything that will lead up to the trip, and everything that will follow when you return home. Describing what the family will do after the trip is most important, so that your child knows she will return home. The last time she flew halfway across the world, she lost everything she had ever known. The fear (and sometimes hope) is that it will happen again.

Do not think that the trip is a bad idea if your child starts to have nightmares before, during, and after. This is a chance for her to reprocess some very early preverbal and precognitive experiences, or experiences in another language, that have been long forgotten. The opportunities for parents to attach during these times of stress—to understand their child's fears and longings, and to be there beside the child—are invaluable and can form lasting bonds that may not have been formed as yet.

If you can afford many trips, make the first a trip to land of birth only. It is always a shock to see other countries for the first time, unless people there are very "Westernized." If your child left the country before she was three or four years old, she does not have many cognitive memories. Vague images are left, but having lost her first language, her memories are hazy and diminishing. Remember, this will be the first chance to establish her own pictures (in her mind) of her country of origin. This is a huge opportunity to establish a real memory, not just what adults have told her.

Thinking About What Came Before

If you traveled to your child's birth country to adopt him, think about taking him on a journey to re-live your adoption trip—but also a journey for him to think about what came before.

Remember: Your child had a previous life *in utero* and in another country. He has a Chinese mommy and a Chinese (or Indian, or Colombian . . .) daddy who created his life, and that is why he looks the way he does. It is important to give him that reality base and to have him hold it as his own. It is also important to talk about your connection to his country and to his birth family, since you are all now an extended family together.

Preparing for the Trip

Depending on your child's age, begin to break down the trip and go over how it will happen in detail, mapped out with calendars and other concrete tools.

At Center for Family Connections (CFFC), we work with the parents concurrently as we work with the children. We spend time helping parents to understand how to regulate their own feelings and how to think in advance of what might be happening in their child's mind. At the same time, another therapist spends time helping the child think about 'packing'. We have kids keep a calendar with the things that will be done leading up to the trip, during the trip, and most importantly, upon returning home. We suggest role playing the plane trip (many hours) and having the child pack her bag, bringing both things to entertain herself and things that are comfort items and transitional objects.

Have your child bring what we at CFFC call *An Emotional First-Aid Kit.* This is filled with things that make her feel safe and calm when she is anxious. Parents could use one as well! Some common items people include are:

- soothing lotions
- music she loves
- games she likes to play
- things she can do by herself (reading, etc.)
- things she can do with others
- a favorite "blanky"
- a toy (no matter how old)
- a favorite pillow case, pillow, and blanket
- pictures of people who cannot come and of your pets.

Be sure she has everything she needs to feel at home while away, and to remember who she is while she thinks about who she was and who she will become as she integrates the past with the present.

Your child's first trip to the United States probably did not have any of these things. She was surrounded by totally new smells, new sensations, and new people. She did not get a chance to bring an emotional first-aid kit.

This time she can redo the trip with her favorite things and people she knows surrounding her. This time she can also bring home the things she may need from her country of origin. Rocks and shells are pieces of the earth where she used to live. Fabrics and photos are reminders of what she saw and felt.

A Pre- and Post-Trip Therapeutic Model

In our pre- and post-trip work with kids and families going back to countries of origin, we always spend time getting to know the child. There is a consultation with the parents first, then with the parents and the child. The therapist who works with the child then does a six-session assessment to learn who the child is and how he thinks. We then meet again with the parents alone to get further insight. The therapist then works with the child to prepare for the trip.

We often talk about what other kids have said to us and what other kids do, because sometimes children feel disloyal if they voice their own interest in their birth family or country. We draw "Journey Maps" of their trip, tracking how they will get to their birth country and how they will get back to their forever home. We make a box for children to keep their feelings in, and provide a chance to understand more about those feelings, and how to regulate them. We offer an opportunity to learn how to identify feelings within one's body, and then how to describe feelings and take care of them.

We meet well before the trip and then have another six-session post-trip workshop with the child, after a meeting with the adults alone to talk about how the trip went.

The relationship that the child is forming with her therapist is an important "container" for thoughts, worries, and the processing of things that are going on internally. The child's therapist is always working with the child to figure out how to share these feelings with her parents, either on their own or in a family session.

Adoption Is Forever . . . And So Is One's Past

We want adoption to be forever. We want permanent plans for all of the children who are in the situation of needing parents other than those who gave them birth. In addition, we want children to feel connected and whole, as well as protected and loved. It is possible that a person who cannot parent can still love and be of importance to a child. We have a responsibility to keep children whole and to protect them only from danger and harm—not from the truth.

Return trips can help adopted children and their parents to learn and face the truth of a child's past and identity. A good therapist can help you and your child prepare for and process this experience—provided that the therapist has a deep understanding of the complexity and joy, as well as the challenges, losses, and possible traumas, that are an integral part of the story of adoptive families.

II

choosing GROUP *or* INDEPENDENT TRAVEL

The Group Travel Experience | 8

Andrea Williams

Early and often—that was my intention before adopting. We'd go back to China when my daughter was still very young and return every two or three years, traveling throughout the country. I'd never been to China, and even after the adoption trip, with most of our time spent in a very comfortable, very Western hotel room, I still felt as though I hadn't really been there. I wanted to explore rural China and I wanted my daughter to see the country before it changed too much, before its cities became not so different from others around the world. There were many places I hoped to explore with her, but I thought it was important that our first international trip be to her birth country.

Then I became a parent. A not-young, single, working parent of an only child. By the time I once again had brain space to even think about international travel, a few years had passed and my daughter was already four—time to get back to China. I knew that neither of us would enjoy spending several weeks without a playmate for her and an adult or two for me, and I also knew exactly who our travel companions should be: my daughter's oldest and dearest friend, who was adopted at the same time from the same orphanage, and her parents. The only problem turned out to be that they weren't on the same mental timetable as I was and felt no need to go back so soon. The concrete advantages of traveling with these friends trumped the abstract idea of returning early, so I decided to wait, hoping or imagining that I could persuade them to go the following year when our girls were five.

Well, my daughter turned five, six, seven, and each year I said, "*This* year we're going to China"—in the spring, in the fall, in the spring—and I believed that we would. I reluctantly accepted that the first trip might have to be without our good friends, yet no alternate companions presented themselves. So when my daughter started asking when *were* we going to go and saying that she really wanted to see what China was like, it was clearly time to swallow my independent traveler pride and just get us there. After repeatedly saying that I didn't want to do the Beijing-Xi'an-Panda thing, that's exactly what we did. Not long after my daughter turned eight, we at last returned to her birth country—a few years behind schedule—on an adoption homeland tour.

The Group Experience

Going with a tour meant not having to arrange *any*thing except getting my daughter's passport and scheduling pre-trip immunizations. We traveled just three or four months after making the decision to go. I booked our flights myself, but even that could have been done for me. It was almost effortless (alas, no one packed for me), and when we were in China I was able to simply be with my daughter rather than obsessively read guidebooks, plan our schedule and arrange activities. My daughter may have loved that aspect—just spending three weeks of focused time with me—as much as she liked seeing China.

We had a congenial and easygoing group of ten variously configured families, led by Michael Han, a charming and thoughtful Chinese man who lives in Oregon. Michael facilitated adoptions for years and now runs homeland tours. The thirteen girls in the group ranged in age from six to thirteen; none had previously been back to China. Three of the families were already friends and there were three sibling pairs, but only my daughter and another girl were from the same orphanage. In fact, learning about this girl had been the decisive factor when I debated joining this tour. Very, very few children are from their orphanage, and the opportunity to visit it with another girl who'd lived there at the same time was too good to pass up.

Having heard accounts of other homeland trips, I'd thought the girls might coalesce into a gang of sorts, and that did happen for some, though not for my daughter. She had fun playing with the other girls and wasn't excluded in any way, but she didn't develop any new friendships or bonds. Though she spent most of her time with me, when I asked her recently what she liked about being on the tour she immediately said, "all the other kids."

Everyone in the group got along well and there were no difficult personalities, but all those people added up to a pack of twenty-nine, a larger group than I'd have liked. Being so many meant that there wasn't much flexibility in our schedule, and we often spent significant time in a holding pattern while someone finished eating, used the bathroom, made a quick purchase, or got an ice cream.

In Xi'an, for example, we were a little behind schedule so had less than half an hour to bike on top of the city walls (which was really, really fun). We were all back on time, but didn't leave for another half hour while everyone used the bathroom or got lost and found, time I'd much rather have spent looking down on the old city from our tandem. And when the girls had their thrilling five minutes with a panda at the reserve in Wolong, there was one fewer panda than eager panda petters. My slightly reticent child didn't claim "her" panda quickly enough and had to share one, giving me a less intimate vicarious encounter than I'd hoped to have (though she didn't seem to mind, and if it hadn't cost $150, I might not have minded either).

On the other hand, being in a large group was occasionally an asset. For example, with at least ten other vegetarians in the group, our dumpling feast in Xi'an included a huge assortment of meatless dumplings in amazing shapes and flavors, ten times the variety I'd have been able to sample on my own. And when we took the overnight train from Beijing to Xi'an, our group nearly filled the sleeping car, creating a pajama party on rails. It was in the jam-packed Beijing train station waiting for that train that I was most glad to be in our tightly herded group, able to enjoy watching the masses of people around us instead of frantically trying to find my way among them.

The Benefit of Guides

Our tour leader, Michael, traveled with us. Although my sole travel problem was an ongoing search for Bank of China ATMs, the only kind that took my card, it was nice knowing that someone I trusted had assumed responsibility for my daughter and me. And Michael was fun to be around: smart, kind, funny, tireless and efficient, cheery even with a killer sinus infection. The girls loved him. He was a good cultural bridge as well, fluent in both American and Chinese cultures, with a dual perspective gained from living in the U.S. since grad school after growing up in Beijing. I could ask him *why* something was the way it was, and he would understand what I was asking in a way that local guides, immersed in their own culture, couldn't always do.

Being in a large group of American families pretty much ensured we wouldn't experience everyday Chinese culture directly (though we *were* living the ordinary Chinese travel experience, minus the matching group hats and bags). However, since I speak fewer than fifty words of Mandarin and my daughter wasn't willing to try her after-school Chinese, we weren't likely to have had many meaningful interactions on our own anyway. The local guides in each city (all of whom had worked with Michael before, some even from when he was facilitating adoptions) were our "real people" connection, and provided glimpses of ordinary life.

In Xi'an, our wonderful twenty-something guide talked about her experience in Xi'an's schools, describing the very long hours in school, homework into the wee hours, and the pressure she felt to do well. In another city, our mid-thirties guide told us about her own experience as a single adoptive mother. While she works, her father takes care of her young daughter in her home city, and her older brothers—who'd had no interest in *her* as a child—dote on their niece. And it was only after adopting her child that she learned from several neighbors that their children were adopted as well. I learned something about the health care system through another guide's story of her mother's recent illness and death; she felt fortunate that, unlike many families, she and her siblings had managed to pay for treatment and hospitalization for their mother.

Scheduled Days

Nothing was left to chance on our trip, which is probably true of any well-run Beijing-Xi'an-Panda-Shanghai (or variant) tour. Whether or not that's a positive feature depends on how you like to travel. It wasn't an adventure. I usually felt rushed in the morning and stalled at various points throughout the day. My daughter had trouble moving quickly from bed to breakfast, but once underway she didn't mind the staggered pace and the inevitable time in limbo.

Everything ran smoothly after the race to breakfast. Most days were scheduled from early morning (8:00 or 8:30) through dinner, sometimes beyond, leaving almost no time to explore on our own. Lunch was a long meal; I'd have preferred to spend some of that time just wandering around. Most days, our bus or vans went from one site to the next to the next, so I couldn't choose to skip the second stop, for example, in order to spend more time at the first.

It wasn't until I desperately needed a battery charger for my video camera that I left the group to find Chengdu's electronics hub. I realized then that I might have done the same thing in other instances, making arrangements to meet up via taxi in order to forgo the embroidery factory, say, and stay longer at the Summer Palace. Then again, my daughter might not have allowed it—when we were on our own in Beijing before the tour began, she hadn't trusted me to take us on the subway without getting lost! She liked the security of being with the group.

With the notable exception of a Chinese-style tour through the Forbidden City (we should have asked for a meeting place and explored by ourselves), the activities Michael had arranged were kid-tested and approved—making a clay figure in Xi'an, flying kites, visiting a Chengdu weekend "enrichment" center and joining a class there, visiting a Beijing kindergarten, and so on.

And though the daily schedule was pretty fixed, there was some flexibility in the overall itinerary. One family skipped Xi'an to go to a daughter's orphanage city. I arranged with Michael to go to Guilin instead of Shanghai for the last few days of the tour, and four other families decided to do the same. Being a smaller group allowed for a somewhat looser schedule, and one family even took a day off to just relax in the hotel.

Visiting the Orphanage

After the scheduled tour, every family went to their daughters' orphanage cities. Michael arranged these visits. I don't know how hard it would have been to do this on my own, but the next time we go back, even if we travel independently, I will have him do it again. On this part of the trip, I liked having all the logistics taken care of for me.

It was good to visit the orphanage and finding site with another family. Even though my daughter had seen the photos I took at her old orphanage (a different building than the current one), she was clearly taken aback by the actual place and actual children, which were decidedly *not* like the pictures in *I Love You Like Crazy Cakes*. When I'd asked her before going to China what she wanted to do when we went to her orphanage, she'd always said, "Play with the babies." Well, when the time came, she stood in the doorway rather than follow me into the rooms. Most of the toddlers and preschoolers now living in the Social Welfare Institute (SWI) have medical or other issues, and there are still very few caregivers. Being there with another girl who'd started life in the same institution and was now, like her, a thriving and cherished daughter living far away, normalized the experience somewhat. And they had each other to play with outside, while their parents spent more (heartbreaking) time looking around inside.

We spent two nights and one day in their city, which was not long enough. One more day would have been good. The orphanage and finding site visits, plus a trip to a department store to buy clothes for the children at the SWI, took up the entire day. There was only about half an hour to walk around the city and try to get a sense of the place; it's on the coast, but we didn't even see the water until a quick detour on our way out of town the next morning. I wonder if we'd have been able to get more information—the adoptive parent's holy grail—from the SWI director if we'd had another day, or to glean something, anything, from a trip to the police station. Next time we'll try, though it may be too late to learn more, if indeed there ever was anything more to tell.

Adding Time to the Trip Pre- or Post-Tour

About half of the families added time on their own in China, either before or after the scheduled tour. My daughter and I spent four and a half days in Beijing before the tour started, and some of my favorite memories of our trip are from those days, when we walked and walked and walked all over (since my daughter didn't allow us to take the subway). We stayed in a traditional courtyard hotel that straddled the border of old and new Beijing: turn left into *hutong*, right to modern street and shops, and straight ahead to an empty lot waiting for its skyscraper. A bicycle repairman was the first person we'd see when we stepped through the great wooden door to the street. We had relaxed breakfasts, ate too-salty octopus on *Wangfujing* snack street, hung out in parks and playgrounds, managed to order meatless dumplings (laughs all around) at a teensy dumpling stand in a *hutong,* and pedaled a boat into a fierce head wind on Qianhai Lake. We had a great time, but after four days my daughter was eager for the arrival of the other kids. And for me, having had those days to just wander and absorb the city a little on our own made it easier to enjoy the structured time that followed.

The Right Choice, This Time

I'm not a convert to tour travel, but the tour that we took turned out to be a great choice for our first trip to China. My daughter enjoyed everything, which is what matters most. When I felt frustrated by group logistics, I reminded myself that this was our introduction to China, a glimpse of some highlights and greatest hits, to be followed by other trips made on our own in my own style of travel. And I learned some things that will make those trips easier—sometimes I'll want to hire guides, for example, even if just to negotiate the train station, and I've really got to learn some Mandarin. I don't *intend* to travel by tour again, but who knows? Expedience may dictate otherwise. Meanwhile, it has been two years since we were in China, I have Mandarin lessons on my iPod, and I'm beginning to plan our next adventure. Now it's time to convince our friends to come, too.

On Our Own

9

Adventures in Independent Travel

Debra Jacobs

Aside from some group adventure trips on bicycles or skis, I've always traveled unencumbered. From back-packing around Europe when I was younger to putting panniers on my bike and riding from Boston to the Berkshires, my inclinations have consistently leaned towards independent travel.

My two adoption trips, of course, proved the exceptions to the rule. On those trips I focused on my babies and gratefully allowed others to plan the itinerary and take care of all logistics. My travel mates and I got on and off the bus, followed the guides, and rarely ventured alone farther than a few blocks from the hotel. Instead of soaking up the local culture, we completed paperwork and fed, changed and cooed at our babies.

When I adopted my older daughter in 1999, a student of mine urged me to contact his wife, who had not yet immigrated to the U.S. She was a TV reporter in one of the cities we visited. I called her when we arrived at the hotel and arranged for her to meet me at our room. I thought we'd walk a block or two to a local restaurant and then I'd be able to drop into bed; I was exhausted and my baby had a bad cold. She had another idea. She wanted us to experience the "real" China, so she drove us two hours out of town to a restaurant overlooking a river, where my mom and I were the only Westerners in sight. On any other trip I would have loved this—even the breath-stopping U-turn she made on a major highway—but on that trip I just wanted to move in the comfort and safety of our group.

Planning for our family's first return trip when my girls were eight and four years old, I knew I wanted a different experience. There would be no new babies this time, only my children and one other family, close friends of ours whose children, ages eight and five, were best buddies with mine. We would be spending part of the time with my older daughter's beloved Chinese Culture Group leader, who was living in Beijing for the year. She would show us around Beijing; then she and her friend would accompany us to the orphanages, acting as translators and guides. For the rest of our trip we would be on our own.

On this trip I did want some of the comforts of home. Staying in Western-style hotels seemed important; I thought my kids would need this comfort after all of the demands put on them by being in a new and different place—and the emotional challenges my older daughter, at least, would certainly face as she visited the country of her birth and the place where she spent the first eight months of her life. But other than that, I wanted to be in China, not in an American bubble in China. I wanted to be able to wander around and not have to be on a bus at a certain time, and to change my plans if we wanted to stay longer somewhere or cut short our visit somewhere else. Independent travel was the only way.

The Importance of Friends

For our family, traveling with friends was crucial. As a single parent, I would have felt compelled to join a group tour if the other family hadn't joined us, if for no other reason than to quell fears of worst-case scenarios (Who will take care of my children if I get sick? What will I do if my money or passport is lost or stolen?). Sharing the trip with good friends—laughing with them, puzzling together through cultural or language misunderstandings, supporting each other through the emotional bumps that go with the territory—made my experience so much richer.

My children would also have had a very different experience if they hadn't been with their friends. They would surely have fought more. Instead, when the younger ones got too tired to walk, the older ones offered piggyback rides, preventing meltdowns when parents weren't able to carry them. The younger ones danced together, made tents out of blankets in the hotel rooms, and engaged with each other in hours and hours of imaginary play. While there were some moments of jealousy and perceived unfairness, the older ones mostly laughed and played together. They supported each other through upsets, often in nonverbal ways. I'll never forget one of them silently rubbing the other's back in the van after an emotionally difficult finding-site visit.

Planning

Planning the trip was half the fun. The two families had more pre-trip dinners together than I can count; after dinner, children played while adults looked up plane and train schedules, hashed out itineraries, pored over maps, made lists of everything we wanted to see and do—and then, slowly and painfully, eliminated many of those places as unrealistic goals in the time we had. Our calendars had more cross-outs than a third grader's math homework.

Adults in the two families worked together to agree on a philosophy of travel: while we had by necessity many places to go, including three orphanage cities and Beijing, we wanted some time just to be, to wander around, to discover. We didn't want to say, "It's Tuesday. We must be in Xi'an." We also wanted to combine urban experiences and the high emotion of the orphanage visits with the peace and beauty of at least one of China's many outdoor, scenic places where we could hike, the children could run along paths in the woods, and we could relax and recharge.

One planning item to keep in mind: If you will be visiting your child's orphanage, you can't just show up. You must notify them in advance and make sure it's okay to come on the date you want. Some provinces are now charging a fee to returning families for the privilege of visiting the orphanage. One way to arrange the orphanage visit is to contact Our Chinese Daughters Foundation (OCDF). You don't have to go on a group tour with them; they will plan just the orphanage part for you if you like, and provide a guide.

I went to the e-mail list for families with children from my daughter's orphanage and asked if anyone knew someone in Changsha who could arrange the visit for me. There, I found out about a travel agent in Changsha who used to arrange adoption trips; now most of her work is to help families on return trips. She was fantastic. She contacted the orphanage, made all my requests (Would we be able to meet any of my daughter's caregivers? Could we look in her file?). She also arranged transportation for us for the two-hour drive out to the orphanage city.

Think about some of the things you want to do, not just where you want to visit. We thought our older girls would enjoy seeing what school was like for children their age in China, so I asked the travel agent if she could arrange this. She connected us with someone who works for the local education department, who arranged for us to visit a school for migrant workers' children. This school had never had visitors before. Our girls didn't get to see a typical school day, but boy, did they feel feted. The teachers and children made them the guests of honor, showing them Chinese games and songs and showering them with gifts as confetti flew out of a cardboard tube. Because we were traveling independently and didn't have a slew of other people with us, the experience was up-close and immediate, and that night we were able to meet some of the teachers and their children for dinner.

Making Mistakes

Unless you speak Mandarin and have lived in China, you will likely make a mistake or two if you travel independently. Ours made for some laughs and good stories.

One mistake we made was in our planning for in-China transportation. We had the romantic notion that we would take the overnight train from Changsha to Nanchang. There was one such train a day. What we didn't realize was that this train was nothing like the luxurious Beijing to Xi'an overnighter, with sleeper cars and Western-style toilets. When our friends, acting as guides and translators, went to get tickets for us, they learned that it was standing-room-only: there were no seats on this train. Can you imagine sitting on your suitcases in a crowded train car for several hours, overnight, with four tired children? We couldn't, so we spent more money than anticipated and hired a driver.

We also had no idea what it would be like buying train tickets. It's *very* different from buying tickets in the U.S.: no polite line in the Amtrak station, but a huge crowd jostling for a space at the window. And so many windows! Which one was right? We did take a couple of trains, and the experience was lovely, but it would have been very difficult without our Chinese-speaking friends. They also warned us about the scene in the train station—just put your head down and forge ahead. My four-year-old nearly got trampled. But the rides themselves were wonderful, including the scenery, the man selling socks (who set them on fire to demonstrate their fire-retardant qualities), and the many people we met along the way who were curious about our families and wanted to talk and take pictures with us.

Another mistake we made was common to Americans: packing too much stuff in suitcases that were too big. When you travel in a group, you can throw your oversized bags in the back of the van and forget about them. When you travel independently, especially on trains, you have to lug them for what seems like miles. I never felt more like an ugly American than when I stepped onto a train and several accommodating people helped me lift my big suitcase onto the overhead rack. They were all carrying small bags. Next time I will lay out everything I want to bring, and then leave half of it home. I will also pack three small bags—one for me and one each for my kids—instead of bringing one big suitcase for the three of us.

One other gaffe we made was in poor planning for our in-the-woods hiking experience. We had selected Lushan, a UNESCO World Heritage site in the mountains a couple of hours drive from Nanchang. Lushan was where Mao summered and was, we read, a popular destination for Chinese people but few Westerners. We looked at photos on the Internet and it seemed exactly what we wanted: footpaths and wooden bridges, huge waterfalls and sparkling lakes. So we asked the travel agent who had helped us arrange the orphanage visit to book us a couple of rooms at a hotel there. (Note: Our travel agent was based in Changsha, Hunan Province; Lushan is in Jiangxi. I don't think the travel agent had ever been there.)

After traveling all morning on a train, we had arranged for a driver to meet us at the train station and take us straight to Lushan. Our Chinese-speaking friends had by that time left us on our own. Of the three adults remaining in our party, one friend had the most Mandarin (about 100 words). She sat in the front of the van and tried to make conversation with the driver. "Lushan is very beautiful, yes?" she said, using her phrase book to find the words she didn't know. He looked at her like she was a bit gaga. "I must have said it incorrectly," she said. Hmm.

So we drove and drove until we finally reached the foot of the mountain. This was March; it was cold and damp, and starting to get dark and to rain as we began our climb. The hairpin turns were a fabulous adventure to some of us (mostly those aged eight and under) and caused breath-stopping terror in others. After nearly an hour of climbing, we pulled up in front of the hotel. My friend went in to register while the rest of us stayed in the van. She came out a few minutes later. "They turned on the lights for me when I walked in," she said. "There's no heat. It doesn't look like anyone else is staying here."

No one had clued us in to the fact that "off season" in Lushan meant "almost completely closed down."

Much to the chagrin of one of my friends, who wanted to head right back down the mountain and into the city, we decided to spend the night. After traveling all day long, there was no way I was going to head back down a steep mountain with a bunch of tired and hungry kids in the dark and the rain. After carrying our bags up the stairs and finding our (freezing) rooms, we went down to the restaurant to get some food. Again, they turned the lights on when we entered. Using the trusty phrase book, we ordered some food and a couple of beers and took them back up to the room. The adults looked at each other, and the absurdity of our mistake hit us in a wave of laughter that verged on uncontrollable. Although I had only taken one sip of beer, one of my daughters turned to me and said, “Mommy, I think you better stop drinking beer.”

One thing this experience made clear was the importance of having a working cell phone (you can rent one for the time you are in China), and if you are without a guide, making sure you have the phone numbers of people who can help you out of a jam. We were very thankful to be able to reach our travel agent in Changsha and have her speak with the hotel staff both in Lushan and Nanchang to change our reservations.

Another thing our adventure in Lushan brought home to me was our pampered life as Americans and our horror when, for example, we didn’t have heat for just one night. The workers in the hotel were dressed like Michelin Tire men, in layer upon layer upon layer. Instead of just bucking up in the cold and dressing warmly, we couldn’t wait to get back to the city, and heat, and being taken care of.

Lushan *was* spectacularly beautiful. We went for a walk in the morning before our driver arrived to take us back to the city. The houses were unique and lovely. The scenery was spectacular. I want to go back on our next trip—in the summer, of course.

Just Wandering

The next morning our driver came for us and we headed back down into Nanchang. The Gloria Hotel never saw guests so happy to arrive. Instead of spending two days in Lushan and three in Nanchang, we spent five days tooling around the city. We never got the hiking and in-the-woods experience we had hoped for, but we loved having so much unplanned time to explore the city’s streets and parks. We found whole segments of city blocks devoted to specific enterprises: spinning yarn, for example, or glass cutting. My children's favorite was what they called "Candy Street," shop after shop after shop selling—you guessed it—candy.

Just walking around for several days was a luxury not often available on a tour. Not just walking around, but walking around with only a few other Americans instead of being cocooned in a group. We spent the better part of a day strolling around People's Park, taking our time to play on the exercise equipment ubiquitous throughout China (meant for adults, but our kids loved them). The two older girls went bungee jumping, one of the highlights of their trip. The bungee cords were attached to the top of a huge metal frame. The vendor pulled down the cords, strapped the girls in (one at a time), then yanked down hard and let them rip. Whoo-eee!

Food was also fun on our own, and we appreciated the fact that once our Chinese-speaking friends left us, we had the adventure of scoping out our own restaurants. We found a favorite place not far from our hotel and went there several nights in a row. The phrase book helped a lot with ordering, but we also pointed to dishes on other customers' tables and on the menu when it was illustrated. We didn't always get what we thought we had ordered, but what we got was always delicious.

Meeting People

One of our main goals as independent rather than group travelers was to meet and interact with people in China whenever possible. Before we left for China, we had made as many Chinese contacts as we could: acquaintances of acquaintances, friends of friends of friends, whoever might be interested in getting together with two American families traveling in their country. On several stops along the way these contacts welcomed us warmly. We were invited to share a typical Shanghai feast (including blood soup); taken on an "insider's" shopping spree in Nanchang; and welcomed into the family home of my younger daughter's "big brother," where we enjoyed a delicious Korean-Chinese-American dinner. (We participate in a university "Big Sibling" program, where Chinese college students pair with children adopted from China.)

We also had spontaneous encounters with people everywhere we went—on trains, in parks, in stores, and in the hotels. In Beijing and Shanghai no one paid us much attention; people in those cities were used to having Westerners in town and with a few exceptions seemed generally unfazed by seeing us with Chinese children. Outside of these large cities, however, we were the main attraction.

Many of the conversations we had with people would not have happened if we had been in a large group surrounded by other Americans. For example, we wandered into a tea store to buy a couple of pots and cups as gifts. With our few words of Mandarin and her nonexistent English, we "conversed" with the proprietor. She invited us into the back of the store and spent the next half hour showing us the proper way to make and serve tea. I don't think more than the three adults and four children in our party would have fit around her small table.

In many of the places we visited, the swarms of people staring at us, asking questions, and even touching the children sometimes seemed overwhelming. At times our children were okay with all the attention and at other times it seemed too much. As much as we adults wanted to stay and communicate with people on the street, we respected our children's need for privacy and abruptly ended conversations when that's what the kids needed us to do. I reminded myself that I wasn't being rude; I was simply protecting my children.

Safety

The crime rate in China is low, although reportedly on the rise. We felt safe walking city streets at night, with so many people out and about. In crowds, however, be aware of your belongings. Our first day in Shanghai we stopped to listen to a band playing on the wide sidewalk outside of a hotel. Our four- and five-year-olds started to dance, and my friend took out her camera to photograph them. Soon a crowd gathered around the kids and became tighter and tighter. We pushed our way in to grab the children, and when we looked up, the camera was gone.

One Step Closer

A group tour would certainly have made the logistics of our trip easier, and if we had been without our friends it would have provided playmates for the children and adult companionship for me. Yet independent travel helped me to feel one step closer to China. I have no illusions that I, or my children, "know" China; that would only be possible if we lived there for many years. Yet by going it alone, making mistakes, sometimes stepping out of our comfort zone, interacting with people and figuring it out for ourselves, we at least made a beginning. Hopefully, we'll do it again. And again. And again.

The Independent Travel Option /10

Unexpected Joys and Complexities of a Personalized Adoption Journey

David Youtz

Chinese Culture and Adoption Issues Intertwined

I believe in heritage visits to China for the same reasons I believe in involvement for adoptive families in Families with Children from China and similar communities. During the years I served as President of FCC of Greater New York (2000–2007), I was frequently asked why the China adopting community feels it is so important to include China and Chinese culture in the lives of our children. Sometimes the question was, "Is there such a thing as *too much* China involvement?" Or, "Has this gone too far?"

We involve our children in Chinese culture because their ethnicity is a real part of who they are and how the world will see them. Through involvement in language and arts classes, holiday celebrations, parades, and heritage visits, we are honoring and acknowledging our children's origins in China, and rejecting the idea that coming from China or being Chinese is second to any other possibility.

Additionally, with so much negative Western news coverage of China, we want our children to have a balanced and proud understanding of their country of origin as a place both dark and light, with poverty and immense challenges, but also with brilliance, culture, and rich history.

Inclusion of culture arose in our community as our understanding of the complex dynamics of adoption also increased: We do this for reasons of self-empowerment, pride, and confidence. In other words, our celebration of Chinese culture is also motivated by our desire to get adoption right. Unlike earlier generations, when parents hid adoption from the world or glossed over it, we take pride in our status (and the transracial aspect of our families would anyway make it foolish to pretend otherwise). At some future point, we also want our children to have the option to search for birthparents if they so choose, with enough language and cultural awareness to make this possible, and to enable their own reconnections with the country of their birth.

At the more day-to-day level, coming together through cultural activities enables kids to know other families that look like theirs and lets parents and kids compare and share their experiences. It also connects kids to Chinese-Americans who might serve as role models or friends. At the same time, we strive to keep the normal balance of any family and, most importantly, follow what best serves the needs of our individual child or children.

Does all this run the risk of being *too much*? That depends, since every family is different, and cultural resources and circumstances vary enormously. Yet I think I understand the reason behind the question. These kids have multiple parts to their identities: adopted person, American, Chinese-born, Chinese-American, boy/girl, soccer player, Barbie fan, horseback rider. Do we do the right thing as parents when we heavily emphasize one part of this identity? This question only increases with the child's age, especially approaching the teen years when the child may ask not to be involved, or gets too busy with other activities, or starts to feel that "Chinese-ness" is yet another thing, in addition to adoption, that keeps him or her from fitting in.

Still, we know that our children must learn to become not only adopted adults, but Chinese Americans. Involvement in Chinese culture and language learning—and heritage trips—can help them along that path.

Heritage visits, which serve as both adoption journey and family vacation, can raise this self-exploration to the next, more mature level. Starting in 2005, FCC of Greater New York began holding an annual event to focus on heritage visits, encouraging and assisting families to go beyond other ways of engaging Chinese culture and to undertake trips to China, and—crucially—to help parents think through the complexities of these visits for the child.

Neither Distant Nor Exotic

In the case of my family, we already were involved with China long before we adopted. My wife and I had both lived in northern China and studied Mandarin before we met in a China studies Master's degree program. We got married and moved to Hong Kong for work (from 1991 to 1996), which included frequent travel in China. Late in our time in Hong Kong we decided to adopt, and China adoption seemed for us an obvious choice.

In the early 1990s, the Hong Kong press carried dire reports about the conditions in Chinese orphanages, and we felt we were well prepared to provide a life for a child that included close connections to her birth culture. For us, China was neither distant nor exotic, and we were experienced enough to know how hard it is to "know" China. We adopted a six-month-old baby in 1995 and lived with her in Hong Kong for another year, then moved back to the United States.

My daughter did most of her growing up in a town in New Jersey with a strong East Asian population and close proximity to New York City. She became a girl with strong American and Jersey/New York identities: a big fan of the Yankees and Radio Z-100, and of Polly Pocket toys and dress-ups, a good traveler, and sociable and at home with a widely diverse (racially and otherwise) group of friends. Like her Chinese-American friends, she joined (and resisted) Saturday Chinese school and participation in the local Chinese community's Lunar New Year programs. She appeared to have a strong sense of her own identity, and a clear sense of where her home was, but the Chinese aspect of her identity was harder to pin down. If anything, we worried that things Chinese might seem to belong more to her non-Chinese Mom and Dad than to her.

Choosing Independent Travel

We planned a return visit to China when my daughter was eight and had both some maturity around her adoption story and some Mandarin language that would enable her to engage with what she saw. The idea was a trip in the company of our Chinese-American sister-in-law that would include time in the homes of her family members in northern China, as well as some travel and a visit to my daughter's hometown in southern China. Alas, the SARS crisis in 2003 scuttled those plans and we rescheduled the visit for the following summer. Our sister-in-law not being available then, we chose to make the trip just as our family alone, rather than joining a tour—and I came to understand clearly both the pros and cons of that choice. Being independent meant flexibility and choosing our own timing, destinations, and purposes for the visit.

The goal for the trip was to reacquaint our daughter with China. She had heard about China her whole life, from her parents' stories and from friends and movies. She had seen the images in our albums about her adoption and our visit to meet her. Now we wanted to make China three-dimensional and real, so that it would belong to her. We wanted to give her opportunities to confront whatever negative or positive stereotypes she had accumulated about her country of origin. We hoped, in particular, to encourage familiarity and pride in the beautiful province she comes from, Guangxi Zhuang Autonomous Region.

We also, naturally, looked forward to a fun family experience together, having earlier enjoyed family travel in the U.S. and Italy. These days, with some planning, American families can travel independently without much difficulty, and we had the benefit of speaking Mandarin and having past China travel experience. My daughter's age also seemed fortuitous, since she had entered a new, more curious stage regarding her own adoption almost immediately upon turning nine.

We chose as a family to leave until later the decision to visit her orphanage or not, since we felt she had a right to at least some control over her own story and the more complicated parts of a visit. There were some practical considerations that guided our choices, as well: We had friends to see in Hong Kong and Beijing; we wanted our daughter to see some of our favorite sites, like the Forbidden City in Beijing and the Li River in Guilin; I wanted to add a return visit of my own to the northern city where I had worked in the early 1980s; and we had to fit the trip into work and other schedules.

One of the obvious benefits of traveling in a tour—especially those tours now available that cater to adoptive families—is having a coterie of kids your child can hang out with. We lacked that, and my daughter certainly would have loved the friendship. On the other hand, we had an extraordinary family adventure that belonged just to us. My daughter got up close to a water buffalo, cycled around the walls of an old walled city with Mom, and tried every kind of Chinese food. She learned how to take photographs, enjoyed swimming pools as long as she wanted on hot days, came to loathe Chinese mosquitoes, and to love the inexpensive stuffed animals that were available. She learned that they have Wal-Marts and Starbucks in China, and she tried speaking Chinese with local people (including trying to explain that, "Yes, these are my Mom and Dad; I'm adopted.").

We had some unforgettable adventures, including eating lunch in a small house in the countryside where frogs were jumping across the cement floor, and getting stuck deep inside a scary cave outside of Guilin when all the lights went out. China is astoundingly diverse, and I think independent travel gets you closer to real life than does a tour. You are much less insulated from the frustrations of travel and odd encounters, but that after all is part of what you want to experience, so you get to know China in all its facets, strange and wonderful and difficult.

Demystifying and Momentous

We did, in the end, visit the city where my daughter spent her first six months, and the orphanage and workers who took care of her. At the last minute, before flying to Nanning in Guangxi, she became very anxious—which was a surprise, I suppose, even though we had tried to anticipate her worries. It was also an important opportunity to talk. Once we arrived in Nanning, she decided she did want to visit the orphanage, but chose *not* to try to meet the foster mother, whom we had met briefly nine years before. In retrospect, I think there may have been confusion about the term "foster mother"—so close to "birth mother"—or maybe this was a way for her to take a little control and postpone until a future time a part of her story that made her anxious. In either case, we respected her choice.

I know many adult adopted persons counsel that parents should let the child (or young adult) own the decision of whether or not to do a search, and therefore should not force the issue while the child is young. That makes sense to me; however, the incredible pace of change in China's towns and cities has also prompted some adoptive parents to undertake a search now rather than wait a decade or more, when many traces of a child's origins may well have been swept away forever. In our case, we took a step towards making the town and orphanage familiar and demystified, without pushing beyond what she was comfortable with at that moment. Being independent travelers gave us as much flexibility as we needed.

With her decision made, we proceeded to have a momentous visit to the orphanage. It turned out that the orphanage founder and the head nurse remembered our daughter—she had been one of the first babies in their new facility in 1995—and that was an unexpected and happy dose of celebrity for her. We had a chance to tour the building, including the wing for special-needs children, a specialty of this orphanage. Seeing these children was a sobering new experience for my daughter (yet another issue to discuss and prepare a child for in advance).

The main baby room, however, was a delight, and my wife and daughter cooed over the extraordinary cuteness in crib after crib. My daughter had rarely shown much interest in babies and never really warmed to the idea of our adopting a little sibling, so I was surprised to hear her gush about how cute the babies were, and then volunteer that she might after all want to adopt a baby sister. A few moments later the founding director of the orphanage took us to see a surprising sight: infant triplets who had just arrived several weeks before—the orphanage's first triplets. And my wife and daughter immediately (and a little later, myself . . .) fell in love with the new idea of bringing those triplet girls into our family and trying to ensure that these sisters were kept together in one family. We talked about this idea for the remaining week of our China visit.

Most heritage trips do not result in an inspiration to adopt again (although Dads should beware of visits to the baby rooms!), much less the idea of adding triplets to your family. The year after the trip was filled with the headaches of the application process and the anxiety-causing likelihood that this unusual adoption would not be possible. To our delight and amazement, we were ultimately matched with the triplet girls we had hoped for and found ourselves making another kind of return visit a year and some months after the first. This time our entourage included other family members to help with our audacious undertaking, and there was little time for tourism or long family conversations. Fortunately, our older daughter remained committed to the idea of this new adoption and another big adventure. My wife's formulation was that this was all about sisters: adopting sisters for our first daughter, and keeping the triplet sisters together to grow up with each other and with a new fellow-Guangxi sister. We brought our expanded family home in the fall of 2005—the year that turned out to be the all-time high point of China adoptions to American families.

Choosing to Move to Asia

There has been a further adventure in our family on top of these: A year and a half after bringing the triplet toddlers home, I was recruited to take a new job in Hong Kong. This was not an easy decision, since adopting our triplets had been predicated in part on the stable environment and good support community we had established in our town in New Jersey. On the other hand, we had always nurtured the idea of living and working again in Asia, and the job was with a wonderful nonprofit organization involved with adoption and the care of women and children in crisis in Hong Kong and China. The issue that helped tip the balance for us was the opportunity for our daughters to grow up in a Chinese city surrounded by other Asians and with many opportunities to re-encounter China.

I remembered watching my daughter during our first heritage visit, when she was mesmerized by seeing that everyone in the ads and drama on TV, and even Chinese-language MTV, were Chinese: For the first time, everyone who was cool, successful, or powerful looked like her. I remembered her in the middle of Beijing turning to tell us, with a sly smile, that we were the only people in the whole street who were not Chinese. For those Dads or Moms who might suspect that this is not a real issue for our transracially adopted kids, a heritage trip can suggest otherwise. So we moved to Hong Kong and have begun to integrate ourselves into new schools and work, new circles of friends, and new identities.

III

making CONNECTIONS *in China*

Roots and Routes

11

A Narrative in Belonging

Sheena Macrae

Roots, Routes and Belonging

Roots and routes—I love this play on words from Scottish sociologist David McCrone. What does it offer our children adopted from China, in terms of their sense of identity and visits back to China? McCrone argues that we all can shape our paths forward, choosing our routes in life—despite our roots. Yet isn't this counterintuitive? Surely, roots are more important? But think about it: Our adopted children from China have damaged or unknown roots. Their development and understanding of their pre-adoptive history are often arrested by fragmentary knowledge of their early lives and of the facts that led to their abandonment.

McCrone's emphasis on the importance of a person's *routes* in life is a useful tool for building our children's self-esteem and sense of identity. It is a healing view of life, and in the long term offers children an autonomous role in shaping their own destinies. And in looking at the routes our children may take, I believe that multiple trips back to where their *roots* once grew enhance the possibility of building new *routes* forward.

Belonging

Making multiple return trips may not be right for every family, either economically or emotionally. In my family, we plan for our trips by stringent saving. We also prepare through lifestory work based on experiences, photos, and DVDs of previous trips. For us, return trips are the right thing to do. Annual trips have helped my daughters strengthen their sense of belonging to our family and have allowed them to gain a degree of comfort and familiarity with China and their first communities of care. Our return visits have given them access to continuing layers of their stories in the present so they can really work out their sense of belonging—they can explore their roots, and can begin to build routes, for themselves.

There are different sorts of belonging. For many adopted children, there can be self-belonging, reliance simply on oneself, as a child erects a wall defending her core self from the world. That shows a hurt self. Both of my daughters, to varying degrees, once displayed this sense of belonging.

To help children move into a more secure sense of belonging, many adoptive parents realize the benefits of creating lifebooks. We help our children with their stories, co-creating the stories with them. In facing the "tough stuff" of their losses with our kids, we create for them the sense that they can explore this difficult emotional terrain from the safety of our storytelling laps.

Facing this "tough stuff" with my kids took my understanding of belonging to a new level. I came to see that however much co-created, a story made up by an adult hijacks the child's view. And so we went back to China within a year of adopting. These early trips in which the children saw their memories come alive convinced them, as one of my daughters said, that they "were not lying in their heads." And I came to see that my children needed vital, live, real connections in China to their past—which they could view through the lens of childhood, year by year, with new views and perspectives, created as often as we had money to take them back.

So that is why I am writing "a narrative in belonging." All of us make sense of who we are by creating a story about our lives. It's what gives us self-esteem—or not. In going back on numerous trips to China with my children, I've come to understand that their sense of belonging—and our identity as a family—grows stronger the more they know of their roots. Going back, paradoxically, has shaped their routes forward to becoming strong, resilient, and balanced children; it has given them a real sense of their own stories. It has essentially created a living lifebook.

While we as parents are making the decision to return to China each year, it's clear that on those trips our children are in the lead, despite being relatively young. The creation of a "living lifebook" allows them to take the lead in reviewing and recreating their stories as new facts and differing perspectives emerge during each trip. And I think these trips have accelerated the development of their ability to reflect and comment on their own roots, as they experience the way things are now in the places of their birth and their first communities of care.

Learning How to Belong

When we adopted our elder daughter in 1998, our first thoughts as anxious first-time parents were naturally to "make her ours." But as we walked as strangers in the city that housed her SWI, her first community of care—and as we learned that it was so young a city that only the children there were its natives—our thinking changed. We saw that her belonging to us could only thrive if we gave her a continuing connection to the city and SWI community that had raised her to toddlerhood. For this community had given her a chance to seize at routes when they sent her papers to the CCAA as a child to be placed by international adoption. With this understanding, so began our commitment to returning to our children's first communities of care, which we have done annually ever since.

Building Connections

Families often worry about what is an appropriate age to take a child back to China and to visit their SWI. Perhaps there's no more a good answer to this question than there is to the question, "How long is a piece of string?" We've found, however, enormous benefit in taking the children back to visit as soon as we could. In fact, we were delighted when we discovered that our daughters were confused about how close Guangzhou was to our home in Guildford, U.K. To them, places in England and in China were simply places that our family knew. As they've grown our daughters have learned how to locate these places, psychologically as well as geographically.

We've made our multiple trips to China as a family. It is simply what our family does; it is part of who we are. It's about revisiting communities that raised our children, and letting the children see for themselves their roots in the children living there today, and in the carers, the doctors and the officials.

What did we do to prepare for visits? Before our first trips to either child's SWI, we began by establishing contact. We sent photographs, we copied the post-placement reports to the SWI, and we sent copies of the children's British Citizenship certificates. We kept the orphanage files vital. In fact, when my older daughter saw her file at age three on her first visit, she was fascinated how these strangers had photos of both her and us in the big envelope!

One advantage of making multiple visits to your child's SWI is that nothing need be hurried, especially on your first visit. There is time to explore relationships, to get a feel for when further questions aren't appropriate. There's time to savor the places where the children were raised, to learn to "read" those places with the mindset of the people who work there. There's time for trust to grow between us and our contacts in China. We've come to understand that it's a very privileged place to be in when orphanage staff will answer direct queries or let us look at our daughters' paperwork. And it takes years to reach that level of trust; at least for us, it did.

Going Back . . . and Back . . . and Back

Why are multiple visits important for our children? Well, for one of my daughters, the import of our first visit sailed right over the top of her head. But she loved being in China and was perfectly comfortable in meeting with the SWI staff.

The second visit, when she was four, was very different. The staff at the SWI wanted to claim her; they called her by her Chinese name and wanted to take her from us, for a walk. A child whose attachment to us was not complete, she found being pulled back to the SWI staff overwhelming. Over the night that followed, she was engulfed in a huge meltdown of emotion. But we found the child who woke the next morning was ours—she claimed us and her place in our family. How did she do this? She made it clear she was her British self, called herself by her British name (which translates her Chinese name, meaning 'purple flower'), and refused her Chinese name.

Was she rejecting part of her identity by wanting her British and not her Chinese name? Names, after all, are very much a part of identity and belonging. No. Rather, it was clear she was working to make sense of her two names—did they name two different selves in the one child? We were relaxed; we had the whole of the year between trips—and the next trip—in which to find out. And we used the time to make sure the SWI knew how our daughter had struggled with their calling her by her Chinese name.

My younger daughter made her first trip back at age two. She toddled her way delightedly round her big sister's city and SWI. But on the way to her own institute, a long drive of five hours, she became less sunny. Was it the drive? Was it the white van? (We found later that she'd been taken from the SWI in a similar white van.) Was the anticipation—that something important was happening—palpable? When big sister changed seats after a toilet trip, my little one was in despair. "Where Dedda?" she called, until she saw her sister ensconced in a different row of the van.

And so we were glad to arrive. The SWI staff was reserved initially, but welcoming. My little daughter clung to me while the managers and I talked of her finding place; the place that professional searchers had suggested to us was wrong, apparently. Out came the SWI log-in book, listing, in careful calligraphy, entrants to the SWI by date, finder and finding place . . . and the SWI staff instantly offered to take us there.

And so the good-byes began; the children upstairs were called to wave good-bye. And that's when the transformation of my daughter began. She realized she was leaving with us, that she belonged with us. I suddenly understood. With a bittersweet understanding of her feelings—and some sense of the feelings of the waving children up on the balcony—I heard my daughter call to them, as she pointed at me: "MY Mum-mum." Roots and routes and belonging.

My older daughter clung closer, too, and we learned another lesson that trip: SWI visits can be invasive and destabilize the children who remain. Our children had left there the day they were adopted, and they leave again after each trip. What does that do to the hearts of the children who remain in the institution? So in going back to visit the children's institutions, I am conscious of not wanting to parade my children's place with us in front of children who haven't been adopted. We simply don't ask to visit the children who remain; we allow the SWI staff to steer us to who and what we may see. Balancing our need to see with respect for, and very few demands on, the staff is, I think, a responsibility of the families who go back as repeat returners. Paradoxically, this respect has won us perhaps more permitted insights than if we had demanded them.

Finding Places

Visiting a child's finding place with one's children stirs up a feeling that has no words. It locates the children, perhaps (for not all the official finding places are genuine), to the final connection with the person who placed them there. There may be dust and dirt; there may be an anguished thought: "Why here, for heaven's sake? This is not a safe place to leave a child." And certainly I have felt that. My older daughter, when finding a dead frog in her finding place, said, "At least, Mum, that isn't me." But later visits bring a better understanding of busy, dirty roads and seemingly inappropriate places. Wherever there are people passing, there is hope for a baby left there. Someone found my daughter, someone took a minute to look, to see her, to bend down and take her to the local police. She was lifted away from the fate of the frog. Just so, my younger daughter was lifted away from the side of a dusty road.

Going back on multiple visits has also helped my children explore with growing understanding that most children in China don't need adoption, let alone international adoption. They have seen some of the circumstances that may lead to relinquishment and abandonment, but they've also seen how families do, mostly, stick together. They've seen begging, poverty, substance abuse, and poor housing conditions. These are tough scenes to witness, but they exist in a larger context. They've also seen Chinese children going to school and playing in nurseries or parks. They've jostled in a queue for tickets for rides in the parks, blown bubbles with Chinese children, and shared balloons with them.

At times, these experiences have made my older daughter very angry that she wasn't considered "worth keeping" by her birthparents. At the same time, both children have had the opportunity to see what it is like to struggle with poverty and disability, to see some of the living conditions in areas where they might have grown up. I've heard my daughters say, "Mum, it must be hard to live there, I am glad to be here right now."

Going back again and again develops our trust in the SWI staff. And it makes for familiarity. My older daughter wrote this last visit: "I felt that I knew my way around the first two floors just as well as I know my way around my own house, because we had been there so many times since I was adopted."

By being known, we've been able to conduct exchanges with our daughters' caregivers. We've been the bearers of gifts from other families who've adopted from our SWIs, taken letters, photos . . . and been able to send back pictures of the gifts delivered. We've been able to have discussions with staff members about issues of attachment and post-adoption problems caused by institutionalization. These have been interesting exchanges, sometimes each party having to work to understand the other!

In gaining trust, we have been allowed over the years to ask to see documents on file about our children. We have been content not to push for a copy, but simply asking again next trip if this might be possible.

And gradually . . . we have been able to extend the information we have about our daughters.

But trust doesn't arrive without work. We have been able to develop our relationship with the children's SWI staff members because of our developing friendships in China. Our third guide was in fact a moonlighting journalist, guiding to improve her English skills. From the start, it was a firm friendship, and the exchanges have deepened over the years. She's brought Chinese school kids to our country and visited us at home. Likewise, we have visited her in her home. And she and another friend made in a similar way have become our children's unofficial aunties, with the children standing as unofficial big sisters to one friend's (One Child) baby son.

These women have themselves developed trusted relationships with the children's orphanages. That helps enormously in making exchanges and visits go smoothly—and, of course, with translations. Our relationships with our Chinese friends have helped us learn how to behave appropriately when visiting an orphanage, to understand occasional negative reactions from staff members and stumbling blocks to our requests for information.

Our Chinese friends also help us set limits on the behavior of some orphanage staff members. Occasionally, caregivers forget that our children are no longer simply "theirs," and treat them as though they'd never left. This behavior is a form of claiming, and it's about roots—but it's hard on our daughters. My friends are able to assist in pointing out that the children have other claims on them now and that they behave differently than a Chinese child might; certainly very differently than an institutionalized child. My daughters belong in our family, and in Britain, as well as having roots in China; they have found and established a place in both.

The Impact of Going Back

For my children, it's a question of understanding "their" China. They get to see its changing face: more cars, more wealth, and—paradoxically—more poverty. They see kids going to school, just like them. They also see kids so not like them that it's painful. They've seen some very difficult sights: beggars, amputees, people searching through garbage cans—but they've also seen the beauty of China and the warmth and friendship of its people.

It's about recognition that the SWI was their first community of care. It gives them an understanding that Chinese people—SWI staff particularly—feel it's natural to invade children's space, to tweak their cheeks and rumple their hair. My children have learned that this physical contact is a custom, and they can bear it now without twisting away. It's about looking at children in the SWI—same-age children, some just about to be adopted—and appreciating what is the same and what is very different about them. As the children grow, their ability to reflect on these issues has grown exponentially.

It's about being able to deal with the past when you are confronted with it. My older child met, by chance, her first primary caregiver on our last visit. We thought this was a wonderful stroke of luck, and supported her obvious emotion with a glad heart that she had made the contact. On coming home, however, she wrote a story in which she details that this meeting was tougher than we'd thought, because of the memories she had of the care she'd received as a toddler. Her narrative completely tore ours apart. She had access in memory to a much tougher story than we'd thought. We're working on the emotional impact of these memories now.

Has the impact of the trips been hard? Yes, at times. A child's poise can be fragile, and an adopted child's even more so. As Bessel van der Kolk says, "the body keeps the score," and sometimes my children have been shaken emotionally—and to the extent of reacting with physical shaking—when they've found the past. But having found the past has, in my daughters' case, allowed real emotional growth and allowed them to put the past in its place—in China. For my children, this experience has been helpful, supported as they are by us and by friends in China. Each family finds its own way of dealing with memories, with the joys and tribulations of the past, and this is ours.

The Story of Belonging

Going back to China is about belonging. What my children have is not the same as living in China, either in birth or foster families or as expatriates. It's not the same as living in the West in an area that reflects their ethnicity or is culturally diverse. It's simply something that allows them to straddle both their worlds, both identities. When they arrive in China and are with the SWI and our friends, they simply are their Chinese names and selves. As the children skip down the aisles of supermarkets, astonished heads turn when we call to reel them in. We are the ones who stand out; the children blend in until we arrive on the scene. As they play in the parks, there's a real feeling of acceptance and comfort.

Will this sense of belonging last until they are able to make trips to China on their own? I think it will. They have a network established for them and some *guanxi* put in hand by me. That's the purpose of going back. No matter if the fit is different, they know they belong. Both here (U.K.) and there (China), they have found a place. They each have a coherent life story. They are the authors and editors of their stories. There are many people in China, friends that we have made there, and indeed Chinese friends here, who also serve as keepers of those stories.

Going back to China multiple times has produced a narrative of its own, and my children own this story in their notebooks, pictures, and memories. I have no doubts that my children have constructed both roots in the past and routes to the future, a sense of belonging and a real sense of perspective, because of our frequent trips to China. My children understand very well the stories we tell to make sense of the past. And through our trips, we narrate these stories in a way that lays foundations and hope for the future.

Resources

Helen Fitzhardinge, "Adoption, Resilience and the Importance of Stories: The Making of a Film about Teenage Adoptees," *Adoption & Fostering* 32, no. 1: www.baaf.org.uk.

David McCrone, "A Matter of Identity," *Edit* 3, no. 1 (winter 2003): http://www.cpa.ed.ac.uk/edit/3.01/026.html.

Bessel van der Kolk, "The Body Keeps the Score: Memory and the Evolving Psychobiology of Post Traumatic Stress," http://www.trauma-pages.com/a/vanderk4.php. Originally published in *Harvard Review of Psychiatry* 1, no. 5 (1994): 253–65.

Joy Rees, *Life Story Books for Adopted Children: A Family Friendly Approach*, illustrated by Jamie Goldberg (Philadelphia: Jessica Kingsley Publishers, 2009).

12

Six Degrees of Separation

Nurturing Networks and Creating Connections in China

Robin Carton

When I was growing up in Maryland, it was considered polite to wave, nod, or say hello to anyone you passed on the street. It was a custom of greeting and an acknowledgment of another's place in our world at that moment. Later, when I left home to go to school in New England, I would use the same way of engaging and acknowledging people on the street. The result was quite different. Rather than the friendly smile, wave, or "good morning" that I was used to, people would avert their eyes, look at the ground, or pretend they had not heard me. This behavior felt rude and dismissive and left me with no frame of reference for what was considered polite and what was intrusive. Fortunately, the longer I lived in Boston the more skilled I became at recognizing when to nod and say hello, when to avert my eyes and when to initiate a conversation with a stranger I passed on the street.

Fast forward over twenty years and my family is about to make a return visit to China. Along with another family, we will be meeting up with friends living in Beijing and traveling around southeastern China, including a visit to my daughter's orphanage in Shangrao. We were not going on an organized tour and would only have the luxury of traveling with our Mandarin-speaking friends for less than half of the trip. For the rest of the time, our family would make our way in the company of another friend, Deb, and her two children. We would be able to communicate with people we met by using our limited Mandarin, pointing, or trying to find the right page in the phrase book.

Even with many years of learning how to interact in New England—a culture different from my birth culture—I was still unsure how we would make connections with people in China. When would it be right to nod and say hello, and when should I avert my eyes? But beyond my concerns about interactions with people on the street, I wanted this trip to be an opportunity for our family to be able to make real connections with adults and children in each of the areas we would visit.

Creating a Network

Here in New England, we have been extremely fortunate to live in a bustling urban community with a large student population. As white parents raising Asian children, we have tried to make it a priority to have friendships that cross race and class. We know that we can never replicate the sense of identity that our children would have had if they were able to grow up in their birth cultures. However, we hope that by spending time with friends who are Asian or Asian-American, our children will develop a sense of self and cultural competency that will enable them to move more freely in the Asian community.

We are part of a terrific Chinese culture group for adopted girls. This connection has given our daughter a cohort of friends who have a similar life experience and a chance to explore, in a safe space, what it means to be transracially adopted. It has also enabled us to participate in a remarkable Big Brother/Big Sister program with young men and women from the Tufts University Chinese Student Association. Of our four Big Sibs, two were born in the United States and two were born in

China. In addition, we have taken advantage of several local Chinese summer camp and after-school experiences. By doing so, we have been able to meet new families and develop strong friendships.

So as we were planning our return trip, we tried to think of everyone we knew who had connections in China. An incredible benefit of the community we have built is that we now have a large network of people who have relatives, friends, or acquaintances in mainland China, Hong Kong or Taiwan. All of our Big Sibs have relatives in China. Many of our friends offered to connect us with their families or give us emergency contact information for our travels. One of my colleagues contacted a former student of his who lived in Shanghai, where our trip would end. After e-mailing back and forth, it turned out that his student, whose English name is Alan, was born in Shangrao and has a good friend named Skip who teaches English in one of the high schools there. After an introduction from Alan, Skip agreed to help us navigate the local customs in Shangrao during our visit and invited us to speak to his students about life in the United States. At the same time, Deb was able to arrange a visit to a local elementary school in Changsha. We also turned to our adoption agency to help reconnect us with the local and national guides we had used on our original trips. So, with our bags packed and our phrase books ready, we left for a two-and-a-half week adventure in China.

Thumbs Up and Photographs

When we got off the plane in Beijing, I was reminded of the culture shock I felt upon moving to New England. But this time, instead of averting their gaze, people on the street would stare at us—three white adults with four Asian children—with great intensity. With my Eurocentric perceptions, I was unsure how to respond to this direct attention. Given that there were generally few facial expressions that accompanied the stares, I was left trying to figure out whether the look was an aggressive challenge or mere curiosity.

As I sorted through my choices of how to react, I decided that I would try a mixture of the friendly greetings from my childhood, combined with a bit of the reserve I had learned in New England. So, when I noticed someone staring, I would make eye contact, smile, nod my head, and say *ni hao*. The results were amazing: For the most part, people would widen their eyes in surprise, smile back, point at our group, and give a thumbs up. In contrast, some of the older people would merely stare in return, although a few would also nod in acknowledgment. This first contact often provided an opening for us to begin a dialogue—with gestures, simple phrases in either Mandarin or English, or just plain smiles.

And once the dialogue began, everywhere we went people asked to take a photograph of themselves with our children. Photographs were taken in shops, on trains, at street corners, and in restaurants. A friend of ours speculated that this attention may have to do with China's "one-child" policy. As our four children played together—clearly some combination of siblings with their American parents—perhaps the longing for more than one child surfaced. And so, time after time, we allowed people to photograph our children playing and laughing and chasing each other, with the big ones giving the little ones piggyback rides and the little ones holding out their hands to the big ones when they needed help.

Making Contact

I then found that I was able to make connections with people in ways that I never expected. No matter where we went, everyone wanted to know where our children were born. Someone would start asking questions, and the rest of the time would be spent in conversation with people who were interested in knowing more about who we were and why we were in China. We spoke with street vendors, shopkeepers, taxi drivers, wait staff in restaurants, railway workers, and people exercising in the parks. Many people had very little understanding of child abandonment and adoption in China. Some of them even asked if we were taking our children to see their parents. Since it is a common Chinese practice for people to raise one another's children, in some ways the question was not so strange.

In a department store in a small city in Hunan province, several clerks tried to discreetly follow us as we took the orphanage director on a shopping spree for diapers, wipes, and soap. As the director went ahead, I stopped and smiled at one of the young clerks who was trailing us. She covered her mouth with her hand, laughed, and encouraged her friends to come join us. As they giggled and blushed, I managed to communicate that while the girls were born in China and my son was born in Cambodia, we all lived in the United States now. They were easily able to distinguish which girl was born in Hunan and which girls were from Jiangxi province. They were very curious about why we were buying so many diapers and pleased when they learned that the diapers were to be used for other children still in their city. After taking several pictures, we said good-bye, and I left feeling as though I had actually managed to make a meaningful connection across our cultural and language divides.

On a surreal train ride from Nanchang to Shangrao, we were the most novel group on the train. Everyone in the car wanted to pass by and get a look at us. Some folks just stood behind our seats. Some came up and smiled. Some took pictures and some took videos with their phones. It was an exhilarating experience to share this four-hour ride with so many people who were interested in making a connection with us and our children.

Connecting with Kids

While many of the connections we made were between adults, we also wanted our children to have the chance to visit with schoolchildren their own age. In Changsha, we spent the morning at a local elementary school, where our children were welcomed warmly. The children we met were learning to speak English and were delighted to have the chance to try out a few sentences on "native" English speakers. Teachers led a paper-cutting activity, showing the children how to make the character for "double happiness," and they demonstrated several different classroom games. In return, our children presented the class with a book they had made in school. The book listed things they liked about their school at home and included questions that their classmates had asked about what school was like in China. The visit sparked a lot of discussion afterward about the similarities and differences between the schools at home and the schools in China.

We also took Skip, our friend of a friend of a friend in Shangrao, up on his invitation to speak with his English language students at the high school. Little did we know that Skip alone had over 500 students and that there were 6,000 students in the school! As we walked onto the campus, students were hanging over the outdoor walkways, looking down at us from every floor. There was giggling, pointing, and smiling. There were a few tentative waves and "hellos." It was the kind of entrance you see on Oscar night or at an arena. Inside the building, the noise was tremendous. Students were all lined up, pushing to go inside. I haven't seen that kind of excitement since I went to a Grateful Dead concert thirty years ago!

Skip and his colleagues had split the students into two groups of about 250, and I took on one group by myself in a large auditorium. When everyone settled in, one of the English teachers introduced me, and I was on my own. I looked out from the stage on row after row of students eagerly waiting to hear what I had to say. This was their first chance to interact with a "native" English speaker and they intended to make the most of it. I had a bag of gifts, and I told the students that each person who asked a question in English would get a prize until the bag was empty. I had small sports notebooks, baseball cards, and chocolates to give out. I then walked up and down the aisles, calling on people to ask questions. It was fascinating. Many people asked what I thought of the television show *Prison Break* (never seen it). One person asked if I knew the actor Orlando Bloom (never met him). Another person asked what kind of music I like (I went through a list of types). Then she asked if I would sing a song! Holy cow! So I stood on the stage and sang *Three Tigers* in Chinese. They applauded as if I had given a Master's concert.

Then one young man in the back told me I would not like his question, but he felt he needed to ask it anyway: "What do you think of the war in Iraq and the number of soldiers that have died? Do you think this was right?" Whoa. I was prepared for movie stars and songs. This was intense. I was even less prepared for the girl who asked me what I thought about the recent U.S. sale of missiles to Taiwan. But then it was back to things like, "Do Americans like to dance?" "Will you dance for us?" (No—I sang but I will not dance!) After I ran out of gifts, students still wanted to ask questions. I finally had to stop when I ran out of voice.

Sharing Meals

After the high school visit, Skip treated our families to a banquet. Local restaurants often have small rooms where people gather to eat on special occasions. Generally, there is a large round table with a lazy susan in the middle. Servers bring out dishes one at a time, with the most expensive ones coming out first. Diners have dessert-sized plates for food and a small bowl for the "discards." Rice, the least expensive item on the menu, is usually served last.

We hosted or were treated to at least one banquet in every place we visited. At each of the three orphanages, we took the directors and some of their staff out for lunch. In Shanghai, Alan and his family introduced us to the local cuisine. In Shangrao, Skip had some of his students and fellow teachers join us. In Changsha, we ate with several teachers from the elementary school we visited, along with some of their children, chatting about childrearing and educational practices in China and the U.S. We ate dishes we would never have known to order and were able to compare regional specialties. It was a wonderful way to share a meal.

How Our Children Connected—Or Not

As transnational and transracial adoptees, however, our children did not share the same frame of reference as the people we met each day. While they physically looked like everyone around them, their clothing, facial expressions, and body movements immediately set them apart. This was a source of great interest to the Chinese and created periods of discomfort for our children. The pointing, stares, head-patting, and rapid-fire questions in Mandarin at times felt overwhelming and intrusive to them. While we were delighted to provide opportunities for our children to interact with people we met, we also knew that we had to give the kids the space to withdraw and regroup. It was a delicate maneuver to negotiate the balance between our desire to mingle and our children's need for privacy.

Eighteen months later, I still feel as though this trip was a pivotal moment in my daughter's life. The opportunity to see China with her own eyes has left a marked impact on her. And the fact that we made real connections with Chinese adults and children allowed my daughter to replace any fantasies she may have had about life in China with real experiences and understanding.

In China, there are people who smile, there are people who stare, there are people who avert their eyes, and there are people who give a big "thumbs up." And while there are some people who turn away, many more are delighted to chat, share a meal, and discover our commonalities. Given the choice between sitting on a tour bus or wandering the streets, I'll take the opportunity to develop a new frame of reference for meeting people any day.

13 Experiencing Life in Rural China

Susan Beth Morgan

On March 28, 2007, I took my two daughters, ages ten and nine, back to China for the first time since their adoptions at age one. We were participating on a Global Volunteers team, teaching conversational English for three weeks in a rural village called An Shang, two hours west of Xi'an in Shaanxi province.

Global Volunteers (www.globalvolunteers.org) is a nongovernmental organization based in the United States, working with local people in countries around the world in a variety of projects utilizing short-term volunteers. This was my fifth GV program in China. My first two, in 2001 and 2002, involved teaching conversational English to children in a summer camp in Bo'ai, outside the city of Xi'an. GV team members stayed at a nearby hotel and drove the short distance to the school by van each day. In 2004 and 2005, I participated in "Project Peace," an initiative to build a much-needed elementary school in the village of An Shang, a farming community of about 400. Following the completion of the school building, the program focused on teaching conversational English.

All four experiences were wonderful, but I enjoyed the rural village the most. For the first time in my visits to China, I was able to get out of a hotel and live among the local people. Other than some accommodations to foreigners that had been made in the two village houses where volunteers stayed—including solar showers and Western-style toilets—we lived the way many people live today in rural China. In the village we could also easily interact with and learn from local people.

For all of those four programs I had traveled by myself, for about a month each time, and left our four children with my husband, David, at home in the U.S. I usually returned to a very tired husband, and as much as I wanted to be in China, it became harder each time for me to leave my family. After my fourth GV program in 2005, I felt that perhaps my two daughters could participate with me and return to the country of their birth for the first time. I was thrilled that we could work out arrangements with our local school district, and with Global Volunteers, to enable this to happen.

Arriving in An Shang Village

The girls and I had several adventures just getting to China, including being bumped from an overbooked flight to Beijing. We finally arrived very late in Shanghai, a day later than planned, and departed the next afternoon for Xi'an, where we started our Global Volunteers orientation. We then traveled as a team of six American volunteers to An Shang, where we would be assisting seventy-five second-year university English majors with their spoken English.

The "red carpet" treatment and celebration that the people of An Shang village always made for us upon our arrival felt even more special to me this time, as Anna and Mary Ruth were by my side. Our students had already arrived and they greeted us, as did many of the villagers who had gathered amidst the sounds of drums and gongs as our van pulled up to the new elementary school. It was wonderful to be back in my "second home," and even more so to have my daughters with me to experience a little bit of life in rural China, in a place and among people that had become very special to me.

Our hosts prepared three home-cooked meals for us each day, hearty village fare that our team enjoyed, consisting primarily of locally grown vegetables. They were delicious. Anna and Mary Ruth always had a good appetite and seemed more willing than they were at home to try new foods. The room that the three of us shared in Brother #2's courtyard house on the third floor was very clean, light, and airy. It overlooked the main street of the village across from the new school, built with the help of local people and Global Volunteers, where we held our English classes. The Western-style toilet and solar shower bathroom that we shared was in the adjoining hallway. I enjoyed greeting our host family each morning on our way to breakfast, as well as throughout the day's comings and goings, in the best Mandarin I could remember, sure in the knowledge that even when I couldn't get it right they appreciated the effort.

Teaching

Beginning on our first full day of teaching, the students were divided into three groups of twenty-five. The six volunteers broke into three teams of two teachers each, including Anna and Mary Ruth, who were each paired with an adult volunteer. After three days, we rotated our class assignments, so that eventually we came to know all of the students and they, likewise, learned about us. We shared personal life stories as well as our respective countries' histories and cultures.

During the first day with each new group of students, Mary Ruth and I began with introductions, one by one, that included individual hobbies and where each of the students was from. Their hometowns ranged from Inner Mongolia to Sichuan province to China's east coast. Before the end of the first class, our students were asking questions about adoption in China, the reasons why I returned so often and what it was like in America for children like Mary Ruth and Anna. It was an interesting discussion, and Mary Ruth, although rather quiet and shy, answered a few questions herself very well.

Some of the students wanted to know how my husband and I "chose" our daughters. I gave the class a general description of the adoption process as I remembered it from our family's experience. They then asked about how children adopted from China were treated in America and how adoptive families helped their children assimilate into the schools and the culture in general. I asked Mary Ruth to talk about her experiences with our local Chinese School, which she and her sister attended weekly back in the States, as well as her school's annual International Cultures Day and other events throughout the year. Soft-spoken and a bit hesitant at first, Mary Ruth soon warmed up to her task and did a great job describing these activities. I'm sure she sensed the students' sincere curiosity about international adoption.

Experiencing Daily Life and Special Events in Rural China

Our second week in the village just happened to coincide with the grand opening of the Chou Chin Folk Arts Festival in An Shang. The festival provided a fantastic opportunity for us (as well as for our students who were ages nineteen to mid-twenties) to learn so much about the history of Chinese folk arts and to meet many of the artists in person as they demonstrated their crafts. Thousands of people from all over China, as well as exchange students from several countries who were studying Mandarin, came for the festival to the small village of An Shang, whose normal population is around 400. The big event brought with it many opportunities to share American culture with the students and the local people, as we interacted with the many vendors who lined the main street, as well as with our host families and their visiting relatives.

Several farmers were selling all kinds of seeds in paper packets spread out on blankets along the roadway. Although, of course, we could not read the labels, we could guess at the plant ultimately produced by the seeds from the colorful pictures on the envelopes. Many of the vegetables were foreign to us. However, the vendors enjoyed our attempts to share the English names of the vegetables we could recognize, as well as our attempts to pronounce the Chinese names of the ones we didn't recognize.

One of the artists, whom I had met on prior visits to An Shang, was delighted to see Anna and Mary Ruth and asked them a few questions. He showed us some of his latest pen-and-ink sketches of rural village life. The girls each picked out a favorite one to purchase and take home to hang in their bedroom. Then, he quickly drew a rough sketch of both girls, heads bent together, which I'll treasure forever.

Anna and Mary Ruth spent one afternoon playing with two other girls their age from the village. Although they did not share a common language, their time together during the Arts Festival was fun for all of them, as well as an important learning opportunity for each.

A day trip to a distant middle school offered another rich experience as we shared American culture and customs and tried to answer questions in many classrooms. The children were at times shy about asking us questions in English, their teachers prodding them to overcome their hesitancy, but all enthusiastically welcomed us to their school. Anna and Mary Ruth participated well, despite not having expected to be in the limelight, nor to be put on the spot with answering questions. We also shared some trends in American education with the principal, teachers, and other staff, and did our best to answer the many questions they asked.

The principal was amazed that Anna and Mary Ruth were able to travel for so long during the school year. He stated that students in China would never be able to do that and miss so much class work. I explained that I had met with each of their schools and received work from their teachers ahead of time. Also, I felt that each day's experiences in China were an education in themselves for all of us, but especially for the girls returning to their homeland.

Anna and Mary Ruth answered questions from many students near their age who wanted to know about life in America. "What is your favorite food?" and "Do you play sports?" were two typical questions. Some questions dealt with things Chinese, including "Do you like Yao Ming?" and "What is your favorite Chinese food?"

Later that day, my daughters and I talked about our experiences. They liked the colorful, and often detailed, drawings on many of the classroom chalkboards. They noted how crowded the rooms were, compared to their classrooms back home, and how almost all were without the technological devices and other resources they were used to. The students were very friendly, however, and welcomed the three of us as if we were visiting royalty. Anna and Mary Ruth felt a little like "rock stars" by the end of the day!

Whenever we could, during our free time, the girls and I took off on walks around the village. Often one or more of our students accompanied us. They would ask for the English word for things we saw, then explain the object's use in Chinese rural life. Once in a while, they were as stumped as we were. Almost all of the students were from urban areas and were unfamiliar with some of the farming tools, as well as with certain plants and other objects usually seen only outside of a city.

During our time spent living in An Shang village, we learned quite a bit about the different kinds of work that families participated in, the foods that they often prepared, and some of their folk customs. We also learned about Shaanxi opera and the arts and crafts of the region, especially during the Chou Chin Folk Arts Festival. We attended, as did many of our students, an evening performance of "shadow puppets," along with well over a hundred local people from An Shang and surrounding areas. Although we could not understand the story being acted out on the small stage lit with bright light from behind, we were fascinated by the dramatic movements of the colorful puppet figures and the high-energy singing of the puppeteers.

Some things in An Shang would have been difficult for the three of us without the extra comforts set up for foreign volunteers, used to modern conveniences. These included hot showers courtesy of solar barrels set up on the roof (at least on sunny days!) and Western bathrooms with indoor plumbing. Laundry and dishes were washed by hand. Water in general was often in short supply in the village, as it is in many places in China. Central heating is not available in almost all rural homes. It can be very cold in An Shang village in fall and winter. The beautiful weather we experienced those three weeks was a plus, since a day of rain would turn the hard-packed earthen streets into mud, making walking difficult. Farmers in China—like those anywhere else, I'm sure—spent long days working hard, especially at harvest time. Most did not have machinery; they planted and brought in their crops by hand.

The girls and I talked about some of these things during our visit. All of us agreed that life in An Shang was harder in many ways for the local people as compared to our lives back in the States. Anna, however, thought that life was better in a lot of ways in An Shang . . . and so did I!

Experiencing Life in Beijing: What a Contrast!

Following three wonderful weeks living in the village of An Shang, we traveled to Beijing, where we spent almost a week in the home of a young couple originally from Hunan province, whose young son was in a boarding school back home. They lived in a new apartment building, among many others like it, off a main road about twenty minutes from central Beijing. The apartment was big. It consisted of two floors, and the rooms were large and spacious, even by American standards. The upscale furnishings and decor were very modern. What a contrast to our living situation of just a few days before!

The girls said that they missed An Shang village—and so did I. We missed the friends we had made there, including the university students who had taken Anna and Mary Ruth under their wings and delighted in their roles as *jie jie* and *ge ge* ("older sister" and "older brother"). I particularly missed the local people, who were like family now from repeated experiences with Global Volunteers in the village. We all missed the wonderfully hearty and delicious home-style meals we had grown accustomed to every day.

The city was filled with a lot of cars and trucks of all sizes, and crossing a street was often a difficult task. Back in the village, there was only one main road, now paved, with very little vehicle traffic. We missed the rural landscape—with its fields of crops in many shades of green and brilliant yellow rapeseed—as well as the old cave homes dug into the cliffs, no longer used.

After some sightseeing, we spent our last three days in China volunteering at China Care, an American organization in Beijing that takes care of infants and children with medical needs from various orphanages in China. Soon after arriving, we befriended a foster family, a Chinese husband and wife who took wonderful care of five young children. The two girls, both with spina bifida, were close in age to Anna and Mary Ruth. The four girls played together for hours over the next several days, and even the three boys in the family joined in on occasion. They played innumerable games of Uno, had Barbie doll fashion shows, and even staged some theatre productions with puppets behind a bedsheet. We all had such fun together that it was hard to leave when our three days at China Care were up and the afternoon flight back home to the States arrived.

Another Trip: This Time, Visiting Orphanages

It wasn't until we were on the plane heading home that I realized that due to being bumped from our incoming China flight, the three vouchers that I had carried around with me over the past five weeks entitled all of us to travel round-trip to China within the coming year. Suddenly, my goal of returning on a homeland journey to the girls' birthplaces was financially within reach.

Six months later, in November 2007, the girls and I again headed to China, for about four weeks. We visited both of the girls' provincial capitals (Nanchang and Hefei), where they had been adopted in 1997 and 1999. This time, however, we also journeyed to Guixi in Jiangxi province and Lu'an City in An'Hui province, places I had been unable to travel to during their adoptions, to visit the orphanages, meet with the SWI officials, look through the orphanage files, and learn as much as possible about each girl's first year.

I really feel that the first time back to China the previous spring, where we lived and worked alongside local people, provided excellent preparation for the girls' homeland journey six months later. Not only did they have a frame of reference for returning to their orphanage city, but they already had answers to many general questions and uncertainties about what China was like. They were eager to travel again, and it definitely seemed to be the right time.

A highlight of our experience was our visit with Anna's foster mother in Guixi, in Jiangxi province, over the course of two days—one spent in her home surrounded by family members and neighbors. This woman, who had cared for Anna from when she was found at four days of age until almost one year later when I arrived in Nanchang to adopt her, couldn't believe that she was seeing her foster daughter again ten years later. She had been heartbroken when the orphanage officials took Anna from her in 1997. She had cried for days afterward. She never thought that she would see Anna again. Anna's reunion with her foster mom was a dream come true for all of us. I just regret that it took ten years to happen. We also met several other foster moms, who were eager to make contact with their foster children who had been adopted by families in the United States.

Both Anna and Mary Ruth were interested in visiting their birthplaces. Anna, in particular, was very happy to meet and spend time with her foster mother who so obviously cared a great deal about her and wondered how she was doing in the United States. Growing up, Anna had always expressed many more questions than her sister about her early life before being adopted. I feel that the first visit back to China enabled both girls to work through any unspoken anxieties they had about what Chinese people and places were like before they returned to their orphanage cities.

We also returned to An Shang village, now our "second home." We missed our students, as well as our fellow Global Volunteers team members, but spent several days enjoying rural village life, renewing friendships, and, of course, eating plenty of delicious home-cooked food. Upon our return to Beijing, we did some more sightseeing and revisited the foster family at China Care. We enjoyed several more games of Uno, while catching up on news since our first visit. We also put together scrapbook pages of photos from our earlier visit to China Care, and—as with Anna's foster mother and others we had met along the way—planned to stay in touch and nurture our growing friendships in China.

During our trips, my daughters and I learned a lot about life in both rural and urban China. The daily struggles and hard physical labor of many rural farmers and their families contrasted with the increasing availability of modern conveniences to wealthier families in the cities. The friendships we made spanned both extremes. We really felt at home in China and look forward to returning.

Of course, we also experienced problems and challenges during these extended visits. Some of the challenges of our China "adventures," as expressed by Mary Ruth in her journal, were:

- to remember to not drink the water from the faucet
- to not eat fruit that can't be peeled
- to always remember that crossing the street is a challenge because cars don't stop for people
- to not eat a lot of Pringles
- to try and read Chinese characters
- to not get in arguments with my sister

Needless to say, there were times when the hardest challenge was the last one. All in all, however, the experiences that the three of us shared on our two journeys to China over a total of about nine weeks were worth any amount of challenges.

Anna and Mary Ruth learned a lot of things about the people, country, and culture of their birthplace. They had the opportunity to actually experience many facts about China: They noted, for example, that "China has a whole lot of people!" Other, more intangible learnings, took place daily in the course of many of our planned activities. For example, experiencing the eagerness of our students in An Shang village to improve their conversational English highlighted the value of education that permeates Chinese culture.

As we traveled back to the States following our two China journeys, memories filled my mind—going back to 1997, when I was in China for the first time for Anna's adoption. I remember standing with her on our last night at the White Swan Hotel, looking out over the Pearl River, moonlight glistening on the boats as they chugged up and down, lulling Anna to sleep in my arms. I vowed that some day we would return together to China. That day arrived as not one or two but three "daughters of China" returned home: Two of them were "daughters of China" by birth, who returned to the land and people they had lived among their first year of life. And I, a "daughter of China" by adoption, returned to the land and people that have come to live forever in my heart.

Heritage Trips for Two Generations

14

J. Meimei Ma

When I take a trip to China, the fact that our only daughter, Jamie, spent her first eleven months at an orphanage in Hunan is one of many reasons to visit. My husband and I are American-born Chinese, so on return trips we explore our own heritage as well as hers. Our reasons for adopting were similar to those of other parents, but because we have relatives living in China, our experiences traveling there are different from those of many other families. I would like to share some observations from Jamie's first three trips back to her homeland.

Family Background

First, a little background about our extended family. I was born and raised in New York City. My husband, Jim, is from the Midwest. Our parents attended college in China and came to America for graduate school before 1949. Both of our immediate families are highly educated, with most adults having Ph.D. degrees. We have relatives all over China, including major cities like Beijing and Shanghai. Most significantly, my mother-in-law is from Hunan. Her hometown is within a hundred miles of where Jamie lived as a baby. Only a few days after we adopted Jamie in Changsha, we met fourteen relatives of all ages. They were excited to meet us for the first time.

Jim and I visited China before our adoption trip in 2001. I have gone more often, nine times in the last twenty years. My Chinese is good enough for simple conversations, but I do not read or write characters. I usually travel independently with the help of relatives.

Trip Experiences

When Jamie never cried on her first flight to Guangzhou, we learned quickly that she is an excellent traveler. We traveled often by car and plane during her first couple of years with us. When Jim had a business trip to Beijing in 2004, it was an easy decision to expand the trip to include the whole family, even though Jamie was only three. I took Jamie to China again in 2005 and 2007, and her next trip will be in 2009. Our trips are two to three weeks long.

Fun for a Preschooler

On the first two trips we traveled independently. The idea was to visit relatives in Beijing, Xi'an, and Hunan, and to gear any sightseeing toward a preschooler's interests. We skipped places like the Forbidden City and museums. We focused on activities that a young child would enjoy and could handle without becoming too tired or cranky.

The clearest memory Jamie has from her first trip was of flying a kite in Tiananmen Square. The spring winds were almost too strong and we were lucky to find the last kite vendor as she was leaving. Jamie was eager to do it again when we were back in Beijing a year later. We managed to fly one briefly before soldiers cleared the skies of kites because of a special event that day.

Other fun activities included playing in the many parks we visited. The exercise equipment in most Chinese parks may not be designed for young children, but they love trying them out anyway. Jamie enjoyed these, and liked simply running around with other children. She had great fun playing at McDonald's Playland in Beijing and Changsha.

What Jamie remembers most from being in her orphanage town as a preschooler was having fun on kiddie rides and feeding fish. The rides outside of department stores provided ten minutes of fun for only one yuan. On the first trip she rode a cow with *Old McDonald* sung in Chinese. On the second trip she chose to ride a tank from among several other choices available. It looked a bit like her father's tractor, and I am not sure she even knew what it was. At the city park with a large lake, people buy uncooked Chinese noodles from a vendor to feed the fish. If you throw the eight-inch noodles in whole, hundreds of huge coi show up in a matter of minutes and go into a complete feeding frenzy. Jamie loved feeding the fish and kept asking to buy more noodles.

When Jamie was four years old, I was willing to take her to climb steps at the Great Wall in the summer heat. We skipped it on the first trip because I would rather walk up steps at the Great Wall than ride a gondola, and I knew at three years old my daughter would need to be carried too much. On the second trip, we hired a private car for the day to take us to Mutianyu, but did not bother with a guide. She ran up a thousand steps with great enthusiasm and liked being up on the Wall, looking through the little windows and seeing the view. We would stop in the towers to cool off and rest. We enjoyed the area for over an hour.

During the second trip Jamie saw Xi'an for the first time. She enjoyed playing with two college-age cousins who speak some English. Jamie liked visiting the Bell and Drum Towers with them, but found the terracotta warriors boring. She also liked the dance show at Tang Paradise, a theme park based on the Tang Dynasty, but the music at the water and light show in front on the Big Goose Pagoda was too loud. We loved all the dumplings in Xi'an, a local specialty.

Visiting Relatives in China

Visiting relatives is what makes repeated trips to the same places in China worthwhile for us. A few cousins have come to the United States for visits, but most have not. Spending time with them and seeing how they live is a special experience.

When I travel independently, usually I visit a few relatives in their homes. The trips we took when Jamie was a preschooler included a few days in a large, modern apartment in Beijing owned by a retired cousin. When there is time, being pampered by relatives is a great way to get over jet lag. In Beijing, I took Jamie to play in the local playground. With her outgoing personality she had little trouble finding friends to play with, in spite of not speaking Chinese. In Xi'an, we ate a few home-cooked meals at my cousin's apartment. Before one dinner, we had a lesson on making dumplings. My elderly aunt enjoyed watching Jamie play.

The relatives we visit generally do not speak English. Jamie takes that in stride. She was more willing to speak Chinese when she was six than when she was younger, since she knew a little from a weekly Chinese language class. However, Jamie is always happier spending time with relatives or guides who speak English. Having traveled internationally with my parents at the same age, I am not surprised.

While Jamie does not remember much from her first trip, I think it made a difference on later trips that we were visiting people she had met before. For example, she has visited a cousin in Hunan on every trip. I call him Jay in English. He lives near Changsha and is a taxi driver who drove trucks in the Chinese army for many years. On the first return trip, Jamie would not let Jay carry her. On the second, she was happy for him to carry her at any time. At one point, she coyly asked me to translate a request for him to buy her something, since he does not speak English. Jay loves to spoil her. She was happy to spend an hour with him and his wife while I went to the Hunan History Museum with his English-speaking daughter. On the third trip, she spontaneously ran to give him a hug when she spotted him, even though it had been two years since the previous visit.

Our relatives in China were supportive of the idea of adoption from the beginning. It is common for Chinese grandparents-to-be to be highly critical of adoption, whether or not the parents have biological children. And when people do decide to adopt, they often feel intense pressure to adopt a boy. While my mother-in-law made a few critical comments, I chose to focus on the positive. Compared to other families, my husband and I were not under much pressure at all. Once we had Jamie in our arms, everyone in the extended family was simply happy that our daughter was a healthy and happy child. Those who have met her are thrilled at her charms and talents.

Visiting the Orphanage

Over the last six years, I have established a relationship with the director of Jamie's orphanage in Yiyang, Hunan. I first met him during a group visit on our adoption trip. Being able to speak a little Chinese is helpful, since I do not need a translator to talk with the director and his staff during a visit. When I am at home, I communicate with the help of Chinese friends and relatives.

The primary reason I maintain contact with the CWI is to provide financial support to improve the lives of the children living at the orphanage. I am co-moderator of an online group for parents of children from the orphanage. I am also the leader of a fundraising committee composed of parent volunteers. The committee coordinates fundraising projects to benefit the two orphanages in Yiyang.

I believe that making repeated visits to the orphanage normalizes the experience for a child, making it less of a big deal. When Jamie was three, she took the visit at face value as she played with a few older children and babies. When we returned the next year, it was to a place she had visited before and remembered. Jamie did not ask adoption questions when she was three or four, but I knew she thought about her adoption at times. At age five, she once stated flatly that "my birthparents are dead." She was six as we prepared for the third trip. A couple of months before we left, she asked if we might meet her birthparents. I have no doubt that the trip generated thoughts and questions about her adoption. However, in Jamie's case, she does not have to deal with strangers asking questions related to adoption all the time because she has parents who look like her and share her Chinese heritage. That may make the intensity of the issues different than for transracial families.

On our last trip we traveled with a group of families whose children were also adopted from Yiyang. At the orphanage the girls all had intrigued and very intense expressions on their faces when watching the babies. I wonder if Jamie thinks of the visits differently than her friends do, because she goes to the orphanage relatively often. Rather than a once-in-a-lifetime experience, perhaps the experience is closer to visiting relatives who are a part of a large extended family who live all over the world.

Sharing the Heritage Advantage

One of the unexpected benefits of adopting from China is making friends with other parents of children adopted from the same city. I enjoy sharing the advantages of being of Chinese heritage with those friends.

In 2007 I arranged a custom heritage tour for a small group of friends. The five girls are about the same age, live within a few hours of each other, and finished kindergarten just before we flew to Beijing in June. The girls are all from Hunan and mostly from Yiyang CWI. We went with a travel agency that specializes in heritage tours. The tour was about two weeks long, with the orphanage visit during the second week. The bonus for Jamie was that she was friends with all the other girls before the trip. She loved having playmates all day long, especially on travel days.

The itinerary included standard sights in Beijing, Xi'an, and Shanghai, plus a few special features. The highlights, apart from the orphanage visit, included the Great Wall, an overnight train ride, biking on the Xi'an city wall, and a day spent in the mountains of northwest Hunan. The train was the Z19, a luxury, nonstop sleeper train from Beijing to

Xi'an. The mountains we visited are part of the Zhangjiajie National Park, which was designated a UNESCO World Heritage site in 1992. Chinese, Japanese, and Korean tour groups visit regularly, but Western tourists are rare.

2007 Trip Highlights

In Beijing, although the Great Wall impressed all the girls, they did not all necessarily like it. We went to Mutianyu, which has far fewer tourists than Badaling. One girl almost did not walk on it at all. The group walked up while she and her mother rode the gondola. It took her a long time to relax enough after getting out of the gondola to take the few steps up onto the wall. A year after the trip, another girl told me that the Great Wall was not one of her favorite sights in Beijing because "it was a little scary."

The overnight train to Xi'an is our favorite way to get there from Beijing. Jamie loves sleeping on the top bunk. I enjoy the Chinese TV and perfectly clean toilet rooms (Western at one end of each train car, Chinese at the other). Our friends readily agree that the train is great fun. Saving time and money compared to flying to Xi'an is a bonus.

As mentioned before, I have close relatives in Xi'an. My mother took me to meet them during my first trip in 1988. The 2007 trip was my fourth visit to Xi'an. I was happy to finally have time to bike on the city wall. The other parents agreed that biking was better than taking the girls to the famous Shaanxi History Museum, since our time was limited. One of the adults rode around the entire wall in under an hour.

We arrived in Zhangjiajie after dark. Leaving the airport was more exciting than expected because the road was under construction and recent rains made it a sea of mud. The next day, we enjoyed walking in the relatively cool, clean air of the mountains away from city crowds. I think the girls will always remember the troop of monkeys with babies next to the paved walk, even if they forget the glass elevator on a cliff.

Contact with Local People

Normally, a tour group has only fleeting contact with local people. They might have a quick conversation, often with the help of the guide. Sometimes I would chat with bystanders who were curious about a group of young Chinese girls with non-Chinese adults. After learning the girls were adopted by Americans, they usually asked if the children spoke Chinese. Since I am an adoptive American parent, my conversations with bystanders are probably different from what a guide might say. For instance, I can answer questions about what children do in America. I could translate for my friends when our guide was busy.

During the week in Hunan, my friends had a chance to spend time with Jay and his wife because I arranged for them to travel with the group. Jay drove to meet us at Zhangjiajie. At one meal, Jay ordered really spicy Hunan food and those who were daring could sample it. Normally, the guide stuck with less spicy dishes. Jay demonstrated the art of bargaining at a small shop selling silk embroidery in Changsha. Two of the men went on an adventure with Jay one morning. He drove them out to the countryside where they found a village and had tea with a family. They did not go to a predetermined destination, so it was an exploration into the unknown.

Traveling with our friends made it more obvious how my visits to China differ from theirs. For the most part, I am a typical tourist when staying in a hotel. However, I do buy food from street vendors or small local eating places. Of course, any adventurous traveler can do that. The more significant difference is that no one takes any notice of Jamie and me when we walk on the street if we are not with non-Chinese friends. There are no stares or questions from strangers that non-Chinese adoptive parents experience. On the other hand, everyone expects us to understand and speak Chinese. If I strike up a conversation with a stranger, often they express the hope that Jamie is learning Chinese.

Conclusion

As a family with Chinese ancestors from many bloodlines, we are likely to visit China as often as practical. Hopefully, Jamie can visit every two or three years. While we are likely to visit Jamie's orphanage, the primary purpose of our trips will be to visit relatives and learn more about China by direct experience. No doubt, spending time with relatives and others who do not speak English will improve our Chinese. Planning a trip to China is great motivation for studying the language.

Heritage tours are worthwhile for many reasons. I hope to continue sharing the experience with friends who have adopted from China.

IV

the HEART *of the* MATTER

Visiting the Orphanage,
Finding Site and Foster Family

Walking My Baby Back Home

15

Traveling Back to China with My Daughters

Bonnie Ward

Returning to China has become a tradition in our family. Every three years, we pack up and trek halfway around the world to reconnect with friends and family and explore the city where my daughters spent the first year of their lives. We do not call Changde their "birth city" any longer, as we know the probability is quite low that they are actually from the place of their orphanage. This is not surprising, as workers come from often far-away places to live in the cities, and Changde is a busy hub for highways, trains and buses. Birthparents make a predictable choice in abandoning their child away from where they are known and recognizable. But, as Changde is where my daughters each spent their first year, and as it is where we visit not only the orphanage and our friends who work there but also the foster family that cared for both of my girls, Changde is "home" in a way that no other city in China can pull on our hearts.

As with most adopting parents, my first visit to China was also my first adoption trip. It was August, 1998, and I was one of a small, ragtag band of first-time parents, rushing headlong into the great unknown called parenthood. It was a trip filled with wonder, fear, joy and tears—as well as a healthy dollop of anxiety, hand-wringing, self-doubt, and a lot of faith. My subsequent four trips have been somewhat different, as I've watched my older daughter's developmental journey through the emotions surrounding her adoption and her loyalty and love for both her foster family and for me.

My daughter's foster parents, YiMah and ShouShou, brought her to me on that first trip. Along with our local guide, they grilled me about who I was, what I did, why I wasn't married, and more. They wanted to be sure I would be a good mom to the child they had found and cared for during the thirteen months since her abandonment, when she was one month old. They gave me their address and asked me to send a photo each year. When I realized they were the people who had found her, I was so moved, and I began writing and sending photos every month. We developed a strong connection that grew out of a shared love for our child.

Adopting Again: The First Visit Back

When I returned in October of 2001, it was as a part of a much larger group, and with my then four-year-old daughter in tow. Not only was I adopting again, but I was getting to see China—and the adoption experience—through the eyes of my child. I had fears, but they were different this time, and the most palpable, the one burning in my heart, was how my daughter would react when we were reunited with YiMah and ShouShou. I wanted her to be happy to see them, of course, but I knew that someone was going to have a broken heart: if she did not run into their open arms, her foster family would be devastated, but if she did, I felt I would fall apart.

As it turned out, none of us were disappointed. My daughter was all smiles as her foster dad (whom we call ShouShou) lifted her high into the air and swung her around and around. And I was relieved to know, to actually *know,* that my daughter was cherished even now, over three years later, by these people who, through her, had become a part of my life.

This fact, probably more than any other, has colored and shaped our return trips to China. No matter where we go when we visit, we always spend a few days in Changde. It is not convenient—Changde is a three-hour drive from Changsha, and planes do not fly from major cities to Changsha every day. So the timing must be worked out and other sightseeing planned carefully to ensure we get to do the things we want to do and still get our time in Changde. After our visit in 2007, I suggested that on our next trip we might focus on some different places in China and perhaps not return to Changde. Big mistake on my part! My daughters—and the sons of our travel-companion family—would hear none of that. All four children voiced the same sentiment: "But if we don't go when we come back again, it will be *six* years until we are in Changde and can see ShouShou and YiMah!"

So, why? Why is their sense of place, their sense of belonging, their sense of family, tied to this place? It goes much deeper than simply because they understand this is the place through which they were adopted.

Shortly after I welcomed home my first daughter, I started thinking about returning to China. Yes, in part because I wanted to adopt again, but even more so because I knew I wanted her to reunite with her foster family, so that they could see her and know that she was well and well-loved. As I was musing about the logistics of such a trip, a friend mentioned that taking her back at age three would be very different from taking her back at age twelve, and when did I think I would be going back?

That comment struck a chord in me. At different ages and stages of her life, my daughter would glean different experiences from what would basically be the same trip. So, when would be the ideal age for a return to China? And, more importantly, was there an "ideal" age at all?

Because I was adopting again—and because through a miracle occurring in the CCAA Matching Room we found ourselves returning to Changde in 2001 to welcome my second daughter—the "ideal" age seemed to be four. I was concerned that my daughter was too young for such a journey, but this was immediately following 9/11, and quite frankly there was no way I was traveling halfway around the world without her at my side.

This first trip back for her was indeed long and tiring, but it was also magical. Driving from the Beijing airport to the Jian Guo Hotel, she had her face pressed against the window, a smile from ear to ear as she pronounced "Momma! China is amazing!" And, indeed, it was. She loved the hotel; she thought Silk Alley was the most wonderful place as she shopped and plied the merchants with her dimpled smile; climbing the Great Wall made her feel like Mulan; and riding in a Dragon Boat at the Summer Palace was the high-point of Beijing for her.

The morning we left for Changsha to meet her new sister was emotional for us both. I scooped her up and carried her into the bathroom for some private time, and we talked about how this was our last day as "just us two," how our lives were going to change, and how we both had some fears about what that meant. It was good to have that talk and for us both to acknowledge our excitement—and our anxiety—about what was about to happen.

After I received the referral for my second daughter, and learned she was from Changde, in the very same orphanage as my older daughter, I called and gave YiMah the information. YiMah, who worked at the orphanage, went to the baby rooms to find her. She asked if she and her husband could care for her until I came; they were denied, but the director did allow them to visit her and even take her to the local hospital for an independent physical. Dr. Tan, who had also had been my older daughter's doctor, said she was healthy but needed more nourishment. So YiMah cooked an egg for her every day and brought it to the baby rooms and fed her, and played with her and held her. ShouShou visited and took photos; their son brought her toys and played with her. They showed her photos of us. Finally, the week before I was to arrive, the orphanage director let them take her home to stay with them. I was able to call them one evening and got to say, "Mama *ai ni*" to her. (My plan had been to sing her a lullaby, but I started to weep when I heard her say "Mama.")

Seeing her new sister in the arms of her ShouShou and YiMah helped my older daughter to understand her adoption in a much more tangible way, and to put their role in her own life into perspective. What she gleaned from this trip was an understanding of family, adoption, and love in a way that made her feel safe and comfortable, a way that words and stories had barely touched.

That first trip sparked many conversations with my older daughter about adoption. She carried around a Little Girl's Bible for weeks and kept asking me to read the story of Moses. I did not understand what was happening until one day, out of the blue, she said, "Moses was adopted just like me." I replied, "Yes, he was," all the while being totally stunned that she had picked up on that at age four and I had never thought of it that way in my whole life! Then she told me, matter-of-factly, "The lady in the grass (bulrushes) is like the lady who grew me in her tummy and Momma, you are like Pharaoh's daughter." Again, you could have knocked me over with a feather. She got the whole picture.

Grappling with Divided Loyalties: Our Second Trip Back

Just before our trip in 2004, when my girls were ages seven and three-and-a-half, they asked me if we could meet their birthparents. I reminded them that we didn't know who they were, and my older daughter grabbed hold of the younger one and said, "We don't want to meet them, Momma. We have you and if we want to see family in China, we have YiMah and ShouShou; that is all we need."

By an unbelievable miracle, confirmed by DNA testing, my girls are biological as well as adoptive siblings. Their biological connection, however, doesn't really play into our trips at all. That they are from the same place makes traveling easier, but they understand that biology is only one piece of what makes them sisters. They feel that they have real family to visit in China because of YiMah and ShouShou.

When we returned again in 2004, we traveled with our dear friend and his eight-year-old son, who was also adopted through Changde. My younger daughter and my friend's son were returning for the first time, and my elder daughter felt like the "old hand" at all of this. My younger daughter was enthralled by China. Climbing the Great Wall held the same fascination for her that it had for her sister. She asked, "Momma, did the wall really keep out all of the bad men who wanted to hurt China? Where are the Huns now?" When we flew to Changsha and then made the long drive to Changde, all of the children were interested in the WuLing Gate, the Wall of Poems, and the life-sized cardboard image of Yao Ming at the local McDonald's. But visiting the orphanage was a different experience.

My younger daughter and my friend's son had spent time at the old orphanage, and we were able to visit their rooms and speak with the *ayi*'s. My older daughter had not spent any time in the orphanage, and she was quite reserved; in fact, she held herself quite distant that day. It was a foreshadowing of difficult times to come.

When YiMah and ShouShou came to visit at our hotel, my elder daughter was quiet, beyond reserved. It was apparent she was uncomfortable. She was acting so polar opposite to how she had behaved during her first return visit, and it was upsetting to her foster family, to me, and to herself. Her foster parents had planned a big birthday celebration for her and my daughter was so overcome with emotions for which neither of us had prepared, it was an incredible disaster. She sat apart from the party, with me by her side, holding her close and trying to be reassuring. YiMah sat cross-legged on the floor, gently stroking my daughter's hand, shoo-ing away all other family members, understanding that this visit was different now, and that patience and compassionate empathy were what she needed.

By the time we had to leave Changde, the emotional rifts were on the mend, but it definitely had not been the robust, rambunctious, fun-filled visit we had expected to have. Quieter times with just us and her immediate foster family (ShouShou, YiMah, and their son) were what made the difference. She needed fewer crowds and more "nuclear family" activities.

After Changde, we headed for Guangzhou and the luxury of the White Swan Hotel. We took the children to the U.S. Embassy and to the Temple of the Six Banyan Trees, recreating as much of the official adoption experience as we could, so that they would understand what those first few days together as a family had been like. We spent a lot of time in the White Swan swimming pool, because, well, kids and water usually result in fun times and build good memories.

On our last night, we treated the kids to a little taste of home: pizza and cold Coca-Cola in the Songbird Café. As it happened, Guangzhou was celebrating being chosen as the site of the 2010 Pan-Asian Games. They marked the occasion with the most spectacular fireworks display I have ever seen, and we had front row seats from our dinner location. The children were mesmerized, and several times throughout the display my elder daughter pointed out to us, "Fireworks were invented by the Chinese, you know."

As we headed to the airport the next day, she started to cry. I asked if she was sad and she told me yes. She said that she missed YiMah and ShouShou; she told me she loved China but that she was happy she was an American now. What I learned on this trip was how conflicted my daughter was feeling about being loved so much by "family" who were so far away. Feeling happy in our new life together also brought on feelings of guilt.

Maturing into Grace: Our Third Trip Back

When planning for our 2007 trip began, I approached the Changde portion of our journey with trepidation. This time we traveled with my friend and *both* of his sons, his youngest being adopted through Wuhan and the same age as my younger daughter (now six-and-a-half). The Great Wall continued to fascinate; kite-flying in Tiananmen Square was hot but fun; the Forbidden City and Summer Palace interesting and tiring. On my eldest's tenth birthday, we held toddler pandas and drank tea in Chengdu; a surprise party at lunch had the entire restaurant staff singing to her, and she actually enjoyed being the center of attention. Our first stop in Hunan included the provincial museum and "Lady Dai, the Diva Mummy." All of the children were captivated and happy to point out that Chinese mummification beat Egyptian mummification hands down! Then came the three-hour trek to Changde and reuniting with YiMah and ShouShou.

Having learned from our last visit, we kept this reunion low-key. Dinners, teas, and trips included YiMah, ShouShou, and their son, with no extended family. My daughter was open, smiling, loving, and receptive. She handled their need to be at her side, their need to hold her hand and hug her almost constantly. She did this with an open heart because she knew it was important to them. And by the end of our visit, she could admit it was important to her without feeling torn. She could let them love her on their terms and love them back on her terms, and understood it was all good.

On this trip, I learned that my daughter is an amazingly strong young woman and that she has a compassionate heart. My pride in her maturity and flexibility on this trip was immense. Three years had made a difference in what she understood, what she could let slide, what she could express. The previous two trips had given her vastly different experiences, and this trip helped her to process and come to terms with that part of her life in a way that gave her and her foster family peace.

We visited the new orphanage and played with the children for hours. Both of my girls and my friend's sons enjoyed blowing bubbles and showing the children how to use Magna-doodles, but the high-point for them was learning to fly a bug (a golden beetle, with a string tied to his legs).

It was a fun trip, and it showed in their giggles and squeals of delight, in the pre-teen rolling of eyes, in the teasing and sharing. Their sense of home and family are tied to this place. Coming back reinforces that sense of belonging, that sense that while there are many wonderful places in China, this place is *home.* YiMah and ShouShou make a big deal out of all four of the children. They cared for both of my girls and brought my friend's elder son to him at uniting, and they have "adopted" his younger son as another nephew, because we all are family and that is how family works!

Our next trip, in 2010, should be interesting. My girls will be thirteen and eight; my friend's sons will be fourteen and eight. There will be a lot more interesting dynamics than simply family and adoption-related emotions going on. But we are ready, and in fact the children started planning for it the day we landed in New Jersey in July 2007.

I think our children have benefited from these multiple return trips by not only developing a sense of place and a sense of family, but also by getting perspective on their adoptions, China, being American, and themselves—in ways that only this type of travel can provide.

16 | A Rock and a Hard Place

The author of this chapter wishes to remain anonymous to protect the privacy of her family.

As a parent of two children adopted from China, I have sometimes felt the burden of providing my kids with experiences that are "equal" to each other. There is probably nowhere that this particular penchant for parental fairness becomes so impossibly out of reach as it does when returning with two children for a homeland visit.

A return to an orphanage or to see a foster family is full of emotional hotspots, for parents as well as children. I offer this window into our return visit experience to share lessons learned, insights gained, and differences celebrated. In writing this, it is my hope that it may help another family prepare to meet the differing experiences that likely await their children.

I have seen people whose one child may receive literally a firecracker welcome upon returning, while another child in the same family receives a perfunctory, sterile tour of their orphanage. While both of my daughters, at ages five and seven, received warm welcomes from their original communities of care, the disparities were enough to cause some struggle. This is our story.

My two children came from relatively fortunate circumstances, in terms of pre-adoptive history. My older daughter came from a small, rural orphanage in a remote mountainous region of China, where the director takes a personal interest in each child. One early example of this was the fact that he gave my daughter a gift on the day of our adoption. It was a small bracelet given to all children adopted from this Social Welfare Institute (SWI), so they might see each other wearing the bracelet in the future, and get connected. He also gave a gift of a traditional minority outfit and told us we were now connected forever as "family." My younger daughter spent her time in the care of a loving and devoted foster mom. In fact, she earned the name "Princess" early on in our family, based on the high expectations she had for love, attention, and comfort, similar to the heroine of the story *The Princess and the Pea*.

Our family had decided a week prior to leaving for our homeland trip that each girl could pick some rocks from our yard and bring her own "American home rocks" to China. Each daughter would deposit her own selected rocks in her individual hometown as a kind of symbolic connection. Since my girls were five and seven at the time of our trip, and a favorite pastime was picking up rocks, this plan "clicked" for them. Rocks of all sorts make it into our house on a regular basis—whether sparkly, or crystal, or coal-looking, each one is a unique discovery and temporary treasure. We'd planned to take two to three small rocks each from our yard and exchange them for some equally interesting ones to bring home to America. Little did I know how important this symbolic exchange of rocks would be in helping us navigate the emotional curves of our trip.

My Older Daughter's Warm Welcome

Before her adoption, my older daughter had spent all her time in a tiny orphanage, one in which the director has made a serious effort to keep babies alive and well in the often harsh conditions of a remote mountainous region. The difficult winters of this area often required multiple visits to the clinic. The average annual income there is around a hundred dollars per year, and a heater may be needed even in mid-July. The SWI, which also cares for the elderly, as well as children who are disabled and orphaned, is tucked away in a nondescript alley in a small rural town. Every day, caregivers record twenty-four hours of each baby's activities on a chart, in an effort to assure a healthy and strong body. Providing individual attention and spending time with any particular baby is not practical.

My older daughter is a sensitive, creative, dynamic personality whose emotional rivers run deep, strong, and quiet. She was intensely excited about this trip and was looking forward to meeting Mr. Li, her orphanage director. Mr. Li is an open-hearted and involved director. Upon our arrival into the capital city, he met us at the airport, and for a couple of days took time out of his schedule to show us around the city and nearby historical areas. He bought both of my daughters some ice cream on our city walks, hugged them, and allowed himself to be photographed dozens of times. He was, in short, a genial and wonderful host.

Mr. Li invited us to share a meal at his home on the first night of our visit to the city, as well as on the last. His wife cooked a wonderful homemade meal, with plenty of dumplings and enough freshly made food to set the standards impossibly high for the five-star hotels and restaurants that were to follow during the course of the trip. Her dumplings became the stuff of legend for the adults on the trip. For the children, they were simply stuffing. Mr. and Mrs. Li would both refill the kids' bowls with more and more dumplings and delightedly watch them eat, then offer them "one more." While the adults were trying to be respectable in their use of chopsticks—since there were no spoons or forks in the house—my older daughter used chopsticks with ease. This fact was not lost on Mr. Li, who was quite pleased about her expert skill.

Following our feast, we sat down with Mr. Li and learned more about the vague expanse of eleven months prior to my daughter's arrival into our home. We learned that she was a quiet baby during her stay at the orphanage. Mr. Li threw back his head and chuckled as he pointed out the high contrast to what he saw now—as my daughters and a four-year-old child visiting their home that evening raced through the apartment living room. At that moment, it looked like my older daughter was hatching some inspired scheme on behalf of her younger sister and the other child. She was the instigator and collaborator for creating much noise, and we all appreciated the irony of his description of her as a young baby.

Before the farewell dinner on the final night of our visit, we shared some gifts from America and received a gift of chopsticks from the Li's. That night we learned that the four-year-old girl visiting in their apartment was in fact a child from the orphanage. She had recently been brought to the city for medical treatment and was staying at their apartment for a few days, until practicality required that she be returned to the orphanage. This director's practice was to bring kids into his home when feasible. Mr. and Mrs. Li taught the orphanage children to call them *Mama* and *Baba*. He also gave each child at the orphanage his surname. He explained that this was done purposely so that orphanage youngsters would be equipped to handle the dynamics of the school yard and would be prepared when a friend asked about the child's mom and dad. The child could truthfully answer with Mr. and Mrs. Li's names. As we departed the apartment that evening, he expressed his wish that this "family" of international children placed all over the world would someday have the ability to reconnect in meaningful ways.

In the days between our wonderful visits to his home, we learned of Mr. Li's involvement in our daughter's life within hours of her abandonment. He shared details that resolved some discrepancies in her paperwork. He gave us specific insights and personal information about my daughter's early days—a gripping piece of our family history told to us by this kind gentleman who oversaw her care for most of her first year of life. Mr. Li also brought us to my older daughter's finding site, where she picked up some rocks, and her mom had some moments of quiet reflection.

My Younger Daughter's Emotional Reunion with Her Foster Mom

The next stop on our trip was my younger daughter's province and hometown area. There, we were able to visit her foster mom on a day trip outside of the main city. My younger daughter had spent all of her time with one devoted foster mommy who, admittedly, did not put the child down except for a few moments each day.

For my younger daughter, it is a rich story with deep and individual love and care. In fact, my daughter spent every day until she met me in the care of her foster mom. In one of life's little ironies, however, the paperwork indicated that she had spent all of her time in the orphanage. We had begun to surmise that the woman we met in the hotel lobby was special, as my daughter cried inconsolably for two days, calling out a word that sounded similar to *Aiya*. Since our initial meeting had taken place without the benefit of a translator, it took us more than two days until we knew that the woman we had met at the hotel lobby was really my daughter's foster mom, and not one of several different nannies who might have cared for her.

Upon arriving at the designated meeting spot in my younger daughter's hometown, I immediately recognized the foster mom from four years earlier. Mrs. Yu came walking up to our designated spot holding a mammoth-sized stuffed panda bear, wrapped in cellophane and a ribbon. The gift bear stood just two inches shorter than my five-year-old daughter. And, of course, she tore it open with delight! Where Mr. Li had treated both girls with great interest, love, and care, my younger daughter's foster mom was focused only on her; my older daughter didn't really matter to her.

Mrs. Yu was thrilled to see my younger daughter and held her every possible moment she could. When she looked at my daughter, it was as though she were intent on never taking her eyes off her again. It seemed to me that she was hoping to memorize every feature, to capture her essence, and somehow keep her close in memory and in spirit.

This didn't surprise me at all. Although I hadn't known my daughter had been in foster care until days after she left the care of this woman, I could tell she had been given the gift of being supremely loved, taken care of, and doted on. I had carried five years of guilt for not knowing who the foster mom was during the chaotic "Gotcha Day" moments. I felt bad for having been insensitive to her loss during the time of my joy at meeting my daughter. In fact, I had never been able to watch our video of that day completely, seeing the tears in this woman's eyes. It was this return trip that actually allowed me to assuage my feelings of guilt and provide a measure of "payback" to the foster mom—by bringing my daughter back at a young age, so she could see her again, four years after having been forced to say goodbye.

During this visit, we were able to get more information and learn that my daughter was the only child Mrs. Yu had ever fostered. I learned that—just as my daughter had done for two days after being separated from her foster mommy—Mrs. Yu had stopped eating for several days as well, and spent every waking hour looking for a way to come to America to see her.

Although it seems that this foster mom's only source of income was doing babysitting for a neighbor's children, it was apparent that my daughter did not spend a moment in her care with a need that was not immediately and fully responded to. My daughter had lived with a high level of expectation for having any need met immediately, upon demand, and with single attentive focus on her. She communicated this healthy high regard for herself and her needs upon meeting me, in a thousand little ways. After several days of intense, painful, deep grieving, her personality began to emerge. I learned that she was playful and precocious and that she had a well-developed sense of humor at fifteen months. She was used to being the apple of someone's eye and liked her place there. This continues to be true to this day. She was accustomed to loving, attentive care that made her the center of the universe, which should be the birthright of all babies.

Following a lunch with cultural exchanges and a video interview regarding my younger daughter's initial months spent in China, the foster mom returned to her favorite sport of carrying and holding my daughter and whispering sweet somethings in Mandarin to her. We received a precious gift of photos of my daughter's first fifteen months of life, and walked to a nearby photo store to have copies made. As a group, we then went on a ride around the city to her finding location. To my younger daughter, we were just driving to a new area in her hometown, which would be a good spot to pick up rocks for her very own "China hometown" rock collection. It was a perfect spot, which provided ample rock-picking opportunities. We spent some time there, visiting and absorbing the area, while some curious Chinese men wondered why several foreigners were looking with interest at this nondescript spot. My younger daughter dropped off her "American rocks" and picked up several interesting new ones from this special spot in China.

Following this activity, we perused a nearby market and met the owner of a market stall who used to watch my daughter when the foster mom had to take care of errands or attend to other business. She fussed over my daughter, who, while normally quite shy around strangers, seemed to intuitively know (maybe remember?) these people who were part of her caring community when she was an infant. She was having the time of her life, being held every moment, and being doted on. During the early part of the trip, each of the adults (mom, aunt, and uncle) had all been worn out from her pleading requests to "hold me" and "carry me" for the several walking expeditions we had done. Now, her foster mom wouldn't let her touch her feet to the ground. My daughter relished the attention and pampering.

As the time of our departure drew near, the depth of the foster mom's personal price for loving my daughter became clear. It became apparent that she hadn't been accurately told or hadn't anticipated our departure time. She began to cry and hold onto my daughter even tighter. She became emotionally distraught and asked us when exactly we would be returning again. She was inconsolable. It was awkward and painful. To ease the transition, we offered to drive our van the short distance back to her apartment. In the van, she stared at my daughter with huge eyes, red from crying, and with a face wet from tears. We were all silent and serious. Once we arrived at her building, she insisted that we visit her apartment and stay a bit longer. I, my younger daughter, and one of the guides visited for ten or fifteen minutes more. My older daughter was content to stay with her aunt and uncle and peruse some nearby shops.

At the apartment, Mrs. Yu showed us the stroller that she had used for my daughter. She showed us some of the toys that my daughter had played with. The apartment was simple, with a small kitchenette and a bed in the main room. She was gracious and warm, and I was again thankful for this kind woman. I saw her pain and couldn't imagine that I could be that selfless to love this deeply, knowing the pain of saying goodbye was inevitable. We finally stated that it was time for us to depart. She walked back to the van with us, and we talked of keeping our connection with her going, now that we had each other's direct contact information.

Mrs. Yu stood at the van window and spread out her palm to the window. With tears streaming down her face, she studied the face of my daughter, who was seated in my lap. I felt as if I was in the midst of two colliding worlds and wanted to protect my daughter, but at the same time, understood the gift of care and love that was being openly shown and shared. I cried big, silent tears as I put my daughter's hand to the window, covered by my larger hand. Traffic seemed to stand still forever, as the three of us sat there enmeshed together, separated by a thin pane of glass. As the van began to pull into traffic, she kept her hand to the van window and ran alongside the van in the bicycle traffic lane. She kept her hand on the glass for the hundred yards or so to the first stoplight. As we paused and then pulled away from this stoplight, the emotions inside the van were palpable and raw, as we all faced the open difficulty and sacrifice this woman had made in giving such love and care to my daughter. I looked back as the van pulled away and saw her standing there in the street, with tears on her face, capturing the last glimpse. I wondered if I could ever feel the enormity of the pain that she had felt when she let go of my daughter that day four years earlier. Again, I found myself humbled and in awe of her gift, made at such a significant personal price, and of her sacrifice.

Processing the Contrast

Later on that night, in the quiet of the hotel room, my older daughter was processing the emotions of the day. She noted the intense personal love and care of the foster mom towards my younger daughter. She compared her experience and realized that no one had displayed a similar personal, emotional connection to her. I didn't need to explain to her the many differences between institutional care and a family setting; she was feeling and sensing the distinction.

The large panda bear gift and the open display of love and affection given to my younger daughter made my older daughter's positive experience with Mr. Li pale in comparison. She shouted at me with anger in the hotel room, "I didn't get a present!" As she cried, it seemed she was also perturbed by the fact that Mr. Li had been equally enthralled with her and her little sister. In that moment, his kind and compassionate affection towards all of us seemed like betrayal to her. Where was her personal gift of connection, her huge panda bear? And where were Mr. Li's tears of sadness at saying goodbye to her? She compared these things and labeled it "unfair."

I took a deep breath and prayed for wisdom. It felt like one of those pivotal parenting moments that you only get to have one "take" on. What could words do to help her? I had a sense that the soft clay of my daughter's emotions would seal an impression on how she processed this dichotomy and perceived "unfairness" in her young life. In this moment that felt like a hard place to be, I reached for the rocks we had selected from each finding spot. As we studied the rocks, I asked them about the unique features of each one they had picked. I asked them how interesting it would be if each rock looked exactly the same. What if there were not charcoal gray ones with little silver streaks? Or what if we weren't able to find any with the glittery, crystal look? How about the smooth, gray stones? Or the brown ones?

I asked, "If each rock looked the same, why would we ever look to discover new ones? And why would you even want to have a collection of them?" I shared my personal faith that the Creator made each girl in my family with a unique design as well as a specific life purpose. We can't have the same experiences, or be the same person if we are each designed to be someone unique and accomplish something different. If one stone was an exact duplicate of another, why would we ever stoop down to pick it up and discover it?

That discussion, along with my older daughter's tears, seemed to assuage her feelings, and as we went to sleep that evening in the hotel room, I reflected on my inspiration to pick rocks as a symbolic vehicle for our journey. I felt like the connections we made on this trip were meant to be. Why had I chosen rocks to symbolically connect my family's two continents? It certainly had been a pivotal symbol to help us all on this journey in my girls' homeland. It provided the opportunity for us as a family to experience in a practical way the truth that we each have a unique life path. We all slept like babies as we settled into sleep that night.

More Processing Post-Trip

Months after the frenetic schedule of travel is over and life is once again in a comfortable routine, I find both of my daughters are still putting together the pieces of their China experiences. My younger daughter, who is an incessant conversationalist, talks often now of her foster mom and has recently wondered aloud, "Where is my foster dad?" (There isn't one). In her own style, with an exceptionally high need for order, she seems to be placing people in their respective boxes inside her mind. Initially, her experience of meeting her foster mom, who clearly loved her dearly, seemed to put the "Who is family?" question a bit up for grabs. We have now defined *foster mom* as "mom for a short time" or "temporary mom." I've always described myself as her *forever mom*, and I think the distinction has clicked, as she has found space in her mind for both foster mom and forever mom. Most days she is good with me in the *forever mom* category. Then, on other days, I fail to meet her expectations or desires: "No, dear, we can't go out to eat pizza for lunch every day." She now has a person to compare me to when "Mom" doesn't perform to her desired standard.

My older daughter, with whom we are working to address neurological deficits (likely a result of institutional care), is grasping that her early life was something less than perfect. She asks about this now. As we work on addressing her neurological issues, which frustrate her, she knows that when a baby lives in a group home, the baby does not get all the hugs and kisses that babies need. She accepts that at face value, although more questions seem to bubble beneath the surface.

Her discussion of China often centers on food, a topic near and dear to her heart. She talks proudly now of how many dumplings Mrs. and

Mr. Li tried to get her to eat while visiting their home. Even when dining on scrambled eggs or other typical American food, she will reach into our buffet hutch and pull out the chopsticks Mr. and Mrs. Li gave us. She comments on her own ability to skillfully use them and announces that she is the best in our house with the sticks. And then she will smile and talk of the dumplings at Mr. Li's house. She also announces to visiting guests that "these chopsticks were given to our family by Mr. Li" and expresses great pride in that fact.

Both of my daughters received a warm welcome from their first communities of care, and for that they are very fortunate. Yet the differences caused some pain, eased a bit by having our rocks—tangible symbols of the girls' connection to China—and using those rocks as an entry point for processing their experiences. As my children mature, I suspect that they will continue to reflect on the ways in which their visits with their early care providers were both deeply meaningful in unique ways. As they count their rocks from China, I think they will also count their individual experiences as unique and rich.

History, Pride, Self-Confidence

17

What My Daughter Learned in China

Sandra E. Lundy

We said good-bye to our tour group and took the plane from Shanghai to Nanchang, the capital of Jiangxi province. When we touched down at the quiet airport in Nanchang, our guide, Joey, was there to greet us. Joey was slight of build and looked to be all of about nineteen. He introduced us to the driver, an older man equal in weight to a couple Joeys, and we set out for the two-hour trip to Ying Tan. Having spent the last two weeks in big cities and resort areas, we were now in a part of China that seemed almost like a different country. Oxen grazed near the dry landscape along the roadway. Occasionally we caught a glimpse of someone laboring in a rice field, or sitting idly in front of a one-story concrete building. Motorcycles and motorized carts carrying dangerous amounts of commercial and human cargo crowded the highway. There was little sign of prosperity.

Joey made sure we knew that he was only doing this translator gig until a job translating business documents came his way. A native of Jiangxi province, he appeared not very impressed with its charms, and he didn't have much to tell us about the area.

That was okay. Ellen, Kate, and I were all preoccupied anyway, knowing that this would be either the most wonderful or the most disappointing trip we would ever take.

Heart-Heaviness around Adoption

Kate was eighteen months old when I adopted her, in 1998. I was single then, and about as unprepared as any forty-five-year-old woman ever could be for the transformations of motherhood. For example, I thought being a mom would give me more time to myself because I'd be home more.

Fortunately, a wonderful and wise woman entered my life soon after Kate and I came home. Ellen became my partner in life and Kate's other mother. She was just emerging from her own daughter's teendom, and she would become, among many other things, my touchstone when I felt overwhelmed or confused by my new role.

By the time we made the decision to visit China, and to return to Kate's orphanage city of Ying Tan, Kate was nine years old. And Kate, whom we'd given veto power over the idea, was eager to go.

Adoption had always been part of our family narrative. From before she could speak English, Kate knew that she was adopted. From the time she was three or so, she began drawing pictures of what she imagined her birthparents to look like. In first grade, she wrote a letter to her birthparents and was crushed when we told her that we didn't have a name or an address to put on the letter. Ellen and I talked endlessly about how to handle the heart-heaviness that seemed to enclose Kate around the issue of adoption. We concluded that the best response was to bear witness with her and not try to chase the sadness away. By the middle of first grade, Kate seemed to have made peace with that sadness. She put her letter away in a memory box and became engrossed with school and school friends.

When I first brought Kate home, and for months thereafter, she would have meltdowns in which she cried so hard I sometimes found myself in the emergency room to make sure she wasn't in physical pain. After about six months, the crying jags subsided, then vanished altogether. Kate grew into a smart, sensitive, and kind child with an abundance of athletic and artistic talents. While she had a lot of friends at school, she was very shy around new children and adults. Her first instinct was to shrink into herself when being addressed by someone she didn't already know. We assumed this was just part of who she was.

We did our best to keep China present for Kate. She'd gone to a Chinese language preschool camp in the summers, and took Mandarin in school. We celebrated Chinese New Year along with the Anglo-Saxon and Jewish new years, and were faithful attendants at the annual dragon boat races at the Charles River.

We wanted Kate to be proud of her Chinese heritage, but it was not until the beginning of third grade that she paid any attention at all to the many Asian children, adopted or otherwise, that made up a third of her elementary school. I don't know exactly what made her start paying more attention to the Asian girls in her class, but I know what strengthened that attention. Two Asian therapists at a local mental health center had decided to start a once-a-week Asian peer group for mid-elementary girls at Kate's school. The nine girls who signed up and two counselors met at lunch-time, talking or doing projects such as drawing on T-shirts. On the days she had the group, Kate always came home excited just to have been a part of it.

That's when we started to think about visiting China.

Visiting Ying Tan

I'm not sure whether it was the thin mattresses of the Ying Tan hotel or the anticipation of going to the Ying Tan Social Welfare Institute that kept us up that night, each of us churning in her own little world. Before we'd left for China, I'd read some discouraging messages from adoptive families who'd returned to Ying Tan and who'd had—at best—bland and uninformative experiences. I had tried to convince myself, and Kate and Ellen, that just seeing the town where Kate spent her babyhood would make the trip worthwhile. I convinced no one.

Kate and Ellen each had fantasies of coming to Ying Tan and being able, as if by magic, to spot Kate's birthparents. Before leaving for China, we had all spent a long time talking about our expectations, realistic or not, optimistic or otherwise. The talking helped calm our nerves, but being in Ying Tan was stirring them up again. We rushed through our huge Chinese breakfast buffet and decided to spend the few hours before we were to go to the orphanage walking around town.

Only it wasn't so easy. Everywhere we walked—the parks, the side streets, in stores and through the main square—we were greeted by stares and pointing and whispered conversations. Clearly, Westerners were still a novelty here, and Westerners with a Chinese girl in tow were even odder. The curiosity was so unabashed and intense it made us uncomfortable. After about an hour we wandered back to the hotel, where Joey was talking with a woman in the lobby.

She turned when we entered and screamed, "Le Leng! Le Leng!" She scooped Kate up in her arms and gave her a crushing hug. Miss Hua (I'll call her), the supervisor of the orphanage section of the Ying Tan Social Welfare Institute (SWI), Joey explained, had come early because she couldn't wait to see her Leng. While Joey translated our hellos, the supervisor held Kate tightly. She stroked Kate's hair and cheeks over and over again, exclaiming how big she'd grown and how pretty she'd become. Kate was smiling radiantly, almost from the inside out. We went upstairs to change for the visit to the orphanage and gather the gifts we'd brought along. Kate chose to wear a beautiful red Chinese dress. We hurried back to the lobby, then to the waiting van.

Ying Tan SWI was on the outskirts of town, in a rather isolated area surrounded by dusty streets. It was not the place where Kate had lived, which was destroyed by floods in the fall of 1998, but as we were ushered into a large meeting room, I recognized many of the women who had come to Nanchang eight years before to bring their charges to meet their American parents. There was Miss Fu, slim and demure in a pink sheath dress, who had grown up in the SWI and gone to work there at eighteen. She was the one who'd first placed Kate in my arms. There was the director of the SWI, a stout woman with a pleasant face, who, when I had asked her eight years ago to tell me about Kate's life in the orphanage, said only that Leng loved to run. There was a deaf young man, about twenty, who had also grown up in the SWI at the time Kate lived there.

And there was chaos. As soon as we entered the room, the young man and the women swarmed to Kate, chattering and hugging her, screeching, "Le Leng! Le Leng!" Le Leng is an affectionate form of her Chinese first name, Leng. Some of them lifted her up and twirled her as if she were a baby.

To our great surprise, Kate didn't recoil. To the contrary, she melted into their embraces, more than happy to have her face stroked, her hair patted, her hands held by all these long-lost strangers. Now we understood what those painful meltdowns had been about when she first came home: Kate had been separated from people who loved her, and whom she loved, dearly. "A beautiful Chinese doll!" one woman exclaimed. "A princess!" One of the women sat Kate in her lap and two others braided her long hair, as they all looked at an album of pictures of Kate's childhood that we'd compiled for the orphanage.

In the corner of the room stood a tall, tanned man with a crew cut, a broad smile across his face. A woman stood beside him, a full foot shorter than he but with the same broad smile. They were the only ones we'd not been introduced to yet. We assumed they worked at the SWI.

Ellen asked Joey to introduce us. After a brief exchange with the couple, Joey informed us that they were Mr. and Mrs. Zhu, Kate's foster parents.

Foster parents! I'd no idea she'd been in foster care. But when we managed to pry Kate away from the orphanage crowd and bring her to the couple, there could be no doubt. The man beamed when Kate made her way over to him. "Le Leng! We've waited so long to see you!" Joey translated. Mr. Zhu bent down to talk to Kate, and he seemed shocked, almost hurt, that she didn't speak (I assume) Mandarin. The woman was crying and laughing as she leafed through the album with Kate. She exclaimed over and over again about a picture of Kate in a chef's hat and apron, stirring something on the stove. Kate took out the picture and gave it to her.

Eventually we all sat down at long tables piled high with lychees, watermelon, grapes, oranges, and strawberries. Something of a tug of war ensued, as Kate sat for a few minutes with one person, then with the next, Joey racing furiously to translate. (Finally, he seemed to settle on the strategy of translating one or two words of English for every ten sentences of Chinese.)

We learned from the Zhu's that they were rice farmers on the outskirts of Ying Tan, who fostered Kate for the first eight months of her life. They'd gotten the call only the day before that Leng would be visiting Ying Tan. Although the day of the visit was one of their two annual rice-planting days, they could not bear the thought of missing the chance to see Leng again.

After the feast in the meeting hall, the director took us into her office to see Kate's file. It contained nothing that we hadn't already seen before: her baby medicals, certificate of abandoned baby, and so on. But on the tour of the orphanage, the ensuing sumptuous luncheon at a local hotel (where Kate's foster mom and the orphanage woman vied to see who could force the most food on her), and a dinner that night, we learned more than we had ever dreamed possible.

At the orphanage we were allowed to visit one of the baby rooms, where ten cribs held about fifteen infants who, to put it mildly, were not too happy that we interrupted their nap. The supervisor pulled Kate aside to the crib of one little girl who looked to be about ten months old. "She has your eyes," she said to Kate, pointing to the baby. "And look, this is what your mouth looked like, just like hers!"

In the orphanage playroom, we were taken to a wall of photos of children who had lived at the orphanage over the years. There we saw a group picture with tiny Leng right in the middle, surrounded by other children and many of the same people in the room with us that day.

We learned from the director that Kate had sometimes stayed with her. We learned from the Zhu's that when they were out in the field, Kate had been in the care of their teenaged daughter and son, who loved to run with her and to carry her around. And we solved the mystery of Kate's Chinese name.

Leng means "cold" in Chinese. Every Chinese-speaking friend or acquaintance in the States to whom we showed the Chinese character of her name was puzzled that she was given such a harsh first name, so unlike the flower names or good-luck names girls typically carried. At first we assumed that *Leng* must refer to the fact that Kate was born in January, but now that we were in Ying Tan, it was clear that this area was sweltering pretty much year-round.

Miss Hua had the answer. "When Leng Leng came to us," she said, using another affectionate form of her name, "she was about two days old. She had boils all over her neck. She had a very high fever. We were afraid for her life. So we named her Leng, to bring the fever down." And with that information, our beautiful daughter's Chinese name became beautiful.

The evening ended with tears and bear hugs. Mr. Zhu wrote a note in Chinese. He told her to be sure she learned Chinese so she could read it. Convinced that she would return to China for college, he told Kate he'd see her in ten years and have a good talk with her.

The next day, we went to the train station where Kate had been found. Before our trip, we had all thought that visiting the train station would be a huge, cathartic event. I know Kate had harbored fantasies of meeting her birth mother there. But after an unsuccessful attempt to locate the train operator listed on Kate's Certificate of Abandoned Baby, we soon left the noisy, crowded, dingy waiting room. Kate was not disappointed; I can only guess it was because she had already found what she was looking for.

Finding Roots, Gaining Confidence

Our visit to Ying Tan gave Kate roots. It gave her a history. It lit up important moments in the otherwise dark void of her history, and it gave her back her Chinese family.

On our return from China, our friends began telling us that Kate looked more confident, more at ease with herself. We heard the same thing from her elementary school teachers when Kate went back to school. It was true. Our visit to China allowed Kate to emerge from a shell that had held her apart from others. Before China, she stopped taking karate, which she was good at, because she hated performing in front of others. After China, she seeks out opportunities to express herself: the school play, piano concerts, circus arts. Maybe this blossoming would have happened anyway, but I can't help believing that knowing more of her personal history played a part.

After the trip, too, Kate has embraced being Chinese with a new sense of pride. It's as if what was abstract about her Chinese identity has now become concrete. Kate now has a Chinese tutor, a Chinese graduate student, who teaches her as much about the history and the day-to-day life of China as she does the correct tones. Kate has learned to type Chinese, and she and the Zhu's have exchanged several letters. (Mr. Zhu's note, it turns out, says how proud he is of her and how he wants her to grow up wonderful.) Many of her closest school friends now are Chinese, and she's started to exchange language lessons with a classmate newly arrived from Taiwan. My Aunt Jen, now deceased, used to light up any time someone said the word *Jewish*. Kate's the same way now with anything Chinese.

She is not alone. One of the marvelous things for Kate about being in China was that "everybody looks like me." For once it was Ellen and me, her parents, who were the obvious outliers. Kate's constant awareness in China that she fit in so seamlessly made Ellen and me understand that, for far too long, Kate had borne the burden of "difference" in our family alone, when in fact it is a burden that we, as a multiethnic family, all should be sharing together. It was not enough to raise Kate as an American who is proud of being Chinese. Her adoption had bonded Ellen and me to China. We too had a Chinese heritage to learn about and embrace. Ellen and I started taking Chinese from Kate's tutor. Next year we plan to return to China, and spend some of our time there volunteering in a school or orphanage. Kate's passion for all things Chinese has become our passion. The trip to China was transformative for all of us, and for our relationship to each other.

A Radiant Smile

A table in our living room holds cherished family photographs. Ellen's grandmother is there, surrounded by a loving horde of children, grandchildren, and great grandchildren on her ninety-fifth birthday. There's a picture of my parents at my brother's wedding. In one picture, the Zhu's, Kate, Ellen, and I all have our arms around each other. In another, Miss Hua is holding Kate in her arms. In each photo from China, Kate is smiling radiantly. It is a smile we'd never seen before we went to China, although we've seen it often since we returned.

18 Through the Crucible

A Difficult Orphanage Visit Somehow Eases the Pain of Loss

The author of this chapter wishes to remain anonymous to protect the privacy of her family.

Visiting the orphanage can be hard. Really hard. Sometimes a horde of caregivers waits with great anticipation to see their beloved charge again, greeting her at the entrance with a banner welcoming her back. Sometimes tearful *ayi*'s fawn over the child, give her gifts, hold her in their laps, and tell her stories about when she was a baby. And sometimes they don't.

We made a return trip when my older daughter, Mei, was eight. The experts recommend leaving the decision to visit the orphanage up to the child, but I believed she needed this visit. If she had strongly objected we wouldn't have gone, but she didn't. Mei had been in great emotional pain for months leading up to our trip, and without knowing how or why, I felt that an orphanage visit might help.

Although not all bad, our visit wasn't easy, especially compared to the warm reception her five-year-old sister, Casey, received a week later at her orphanage. I felt at the time as if I had made a huge mistake, that my insistence on taking Mei to the Children's Welfare Institute (CWI) where she had lived as an infant, and to her finding site, would leave a permanent, negative mark on her soul.

Yet when we arrived home Mei seemed lighter, happier, as if she had reached some kind of resolution to the questions that had been dogging her all year. “Now I know what it looks like,” she said. “I don’t have to make up pictures in my mind.”

The Year of Living Dangerously

The best thing I can say about the year leading up to our trip is that it’s over. My sweet girl—who gave her little sister presents and told her stories and worried about her if she walked too far ahead of us in the park—turned overnight into a raging bully. She whacked her sister, hard and often. When we played our nightly game of Uno or Checkers and Casey touched the edge of the board by mistake, Mei would go after her with murder in her eyes.

This was our new normal: waiting on edge for the nightly outburst of violence; holding my breath, afraid if I exhaled I’d unleash the rage. When Casey coughed the wrong way or jumped when Mei wanted quiet, or—more often—when I hugged Casey or kissed her or showed her any affection, Mei would turn in a fraction of a second and be at her, legs kicking to injure, fists flying, even (at age eight) teeth bared and seeking flesh.

Whenever Mei lunged I’d scoop Casey up to protect her and say (okay, sometimes yell), “What are you doing? Leave her alone, you’re going to hurt her!” This wasn’t helpful; if I showed even the most subtle sign of anger, you could almost feel the wind being sucked out of the atmosphere before the tsunami hit. Then Mei would unleash a major wave of fury, kicking, screaming, throwing down the dining room chairs, ripping things, including her beloved teddy bear. It would always end, eventually, with her sobbing in my arms and me bewildered, worried beyond worry, heartbroken for her and for her sister, not knowing what to do.

This went on night after night. We tried therapy. It may have helped a bit, but just a bit. Mei didn't want to go and once curled up in a fetal position, head in my lap, for the entire session. Our daily drama ended sooner when I was well-rested (ha!) and I could remember to breathe and keep my voice calm. Most of the time, though, I was on edge, exhausted, pushed beyond calm.

One night, several months into this stressful and bewildering period in our lives, Mei was snuggling in my lap. She asked me if I would still know her when she went to college. "Of course I'll still know you!" I replied. "You're my daughter, I'll know you and love you for ever and ever."

"But my birth mother doesn't know me anymore." After a bit of crying about this, and more snuggling, she added, "But you love Casey."

I finally got it. "Oh," I said, "you're worried that because I love your sister I don't love you anymore? Because your birth mother couldn't take care of you, maybe I can take care of your sister but not you?" In hindsight it's so obvious, yet I had been clueless until that moment.

I can't remember who once suggested using a rubber band as a metaphor for love, but it stuck in my head and I used it now. "This is what love is like," I told her, the rubber band in the palm of my hand. "When our family was just you and me, I loved you so, so much. Then your sister came along." I stretched the rubber band. "Guess what? My love got bigger. It didn't break. I still love you so, so much, and I also have room to love your sister. Love grows; we can love more than one person at a time."

I'd like to report that this breakthrough ended our difficulties, but it didn't. What it did do was help me to understand my daughter, to tame the mother-bear that roared up in protection of my five-year-old, and to move into empathy instead of anger. Now I was able (most of the time) to give Mei a hug when she hit her sister, to say, "I can see that you're really angry. Hitting is never okay, but I'm here to talk about it when you're ready. I love you."

The girl who was out to hurt her sister is not who Mei usually is. Instead, she's the one whose kindergarten teacher told me, "You know, you have a remarkable child. She's the glue that holds this class together."

She's the one who, when her friend was teased on the playground, took her by the hand and said, "Let's go talk to those kids." And they did. Mei, at age six, told them they hurt her friend's feelings and not to do it again. She's the one who, in the parent co-op preschool she attended, was sitting at a small table with three of her friends, painting. Another child wanted to join them. I told the child that as soon as someone was finished and left the table, he could paint, too. Mei saw him about to cry and, without saying a word, dragged over another table, pulled up a chair, set down a piece of paper, brought him by the hand, and sat him down. Problem solved by a four-year-old.

So it wasn't a bossy, mean-spirited child beating up her sister every night. It was a child intensely tuned in to the social environment and to others' feelings. It was a child whose way of being in the world was not so much to take care of others, but to understand them, empathize with them, and figure out how to set things right, to ease the pain.

In a very deep and painful way, Mei was struggling with her new understanding of just what the loss of her birth mother meant—and with her terror that she would lose my love, too. She wasn't yet mature enough to express her fear directly, so it came out in rage against her sister. These were the conditions in which our family boarded the plane for our return trip.

A Cool Reception

Mostly, we had a fantastic time in China. My kids loved climbing the Great Wall, trying out the exercise equipment in the many public parks we visited, eating *zha mantou* (the doughnuts dipped in condensed milk that came at the end of some of our meals), exploring city streets, and visiting friends who were living in China. The adults in our small group marveled at how much fun the children were having with each other, and how different our trip would have been if they didn't have playmates.

The morning of our orphanage visit, Mei seemed nervous (visiting the bathroom several times before boarding the van for a one-hour trip on the new freeway to the Children's Welfare Institute), but happy.

One other family joined us, along with two (adult) friends. On the way, the kids sang songs, played clapping games and laughed together in the back of the van. As we entered Mei's orphanage city and drove along the gritty streets—tiny shops spilling out onto the sidewalk, punctuated by the ubiquitous China Mobile storefronts every few blocks—everyone stopped talking.

We pulled into the orphanage courtyard and piled out of the van. A well-dressed woman with a reserved manner met us at the gates—no banner, no reception committee, no warm greeting or *ayi* wanting to hug and touch my daughter. The woman, Ms. Zhou, was an administrator who had worked at the CWI when Mei was a baby. While cordial, she expressed no warmth or delight at seeing Mei, but she did give her what turned out to be the greatest gift of the day: She remembered her. She told Mei that she had been a beautiful baby. Later, when pushed for more information, Ms. Zhou also told Mei that the *ayi's* wanted to hold her all the time because she was such a good baby and rarely cried. I wasn't sure I liked hearing that message: would Mei think she was loved only when she was "good?"

Mei attached her body to mine in that courtyard and held onto me with a death grip that she rarely relaxed during the next few hours. She smiled from ear to ear when Ms. Zhou told her what she remembered; in looking at the video my friend took that day, though, I don't see another smile on her face. She was serious, scared, and a little bored when the orphanage director made a long and bloodless speech welcoming us. He talked about how far the CWI had come, yet how much work there still was to do, and how improvements come from the generosity of adoptive parents. Was he thanking me for the donations and fundraising I had done on behalf of organizations working to help the children in this CWI? Perhaps. His words could also be interpreted as a plea for additional donations.

In the conference room with Ms. Zhou and the director, Mr. Wang, I had the opportunity to ask questions. We wanted to confirm that Mei had, indeed, been found at the gates to the old orphanage (where I believe she lived for a month or two before moving to the new one) and to hear details about the circumstances in which Mr. Wang had found her. He couldn't remember, and there was some scrambling through documents before he found the paper he was looking for and said, yes, he was the one who had found her at the gates of the old building.

His vague response was very understandable: He must have found many babies at the gates of the orphanage, it was eight years ago, and he couldn't be expected to remember every single one. Still, that response was just what Mei didn't need. In the fantasy (mine, at least) he would have said, "Yes, of course I remember finding you when I opened the gates in the morning!" As in: "How could anyone ever forget *you*?"

Another disappointment was that all of the *ayi*'s who had worked at the orphanage when Mei was a baby were no longer there. I asked repeatedly for at least a name, so she would have something to hold onto, some connection to a shred of love from her past, but came up empty-handed. "We have no records. All the caregivers from those days have left. We have no contact with them. We don't know their names." All Mei had was Ms. Zhou, who had not provided direct care and whose reserved manner said anything but "I loved you."

I also asked if we could look in Mei's file. The travel agent who had arranged our visit to the CWI assured me that the director had agreed that we would be able to see the documents in the file. When we were there, however, Mr. Wang did not give us access. "You already have everything in here," he said. I didn't push it—we were their guests, after all—but I regret that now.

After our meeting in the conference room, we went downstairs to the new playroom where we spent some time with the *ayi*'s and the babies. Still wrapped tightly around me, Mei handed out chocolates to the children old enough to eat them. I was gratified to see the differences between the care provided now and what I had witnessed eight years ago, when seven or eight babies were lined up in a row, strapped to potty chairs, with one *ayi* sitting at the end of the row paying scant attention to the babies. Now the caregivers were on the floor with the children, playing with them, holding them and talking to them. The children seemed to be developmentally on target, and interacted with us—strangers—in appropriate ways, some hiding shyly behind their *ayi*'s and others running up to greet us.

We then visited a special-needs classroom and went to see the rooms where the babies slept. These rooms looked very similar to those I remembered from eight years ago, with six or seven small wooden cribs to a room. Then we returned to the conference room for photographs. Mr. Wang gave each of the children a little gift, an embroidered hankie, offering nothing to Mei that marked her as special or acknowledged that she was the guest of honor.

The Toughest Moment

Ms. Zhou accompanied us to Mei's finding site, the gates of the old orphanage. People were outside on the corner playing cards; others were walking by. I could see why Mei's birthparents, or whoever left her there, chose that spot. Not only was it an orphanage, where she would surely be found and cared for, but it was on a relatively busy street where there was no chance of her being left alone for long. Still, the heartbreak of her parents having to leave my beautiful baby *anywhere* seemed overwhelming. The heartbreak of having been left—the pain that Mei had been feeling all year—seemed unbearable.

The building itself was boarded up and dark, and Mei later told me that this is what bothered her most. That, and being looked at. Mei started crying and so did I. I picked her up, she buried her head in my neck, and we stood there sobbing. People were curious and gathered around; this kind of attention felt excruciating to Mei. Ms. Zhou seemed visibly uncomfortable; our Western show of emotion was likely unfamiliar and perhaps incomprehensible to her.

Later, Mei said that she was glad she had gone there, despite the upset. While she might want to visit the orphanage again—to see how the babies are doing—she's now done with the finding site. Once was enough.

The rest of the afternoon was emotionally lighter, including a shopping spree on behalf of the orphanage at a local department store (using money we had gathered from the other families in Mei's travel group to fulfill Mr. Wang and Ms. Zhou's request for diapers, toilet paper, and baby lotion) and a luncheon with Ms. Zhou and another CWI administrator. Mr. Wang was too busy to join us.

When it was time to say goodbye, Mei—on her own—went over to give Ms. Zhou a hug. It was the first time all morning that they had touched. To her credit, Ms. Zhou returned the hug with a big smile and the wish that Mei would visit again (and learn Chinese so they could speak directly to each other).

Tough Stuff, But It Eased the Pain

When we later visited Casey's orphanage and she was greeted as a returning queen, and we had the opportunity to meet her foster mother, Mei clearly felt jealous. Instead of acting on her jealousy, however, she was somehow now able to express it: "It's not fair. Casey got a present and I didn't. She got to meet her foster mother and I didn't even get to meet my *ayi.*" You're right, baby, it's not fair. It's just the way it is.

It was the contrast between the two experiences—one child showered with love while the other, who needed love the most, got crumbs—more than anything else that gave me a tight-fist-in-the-stomach feeling, a sense that I had made a major mistake and shouldn't have exposed Mei to the pain of facing the truth. I came home from China really not knowing if our experience had harmed her or not. I worried that she hadn't gotten what she needed, that no one had stepped up and said, "I took care of you. I miss you. I loved you." That the void in her life would get bigger, not smaller. That visiting the finding site had been too much too soon.

But when we returned, the heavy shadow of the previous months lifted. The difference between pre- and post-trip was pretty amazing. The crying jags, the throwing of things, the sobbing as if her heart were breaking—and it was—disappeared. *Poof!* The kid who came home from China was calmer. She was in many ways her old self, sweet and funny and loving and kind. Did she still get angry with her sister? Yes. Often. But after the trip their fights seemed so, well, *normal.* They were typical sibling squabbles, and they dissipated quickly. The murderous rage was gone. I could leave them alone together again without fearing for my younger one's safety. This was a *huge* relief.

We often talk about all the wondrous things we saw and did on our trip, and we sometimes talk about the orphanage and what was difficult—or not—about our visit. Mei says that what she liked about her orphanage is that the *ayi*'s take good care of the babies. This gives her comfort. Somehow seeing it for herself has enabled her to move (for now at least) beyond the pain.

A couple of months after our trip, Casey started asking frequently about her birth family. One night Mei started teasing her about this. "Wait a minute," I said. "It's okay for her to miss her birth mother. You miss yours sometimes, too."

"Not anymore," she replied.

Was it the trip? A new level of maturity? Both? I don't know. I marvel at her bravery, at the deep level of pain she endured and her ability, somehow, to finally let it go. I suspect that, at different points in her life, the sense of loss she struggled with before our trip will bubble up again, and I can only hope that she will find ways once again to move through it and come out the other side.

Walking Down the Village Path

19

***Jane Liedtke,* Ph.D.**

I have watched the faces of the parents who attend my talks about "What's in an Orphanage File" as they listen to what information is inside (and sometimes not inside) the file. I see interest and agony as we discuss how information in the file can lead to finding the abandonment site. We sigh a collective sigh of grief when we discuss the notes and messages found within the files. And I see huge tears fall from both moms and dads as I share the story of one family who followed the trail in their daughter's file, a trail that led them down a special village path—to the door of their daughter's abandonment site and to the people who found her, people who know their daughter's birthparents.

When I tell this true story of a family from one of our tours, I also share the following statements: "It's a one-in-a-million chance, like finding the needle in a haystack; the chances are that it will never happen to you." But it does happen. Eleven families I know have either met birthparents or had the chance to meet them but elected not to do so at that time. I then follow up the discussion by having parents seriously consider the following questions:

- Why do you want to see your daughter or son's abandonment site? What do you expect to find there that you don't already know? Does your daughter or son wish to see this location, or is the trip for you as a parent?
- Will you want to take a photo of your child standing at the scene—the scene of a criminal activity? How will that impact her or him?
- How would you handle yourself as an unannounced visitor at the village home of the person who found your child?
- How would you feel to have this really happen to you—locating your child's birthparents when you only expected to visit the abandonment site? If you wanted the birthparent connection to happen, how would you handle yourself and the situation? If you had never anticipated this happening and the situation began to unfold before you, how would you handle it?
- How prepared is your family to have a relationship with a rural family who may not have much education, who have no ability to communicate with you in English (or you with them in Chinese), who may be very poor and without knowledge/understanding of international adoption, and who have other children who are your child's sister(s) and/or brother(s)?
- How prepared is your child to process this connection to her birthparents and siblings, should it happen? How will other children in your family handle it if this happens to one child, but not the other (especially if you have more than one adopted child)?
- What expectations will the birthparents have when they realize they are now reconnected to a child they abandoned—and that she/he now lives with a family in America? Will their expectations match your reality?
- How far down that path do you want to walk? How far are you prepared to go? What is going to be right for your family and also right for the birth family (respecting their privacy in order to protect them from possible social or legal problems)?

For those families with children abandoned in urban areas—a hospital, police station, train station—the path will not likely lead to a village. It will be easy to tell your child, "We don't know how to find your birthparents," or "It's just not possible to do so." You will have no options to consider. But, for those who discover in their daughter's police report/certificate of abandonment a village name or a doorstep of a family's home or a hamlet so small that everyone for miles around knows everyone else, the walk down that path could be more amazing than you could ever imagine!

Over the last year I've told this one story about the walk down the path for this one special family and their children. Emotionally and intellectually, I considered that this was a "one in a million" situation. I expected that an experience so rare would not be something most adoptive parents would anticipate, nor need to worry about, because it just wasn't going to happen like that again.

I was wrong. Not long ago, another family visited their child's home village after their orphanage visit and—through a series of amazing twists of fate—they found themselves face to face with their daughter's birth family. The connection was made without their searching for it. I won't share the details of this story, nor any of the other stories I now know about adoptive families finding birthparents at this time. How it happened, who it happened to, and why it was possible are their private stories to tell in their own time and in their own voice.

I share this information that birthparents have been found because I want you to realize that it's not going to happen often. It's very, very rare. None of these families were actually looking for birthparents at the time. I think there is something important in that message: When these families went down the path to the home village, none of them were expecting to find their child's birthparents. None of the adoptive parents were prepared for what they found; nor were their children. For the three families I know, it was emotionally draining and a complete shock.

Does this mean that everyone should run over to China on the next flight and weed through orphanage files to find the exact abandonment site, so that they can find birthparents for their child? No, that would be irresponsible to suggest. Am I suggesting that finding birthparents is what all our children need? No, I am not saying that either—it's a family-based decision that should reflect what *your child* really needs and wants. Do some children have a high desire or need to reconnect to their birthparents? Yes, some do. Do they all? No, it's an individual need and one cannot generalize to the entire population of adopted children from China. Some children may have this need at different times in their personal development—based on their personalities, their family environment, the impacts of institutionalization, and the child's emotional development.

What Am I Suggesting Then?

I am reminding adoptive parents that you must think about and take responsibility for your actions *before* walking down the path to your child's home village. Remember that meeting birthparents is not just another sightseeing stop on an itinerary. It is not a walk for curiosity seekers, and it is not your entitlement as an adoptive parent. It is not a photoshoot, nor a quick "Kodak moment." The chance of meeting your child's birthparents could be a life-changing event—for you and your child.

That's why you should have strategies in place before you take the walk to the village: Be prepared for not meeting the finding person, be prepared for no connection resulting, and also be very prepared in case a connection does unfold before your very eyes. Whatever reality you encounter in your child's home village will return home with you—whether the birthparents are part of the picture or not. Here are some of the realities you might encounter on such a visit:

- In general, people in rural China can be extremely poor and live in substandard housing. However, some are doing okay and have experienced improvements in their lives since the birth of your adopted child.
- For the most part, people in rural China do not know anything about adoption in general and international adoption in particular, though one might expect they would. It's not like

adoption is featured often on national TV in China; sometimes it is, but the chances that a rural farmer is going to be watching TV are again rare.

- Some people in rural China might expect that having a connection to their child's adoptive parents in America will give them status within the community, while others might worry that they will be fined—or worse—for having abandoned a child.
- It is not possible to get birthparents visas to visit the United States, nor to help them immigrate to the U.S. Be prepared to explain the real situation with regard to government regulations.
- Likely, you are not a family who would elect to live in China. If you are, you cannot imagine in advance the new connection you would then have to people in China: An entire rural village (and not just one rural family) would hold a key to your life.

Recently I met with a family who walked down the path to the village and met their daughter's birthparents and one of two siblings. They were visibly drained from the experience. They were concerned for the rural family. They were thankful for having met them. They returned home with a deep understanding of what had happened to their daughter—from the time she was born until they received her. However, they also returned home with the heavy burden of trying to figure out the right thing to do next, aside from the obvious need to keep in contact with their daughter's birth family.

This is more information than the vast majority of us will ever know. Some adoptive parents don't even want to know about their child's birthparents—and there are days when I personally waver between which is better—knowing or not knowing. I wonder for my own daughter what that connection with her birthparents would be like. What would it be like for me? When I think about the details of the stories I know, tears run down my face too. Every time I tell other adoptive parents the story that begins this chapter, I cry—and everyone in the audience does too—because we know that if we were in that family's shoes, it would be the hardest day of our lives. We know it had to be tough for them. We know that, in a situation like that, we might not be as strong as we needed to be for our child's sake. We know we would be opening a Pandora's box for everyone—the birth family, as well as our adoptive family. We know that none of our family relationships would ever be the same. We know these things, yet—with amazement and great curiosity—we still want to walk down that village path.

›out in China—

20

›ut

How to Present Our Family at the Orphanage

The author of this chapter wishes to remain anonymous to protect the privacy of her family.

Emily and I both expected to be parents one day. Life partners, we met in the 1980s when we were in our mid-twenties. By the time we were in our mid-thirties and had worked through the kinks in our relationship, satisfied our wanderlust and attended graduate school, we knew it was time to have kids.

As a same-sex couple, we had to decide *how* we were going to become parents. At the time, artificial insemination was the conventional route to parenthood for most lesbian couples we knew. We had discussed this option over the years, including reviewing donor profiles from sperm banks and thinking about who might be a good match. We debated many logistical questions: Who would get pregnant? Would we each get pregnant with one child, using the same donor? What did we want the racial and ethnic background of the donor to be? Between us we underwent genetic testing, fertility testing, and recovery from a serious car accident. We even went as far as contemplating one of us carrying a child from the other's eggs.

It finally became clear that neither one of us was a good candidate for pregnancy. In the end it seemed silly that we were placing so much emphasis on a biological connection to a child. Realizing that adoption was the best option for us was such a relief!

The decision of how to adopt was no less complex than the decision to adopt. At first we pursued domestic adoption but were turned down by several agencies because we were an "out" gay couple. We considered and then decided not to follow up on a foster-care-to-adoption process. That left international adoption, but we hesitated at the notion of separating a child from his or her birth culture. After deepening our understanding about the desperate situation for many abandoned girls in China, however, we began to feel that international adoption from China was a possibility. When a close family member adopted a child from China, we were convinced. Once we found an adoption agency and a social worker willing to work with us as a couple, we were on our way to expanding our family.

Fostering a Sense of Identity

When we adopted Julie we knew that we would visit China with her in the future, but we were naïve about the childrearing adventure we were embarking on. As parenting overachievers, we started reading everything we could get our hands on about international and transracial adoption. As a result, we began to worry about the impact on our child of being raised by white, lesbian parents, and we thought deeply about how we could raise her to not just look but also *feel* like a Chinese-American child.

Friendly and engaging from the very beginning, Julie startled us at breakfast one morning, when she was just two years old, by asking about her birthparents. "Where are my parents?" she asked.

We responded with, "Why, we're right here, honey, we are your parents."

"No, I mean my other parents."

"You mean your birthparents?"

"Yes, them, can I meet them?"

And so the adventure began. We knew that understanding Chinese culture and language and having strong Chinese role models would be important in developing Julie's self-esteem. Fortunately, we live in a large urban area with vibrant Chinese-American and Chinese adoptive communities. We started reaching out to other adoptive families and building close relationships with Chinese-American families in our neighborhood. We formed relationships with Asian-American students at a local university, traveled to cultural events, shopped at Asian markets, learned to cook Chinese food, and studied Mandarin. We talked and read and attended workshops. Most importantly, we talked with Julie about her birthparents, China, and adoption.

Through it all, we hoped we were doing the right thing and that these activities would be enough to foster a sense of identity in our curious and insightful child. We began to understand that we would be going back to China more than once, and it became clear that our first return trip would be happening sooner rather than later. In addition to sightseeing in China, the first trip would definitely include a visit to Julie's orphanage. We had not been permitted to visit the orphanage or even the orphanage city on our adoption trip. Instead, eight-month-old Julie had traveled ten hours by van, with three other girls and caregivers, to meet us at our hotel in the provincial capital.

All One Family?

While we debated some about *when* to visit China, the more complex question became *how*, as a two-mom family, to travel in China—and how to represent our family while we were there, especially at our daughter's orphanage. Even though Emily and I had celebrated seventeen years together the day we left for China to adopt Julie, I adopted her as a single mom.

It is important to understand that Emily and I are raising our children in an environment where we never make apologies or give explanations for who we are—a lesbian-parented, transracially adoptive, Jewish family. We are also lucky to live in an area where being a family like ours is not unique. When Julie was in preschool, she was playing house with a group of friends. One little boy volunteered to be the dad. The response from the other kids was, "We're not playing that kind of family. Our family has two moms, so you can be a brother or a cousin." It is not that our kids *never* get questioned about the configuration of our family, but there *are* other kids in their school and friendship circles who also come from families like ours.

Julie handles questions about her two moms matter-of-factly, just like she handles the inevitable adoption questions: "Is that your Mom? Why don't you look like her?" We understood that people in China view same-sex parenthood differently than members of our progressive, urban community in the United States do, and we were concerned about the reactions our family configuration could generate—and the impact these reactions might have on our children while we traveled.

As experienced travelers, we knew that we would prefer to travel independently rather than join a tour. Meeting people and making intimate connections with the culture and customs of her birth country were things we wanted our daughter to experience. Ultimately we teamed up with close family friends to plan our trip together. I knew that by traveling with other families, as well as meeting up with friends in China, we would stand out most by the racial make-up of our group: a mixture of adult women, both white and Chinese-American, and our Asian kids. In fact, the most pointed questions from people we met in China were about Cody, my non-Chinese son. People knew immediately that the girls were Chinese, but they would always point at him and ask, "Where is he from?" People would also frequently ask us if the children were ours, and would always say how lucky they were, but we were never asked where their fathers were or which mother went with which child.

Our very first encounter in China was with the customs official at the Beijing airport. Our family shares one last name. The customs official looked over our passports carefully, glancing up at our family occasionally, as Emily and I held our breath. After what felt like an eternity he asked, "All one family?" We both answered, "Yes!" We were handed our passports and told to enjoy our trip. As we exhaled, we smiled, nodded and said, *"Xie xie"* (thank you).

Deciding How to Present Ourselves at the Orphanage

After almost a week in China we were still debating how to present our family when we visited our daughter's orphanage. We felt that we had two choices in the matter—being the family we always are and not worrying about what suspicions the orphanage staff might have, or presenting one of us as the "mom" and the other as a friend of the family.

After an exhausting day of travel we arrived in the city where our daughter had lived until she was eight months old. The orphanage visit was scheduled for first thing the next morning. On the train ride from the provincial capital, we realized that "coming out" at the orphanage would not be in Julie's best interest.

Even though China is modernizing at a rapid pace, social policy and understanding of diversity there remain very far behind what is accepted in the U.S. As we traveled deeper into the province and away from the provincial capital, we felt like time travelers leaving modern China behind. From the train window we could see people working in the fields, as they had for centuries. As we went further into the countryside and interacted with other passengers on the train, we believed that the people at Julie's orphanage wouldn't understand our family configuration.

Our goal for visiting Julie's orphanage was for her to come away with a deeper understanding of her roots in China. We also hoped, but had no expectation, that the visit would be a positive experience for her. While traveling in other parts of China we were not so concerned about how our family was perceived. However, in the intimate setting of the orphanage, where the visit was all about Julie, we were concerned that presenting ourselves as a gay-parented family would compromise her experience by impacting how the people at the orphanage would treat her. So we made the decision that at the orphanage we would be a single-parent family.

Explaining Our Decision

Once we made the decision not to "come out" at the orphanage, we had to explain that decision to Julie. We needed to tell her that during the visit I would be her mom, just like I was for her adoption. The discussion was a brief one at bedtime in a funky hotel at the end of an exhausting travel day. Fortunately, Julie had always known that I was the one who adopted her in China and this eased the impact of the decision. I explained again that China is more old-fashioned than home. She took my explanation at face value, partly due to exhaustion and anxiety about the upcoming visit, and we all went to bed. Even though we knew the decision was the right one for Julie, it was still difficult for Emily to agree to stand in the background for what we knew would be a powerfully emotional day.

Visiting the Orphanage

Our orphanage visit the next day was wonderful. Julie's memory of that day is that they treated her like a princess. When we arrived at the Social Welfare Institute, a crowd was waiting on the porch under a handwritten banner welcoming my daughter by her Chinese name. Many of the people greeting us had been there when Julie was a baby. Everyone wanted to hold her and touch her. Elderly residents came by to see what all the commotion was about. Some of them had also been living there when Julie was a baby.

Once inside, Julie, now eight, sat in my lap while we looked at files and greeted people. As we flipped through the book with all of her documents, there was the same picture of me holding Julie that was on her adoption papers. Everyone smiled and pointed at the two of us, me with more gray hair now and Julie so grown up. Thank goodness we hadn't decided to have Emily be the "mom" this time. As Julie and I were chatting, Emily was busy documenting the event, taking pictures and videotaping. Julie's caregiver clearly recognized Emily from our adoption trip. Perhaps because of language barriers, but also because Julie was the focus of everyone's attention that day, there was no need to lie or to introduce Emily as a friend or relative. Both Emily and I quickly faded into the background. Julie's caregiver took Julie onto her lap and peeled her one banana after another. Julie ate them all, even though she hasn't liked the taste of bananas since she was two years old.

As we toured the orphanage and stood outside for picture after picture with various orphanage personnel, Julie became distressed that Emily was not in any of the photographs. Digital photography is a wonderful thing! I immediately showed Julie that Emily had in fact been photographed in almost every picture, including a family picture with Julie's caregiver where Emily had her arm around the caregiver's back.

Julie continued to be the center of attention for the rest of the day. After the orphanage visit we took the director and some of the caregivers out for a banquet. On the drive from the banquet to go shopping for the orphanage, Julie sat in the front seat of the van in the assistant director's lap. (Did I mention that there are no car seats or seat belts in China?)

At the Finding Site: One Family

Shortly after we adopted Julie, the orphanage moved to a new facility and the old one was abandoned. Part of our itinerary for the day was to visit the site of the old orphanage because this was also Julie's finding location. The director drove us there even though she didn't understand our desire to go. As we jounced down an old dirt road on the outskirts of the city, to the remains of what had once been the orphanage where Julie lived, I imagined someone from her birth family walking the same road holding a swaddled infant in their arms. As we got out of the van neither Emily nor I left Julie's side. We were no longer in the background as her parents. In almost all of the pictures of her at the remains of the old orphanage, she is between us with our arms around her shoulders.

This was an important moment for her and a family moment for all of us. We were together in the spot where the transition from her first family to our family began.

Processing the Decision and the Day

Back in the hotel after the visit, we discussed our day. Even though she felt overwhelmingly positive about the visit, Julie was sad and confused about why Emily couldn't be her mom during the visit. When we were talking about the speech that I had made to the director at the banquet, Julie said, "It kind of made me feel happy and kind of made me feel bad because Mommy was pretending to be my only mom because of the rule."

When we discussed the orphanage visit, Julie had this to say: "I felt bad there because Mama didn't get to be a in a lot of pictures. The people there know that Mommy was my mom. She is the one that signed the papers. That is what they know. It's just that this hasn't been so important since when I came from here. It just hasn't felt like that big a deal just having two moms until today when I came here. It just wasn't that important until today. So, yeah, I especially noticed that today."

While the orphanage visit was emotionally exhausting and has impacted her life in many ways, the fact that Emily and I could not openly represent ourselves as Julie's parents on that day was her biggest negative response to the visit.

As Julie matures and revisits her memories of the trip, we have talked more about who gets to know information about our family. When I asked her what name she wanted me to use for her in this chapter, she told me that I could use her real name, that she didn't mind people knowing her story. Our hope is that someday people in China will accept our family as it is and understand that gay people are loving and good parents, with no negative consequences for their children. I explained to her that this was not yet the case and that I had to use different names in this chapter in order to protect the people who had helped us adopt her. I also wanted to make sure that people in China wouldn't treat her differently—because she has two moms—when she visits again. It is up to her to decide if, when, and how to tell people her family story.

Ten years old now, Julie still occasionally asks me to retell the story of her adoption and to explain who knew the truth about Emily and me being partners. These discussions—and the others we have about her forever family, her birth family, and her origins in China—are all part of the rich complexity of Julie's life story.

21 There's No Place Like Home

Mitchell Klein,
with contributions from **Lee Klein**

My son Lee and I are both experienced and prolific travelers. In discussing plans for the winter's holiday, Lee offered little enthusiasm to my overtures: a safari, a tour of European capitals, or an American adventure. In thinking about alternatives, the answer really could not have been more obvious.

"Would you like to go to China?"

"Yes, Dad, yes."

So in March 2008, when Lee was thirteen years old, we headed to China after an absence of, well, almost thirteen years. School and work were both in full swing; we left anyway. A single father, I adopted Lee when he was seven months old. While I remain single, we have had a series of (mostly) extraordinary babysitters and au-pairs to round out our home. Lee and I have a great life together.

The trip had been carefully planned—we would take a homeland heritage tour. Our experience as travelers is logistical; Lee and I are good at moving around, seeing the sights, and enjoying new encounters.

However, we know our limits. We wanted the convenience and security of being accompanied by native speakers in a country where we could not even decipher the written language. Traveling in a small group, we would see some of the most important cultural sites and cities in China. Then each family would return to the city of their child's origin.

Bridging Divides

Happily ensconced in our frequent-flier first-class upgrade, we flew fourteen hours direct from Newark, over the North Pole, to Beijing. Having worked ferociously to both free up my schedule and prepare for the trip, I slept most of the way; Lee made time with the flight attendants while watching an endless loop of TV shows and videos.

We spent the first few days with our guide, negotiating Beijing while trying to recover from jet lag. Lee quickly bridged the cultural divide with a game of billiards in the local pool hall with our driver, Mr. Chen. Coincidentally, in the next two cities our drivers were also named Mr. Chen. Although they spoke not a word of English, all of these men were extraordinarily generous in spirit and deed, establishing a distinctly male bond with Lee.

I suppose the time in the pool hall made up for all the carefully prearranged cultural performances where Lee fell asleep immediately after the lights went down. I, on the other hand, spent many hours persevering in my search for the contemporary art scene. Despite the fact that I went to Beijing armed with gallery addresses, it took a while to realize that our guide could not understand why I would want to go there. The concept of "avant-garde" was incomprehensible to her, even after we arrived at the galleries and saw an amazing array of new art. A recurring observation on this trip was an overwhelming sense of traditional social conformity and uniformity, existing at startling odds with the glimmering shops, such as Tiffany's and Gucci, and the emerging skyline of the New China. Yet Beijing was fascinating and thriving, brimming with contrasts and energy.

Traveling with the Group

With five cities and a thousand miles in front of us, we joined our traveling companions: another single parent with her thirteen-year-old daughter, from Denver, and two moms with their eleven-year-old daughter, from San Diego. The kids forged fast friendships over hand-held electronic devices and text messages home (at fifty cents a message—there was a reckoning upon our return), while the parents began to compare thoughts on the physical and emotional logistics of the journey ahead.

Highlights of our touring included the San Diego Padres playing the Los Angeles Dodgers in Beijing, the Forbidden City, the Great Wall, the terra-cotta soldiers, the ancient walled capital of Xi'an, and a chance to hold a real live panda bear in our laps. We moved from city to city, mostly by overnight sleeper train, with no signs or announcements in English—now whose turn was it to stay awake all night?

American Openness

Frequently, someone would look at Lee and me as we stood beside each other and ask—or mime—"Your son?" We would both nod politely; at first we were wary, but then realized that we were always, without fail, smiled upon in return. At no time was Lee mistaken for a resident. More than once I asked about this and was told that he was so obviously "open" that he could not have been raised in China. I think people meant that through his physical manner Lee exposed himself in a way that, without intention or pretension, did not comport with the norms of Chinese society—conformity in thought and action.

Individuality is a value so imbued in Western culture that it is hardly conspicuous in the U.S., yet in China it instantly revealed the bearer as foreign. Despite this difference, I did not once encounter any resentment; quite the contrary, with their eyes and gestures people expressed to us the same hope for a bright future that we all share for our beloved children.

On Our Own

Our group split up in Chengdu, capital of the frontier Sichuan province, home of the pandas, and site of the devastating 2008 earthquake (which occurred after our departure). Another late-night traveling adventure landed us in Changsha, capital of Hunan province. Only this time we were on our own.

The Dolton Hotel in Changsha is the crossroads of international adoption in this part of China. Its staff is familiar with the needs of Western travelers meeting their children for the first time. Our room was fully equipped with a crib, a bassinet, a baby-food spoon and bowl—and a Barbie doll posing as an adoptive mother holding her Chinese baby. Lee was insulted and appalled. As if matters could be made worse, we were located directly across the hall from a playroom with life-sized stuffed dolls and pandas that would put FAO Schwartz to shame. This was a completely unsuitable welcome for his long-awaited trip; could our host hotel not distinguish the needs of a returning adoptee from those of a family adopting an infant? Indignant, Lee insisted on a new room, in fact a new floor—the crib, the bassinet, and the stuffed animals had to go immediately! Barbie is still with us, though—my reward for our successful relocation.

We woke the next morning knowing we were within driving distance of Lee's village, Yue Yang. For the first time on this trip, I was going to retrace steps I had taken thirteen years ago. Now, just as then, the excitement of being so close to our destination was palpable. The sense of being tourists on vacation was gone as quickly as our change of clothing.

But first we were scheduled for a day of touring in Changsha. The time Lee and I spent there was much more intense than the previous days, partly because we had left our traveling companions and partly because we were closing in on Yue Yang. Looking back, it now feels as if we each were in need of comfort and connection. We found satisfaction in playing out some of our favorite traveling rituals—inspecting the variety of room offerings and sussing out the late night snack and entertainment options; in this case it was a room full of ping-pong tables adjacent to the bowling alley.

Changsha is the city where Mao grew up, and we arranged a visit to the primary school he had attended. We had brought gifts from New York: miniature replicas of the Statue of Liberty and pencils with pictures of the Empire State Building. We were looking forward to mingling with kids close to Lee's age in their own environment. Lee and I joined an English lesson in a class of sixty fifth-graders, in which students were learning the English names of food items such as chicken, eggs, and vegetables. (When I discussed this chapter with Lee, he recalled—with envy and dismay—the boy in the red shirt who could not contain his excitement, his hand shooting up ready to be first to name each new picture we would display.) We all laughed about our common love of fast-food and sugary snacks, while pantomiming that same common knowledge of expanding waistlines and cavities.

Uncovering another cultural divide, we discovered that hamburgers are strictly "out-to-eat" food in China, just as dumplings are in the U.S. Everyone, including the teacher, was truly amazed that you could make a hamburger at home! The kids pored over the souvenirs we had brought as if they were exotic treasures. We were rushed by those wanting to get a closer look, while others didn't want to look at all; a few students wrote us notes with their names—kids are kids and school is school. For some, the class ended too quickly and for others not quickly enough.

Off to Yue Yang, Finally

The drive through the countryside was nothing like it had been thirteen years ago. I have frighteningly clear memories of the one-lane road from Changsha to Yue Yang (that's one lane in total, not one in each direction), with no one slowing down. Now we were on a four-lane highway, nary a pagoda hat to be found; we saw no one bent over working the fields, yet the fields were in perfect condition. Apart from our purposeful mood, we could have been on vacation driving in Oregon.

As our trip seemed to descend into slow motion, I could only imagine what was in Lee's mind. Some have speculated that a primal yearning had to have been at play. I just don't know; as connected as I am to my son, at this moment even to speculate seemed intrusive. Yet I did sense in Lee a pensive apprehension—so I stepped in as father and protector. Reviewing the itinerary first with myself and then with the guide I became clear: I know my child's psyche and sensitivities. Standard fare in this part of the homeland experience is a retracing of events that are speculative at best. I would not conform. The connection between Lee and me has always existed, it is bedrock—there was no need for grim discussion of imagined separations, abandonment locations, and miraculous or mundane findings.

Yue Yang, with 1.6 million people, is considered a small, remote provincial city. To us it looked (and smelled) like Paris. The years had consumed the bicyclists teetering on the dirt road's edge. The four-lane highway opened onto a glorious boulevard lined with arches, heralding our arrival at the feet of the great Chairman Mao. This was definitely not the place I remember.

We proceeded directly to a restaurant where we were scheduled to have lunch with workers from the Yue Yang Social Welfare Institute #6. Another cultural divide: Lee had spent his first months of life in what the Chinese call a Social Welfare Institute (SWI), which is a compound housing a population in need of care—including infants, toddlers, teenagers, and the elderly. To my understanding, *orphanage* was a Western construct. I have subsequently learned, through my work on this chapter, that orphanages do have a corollary in China—Children's Welfare Institutes. The difference is subtle, perhaps convenient or particular to Lee's story, but, to me, the idea of a compound, buzzing with people from young to old, feels less lonely and less isolated than an orphanage.

We arrive at the restaurant, wash up, and are introduced to the current director of the SWI, who thirteen years ago had worked in accounting. We next meet two women who had always worked in the nursery. Since Lee was one of only seven infant boys to have ever crossed their door, these women actually remember Lee. I, of course, start to cry.

Having just washed up and not wanting to offend our lunch guests, I could not excuse myself from the table—so I must choke back this tidal wave of emotion lest I scare or embarrass my son, who I know is having his own experience. This is a loaded moment. I look at Lee; Lee looks at me. Somewhat uncomprehendingly, with slight disdain, but at least in a whisper he says, "What's the matter with you? What in the world are you crying about?" A year later, assembling our chapter, Lee still finds this amusing.

Clinking glasses throughout an extended lunch, everyone took a turn standing to toast our good health, good fortune, and good travels. (Another universal truth is finding a good excuse for an extra-long out-to-lunch on a workday.) Translations ensued, more clinking, a little more crying, some photos, and lunch was over. Lee's summary: "That was weird; meeting people who knew me while I was waiting for my Dad." He loves the idea that he was one of only seven boys and the only one to ever come back to visit. A few more tears for me, then—and even now as I write.

After leaving our luncheon, we needed some time to decompress. Yue Yang is the home of a great medieval fortress, which had been upgraded in every successive dynasty. We wandered through the fort and imagined having to protect the city from Mongols invading from the north.

There was one more stop to make before leaving Yue Yang. We drove to the gates of the SWI, knowing we would not go inside. This part of the city had not seen the same benefits as the grand boulevard and felt much more familiar to my memory. Neither of us felt a strong connection to this spot, but we needed to see it, and there it was. Looking back, it seems odd to feel void of connection to this particular location. Standing at the gates, of course I remembered the night I first held Lee. But the story of our coming together did not begin here any more than a hospital could represent the story of a child's conception. Recalling the conversation I had with our guide on the drive to Yue Yang, I feel that our trip is not a story of abandonment or discovery, but rather a confirmation of the lives we live.

The drive from Yue Yang back to Changsha was quiet. We were tired, physically and emotionally. Unlike the outbound journey, this time I was sure of my job—quiet reassurance. Lee is a child of not-so-many-words, and we had just been through an experience for which not-so-many-words have been formed. So I was quietly reassuring—sometimes I took Lee's hand; sometimes we pressed against each other looking out opposite windows. Even writing a year later I am not clear of all my own feelings, although I think Lee may be closer to his.

It wasn't long before we were back in the city. We stopped at a supermarket; we were hungry and another overnight train ride was scheduled for the next night. Doritos or Oreos topped the list of comfort foods we hoped to find; the best we could do were Kit-Kat bars and Ramen-like noodles. On the way back to the hotel we contemplated switching rooms, then demurred, returning to what had now become *our* ping-pong table. We played until closing and so we returned together again, back to our room. Bedrock.

There's No Place Like Home

Our trip lasted several more days. We visited southern China, where the landscape and the people were strikingly different from the north. Lee reminds me that by this time all he wanted to do was go home. In many ways the sheer quantity and accumulation of new experiences—personal, emotional, historical, educational and logistical—was overwhelming. Lee discovered for himself a clear affirmation of his home. In his mind, China was his birthplace, but not his home. Lee was and remains steadfast about this. Frankly, I was more willing to be expansive, to accept the possibility of a new, unimagined paradigm. Yet, just as Lee was not mistaken for a resident, Lee did not mistake China for home.

We reconnected with our group in Guangzhou and spent one last day touring, shopping, and eating before heading home. Our route included a change of planes in Guam and a few days in Hawaii. Hawaii was a hedge against hitting the ground running immediately upon our return to New York; if there was some unraveling to be done upon re-entry, perhaps a few days on an American beach was the place to do it. While Hawaii was lovely and certainly lush in comparison to China, in the end it just contributed to more body-clock confusion, at least for me. When we finally got home, Lee bounced back immediately, wanting to go directly from the airport to school to see his friends; I had to sleep for a month.

It is now exactly a year since our trip began. More than anything I feel like Lee's story has now been illustrated. The country of his birth is no longer a concept, but a place; a place not home, but not just any place either. In our lives I have always been mindful that this story belongs to Lee; it is part of him. When we were offered the opportunity to contribute to this book, I first asked what he thought—he loved the idea that we might be famous. Famous or not, I knew that I would not try to write this without him and would not submit the final product without his consent. He has read and commented several times, adding his own color and texture. So much so, that I asked if he wanted to share his thoughts and write the last paragraph. This is what he wrote:

When I went to China I thought it would be different than it was—I thought people would think I was from China but I was wrong. In some parts it looked dirty and gross and I did not want to be there but in some parts it was really nice.

I had a great time on this trip. I want to go back when I get older and when I have my own family.

China was great and it will always be a part of me. I think that China will always be the same in my mind, even though I know it has to change in the real world.

For me America is home. I know the culture and the way of life. I have my family and my friends, my house and my dog. All that makes it home. My home.

My Second Trip of a Lifetime

22

Rose A. Lewis

My trip to China to adopt my daughter was the trip of a lifetime. After all, how could anything compare to meeting your child for the first time? I thought nothing could possibly be more meaningful, until my daughter and I returned to China together eleven years later.

November 1996

It was a drizzly, cool morning in November of 1996, when my daughter Ming-Ming, my mother and I, along with seven other families, boarded a bus for the airport to begin our trips home from China. We had become parents together in an instant and supported each other through our first days with our children, and now we were on our way to becoming families on our own. I remember sitting in my seat with my arms wrapped around my daughter, feeling both excited and a bit scared about our new life together.

Then I thought back to the day two weeks earlier when my mother and I had landed in Hong Kong to meet the other families. I had started to cry when the plane landed because I realized that I was closer to holding my daughter than I had ever been. Likewise, on this day of departure, as I held my daughter close, I realized I would be taking her farther away from her homeland than she had ever been. Fighting back tears, I leaned down and whispered into Ming's ear, "We'll be back someday, I promise."

Planning Our Trip

I kept that promise. I made the decision to return to China with Ming just after her tenth birthday. I had heard that a good time to make a return visit was when children were between the ages of nine and eleven, when they are old enough to appreciate the trip and not yet too embarrassed to be seen in public with their parents. I spent a lot of time researching options and asking others who had gone before us, as I wanted it to be just right. I didn't want Ming to just see China; I wanted her to *feel* it. How could I make this happen? I couldn't, really. I could only hope that those who helped us navigate through this tremendous country and its people would understand that this was a mission of sorts, a mission of discovery.

We began our two-and-a-half week visit traveling with other families who had adopted children from China. We signed up for a one-week trip with Our Chinese Daughters Foundation (OCDF), followed by ten days on our own that included a visit to Ming's orphanage, the Xi'an Social Welfare Institute in Xianning.

At the beginning of my planning I had thought of traveling alone with Ming and a guide. But then I realized it would be nice to share this experience with other children and their parents, who were also making their first return trip to China. It turned out just as I had hoped. Within hours of meeting, the children claimed the back of the bus, the adults the middle and front. We adults fell into comfortable conversations about our experiences with our children and our hopes that seeing

China would help them develop a real connection to their birth country. The children stuck together, the older ones helping the younger ones when necessary. They enjoyed the freedom of exploring China with new friends—and with their parents at arm's length. I remember the day the group trip ended. We all gathered in the lobby of the hotel and hugged one another good-bye as, one by one, each family left for the airport to go to their orphanage city and other parts of China. It was a little sad to say good-bye, and I admit Ming and I were both in a bit of a funk for the rest of the day.

Grandmas in the Park

The most valuable advice I received before making our return trip was from a friend who implored me not to take a nap or a swim in the hotel pool after a long, tiring day of sightseeing. She told us to be sure to walk around the city and go to the parks, where we would meet people and feel what China is all about. How right she was! Ming and I, despite our exhaustion on some days, always ventured out to meet people. Chinese people seem to use their parks as communal living rooms—visiting with friends, taking dancing lessons, or playing games. One of our late afternoons in the park was particularly memorable.

After a long and very hot visit to the magnificent terra-cotta warriors and horses in Xi'an, Ming and I headed to the park near our hotel. There we encountered four grandmas caring for their grandchildren. They looked at us with great curiosity and a little concern. Finally Ming informed them in Mandarin that I was her mother, and there were instant smiles all around. I think they really marveled at this unusual pairing. While we in the United States may think the Chinese must see the thousands of families who adopt each year, we forget that China is so big there are few Chinese people who actually see families like us on the street.

In the park Ming sang a song for the grandmas and won their hearts, particularly one of them who made an uncanny connection with Ming. She hugged her gently and stood with her arm around her for quite some time. The photo I took of the two of them smiling is among my favorite photographs from our return trip.

Not surprisingly, the major breakthrough came when I handed Ming a photograph to show the grandmas. It was a photo I had taken just two weeks earlier of Ming standing with China's number-one athlete and overall superstar, the seven-foot-six-inch Yao Ming. Ming had met Yao Ming through the generosity of a man we had met at a Red Sox game the summer before. He marveled at Ming's baseball knowledge (she was explaining something about a player to me) and then asked her what other sports she liked. "Basketball," she answered. And when he asked who her favorite player was, she answered without hesitation, "Yao Ming."

The man replied, "I know Yao Ming. I help design his basketball shoes at Reebok." Months later, seemingly out of the blue, this man called me at my office to say he had tickets for a Celtics-Rockets game the next evening and oh, by the way, he had made arrangements for Ming to meet Yao Ming. I am not sure who was more excited, Ming or I, but she is the one who got to sit and talk with Yao Ming by herself for a good ten minutes, while I nervously photographed the two of them. I was a professional photographer for many years. I have photographed presidents, rock stars, and even the Pope, but this was the most nerve-wracking assignment ever. Luckily, I got more than my share of good shots and managed to have a nice conversation with Yao myself.

After the meeting I asked Ming if she realized what an honor this was, as there were 1.2 billion people in China who would love to meet Yao Ming. She said yes, but I don't think it was until she saw how people in China reacted to the photo of her standing next to him that she truly understood the enormity of it all. This one photograph seemed to get us closer to the people than we ever imagined.

The Road to Xianning, Ming's Orphanage City

We landed in Wuhan on a very hot, humid April day. A guide and a driver met us at the airport, and because a portion of the highway was closed, we had to take a circuitous route to Xianning, one that took us through various villages and smaller cities. I marveled at the countryside. Like most people who visit China, I was struck by the juxtaposition of old-fashioned taxis on the same streets as Western vehicles. While tired and a bit lonesome for the friends she had made during our week-long group tour, Ming rallied and kept her nose pressed to the window to watch the scenery—which included chickens in the road at one moment and then, suddenly, rows of storefronts with the logos of American computer companies the next. It was like watching a live slide show of the old country quickly dissolving to the new and then back again.

After checking into our hotel, we quickly changed for dinner and then went to the hotel restaurant to meet the parents of a Chinese student with whom we had connected via the Internet. This student, whose American name is Charley, had been born and raised in Xianning. He and his wife, Apple, were now graduate students in Illinois. Charley's mother had recently made her first trip to America to care for their new baby. A few months later she had brought the baby back to China, where she and her husband cared for him while his parents completed their graduate degrees. So it was our good fortune to not only have dinner with Charley's parents, but to meet Charley and Apple's baby, David, as well.

Charley's father is a high-ranking official in the police department of this "small" city of 1.2 million people. It was a lovely dinner, and through our interpreter I began asking Charley's father about the city. What did I hope to learn from him? Perhaps a hint about Ming's parents? I noticed Ming listening intently as well. I tried asking about abandoned children, but it was obvious that Charley's dad was uncomfortable with this topic. As a member of the police force he certainly must have seen many children abandoned at the police station or brought there from somewhere else. I am rarely shy about asking questions, but when you are a guest in someone else's country it's amazing how quickly you begin to edit yourself at the slightest hint of hesitation from your host. I really wanted to know if there was any hope of finding Ming's parents. Intellectually I knew the answer but my heart remained just a little bit hopeful, as had Ming's at one time.

When I first mentioned to Ming the idea of traveling back to China she was very excited. Ming had always wondered about where she came from. She was only six when she first asked me why her mother couldn't raise her. When we started talking about making our return trip, she asked me if it would be all right if she made a big poster with her name in Chinese and English. She would carry it around just in case her mother in China recognized her name. "Yes, of course," I told her. "But I must tell you that there are more than a billion people in China and it's unlikely you will find her, but you can make a sign and I will be glad to help you. I would like to meet her, too." A year later, Ming either forgot about the idea or simply realized it probably wasn't going to help her find her mother.

The Orphanage Visit

The next morning was gray and rainy. We were excited—and, yes, a little bit scared—about our visit to Ming's orphanage. While I was still in bed, I noticed Ming was up, looking out the window at the city below and quietly singing "Somewhere Over The Rainbow." Ming had played Dorothy in *The Wizard of Oz* at camp the summer before and she was practicing this song in case there was an opportunity to sing to the children at the orphanage. Suddenly I started worrying about our visit. My daughter was about to be confronted with the reality of an earlier life that did not include her current family and would most likely not provide any clues to her former one. I braced myself for what was likely to be a very emotional day.

With two duffel bags full of knitted hats, scarves, booties, and sweaters Ming had collected through her project, "Knitting to China," we were on our way. Ming had e-mailed friends and family months before our departure asking them to knit things for the children in the orphanage. We had decided on this together after I suggested that our return trip would be more meaningful if Ming had a project that would connect her to her orphanage. We will always be grateful to the family members, friends, and even strangers who cared enough to spend their free time creating this incredible bounty.

As we approached the orphanage, I could barely breathe. Ming was quiet with anticipation. The orphanage was a huge complex behind an iron gate. Like many in China, this Social Welfare Institute takes care of both children and the elderly. We announced our arrival and the gate opened to let us drive into a huge courtyard that had nothing but a large empty swing set. I immediately began to wonder, "Where are the children?" This was not the original orphanage building where Ming had lived the first seven months of her life, but was actually the third location of the SWI. Ming had been at the first one, which was still standing but no longer an orphanage. We would visit that one later.

We were greeted in the courtyard by orphanage director Lu and a provincial official. Mr. Lu escorted us to an elevator that brought us up to the third floor. There, a huge sign in Chinese and English read, "Welcome Fang Xiang Ming (Ming's Chinese name) go back home." We smiled at each other and knew they meant to say, "Welcome home." We all sat down and the provincial official read us a welcoming statement in Chinese that, simply translated, welcomed us to the orphanage and welcomed Ming back to her country.

We presented Mr. Lu and his assistant with our duffel bags filled with knitted goods, and we will never, ever forget the smiles and laughter this gift brought to Mr. Lu and his staff. After our welcoming ceremony, Mr. Lu and others traveled with us to the second location of the orphanage. When we arrived the children, who were around three and four years old, giggled and stared at Ming and me. The children clearly knew Mr. Lu and greeted him warmly. They sang us a song and then Ming sang "Somewhere Over The Rainbow." Mr. Lu could not take his eyes off of Ming, and again I wondered what he was thinking.

A little girl wearing a Disney jacket led her class in applause and the teacher asked for another song. Ming sang "God Bless America," and I marveled at this moment. Here was my daughter, now in the city where she had once lived, singing "God Bless America" to a group of children she might have been among were it not for some remarkable twist of fate.

The Finding Spot

We all tumbled into the van once again and made our way on a winding dirt road to the spot where Ming was found and the original site of the Xi'an District Social Welfare Institute, the orphanage where Ming had actually lived. The drivers parked the vans at the bottom of a small hill. We started walking up a short distance to the finding spot. As we approached the top, we were greeted by two barking dogs and a curious young man who came out of a tiny brick structure to see what the commotion was all about. We learned that there had once been six of these little brick buildings, part of a textile machine factory, but only three were now standing. Little by little, other people also came out of their homes. It was lunchtime and most of them were standing with chopsticks and bowls of rice in their hands—eating, smiling, and staring at us.

I was right behind Ming and Mr. Lu when they reached the top. Mr. Lu pointed. "There," he said through the interpreter. "There. This is where a worker found you."

"There" was on the ground in front of a simple white door that led to an abandoned one-room brick structure with a barred window. The structure was framed by a very tall tree growing out of cement. Ming and I stood together for a moment, just looking, and then suddenly, with sheer determination, Ming walked right up to the door. We all watched and took pictures as Ming explored the brick structure. She looked up at the top of the door and then slowly made her way to the bottom, as if etching every inch of this door in her memory so she would always know where someone had placed her to be found. Then Ming stood on her tiptoes to peek through the bars on the window to see what was inside.

It was a poignant moment for all of us. I tried to visualize Ming as a newborn, bundled up against the April chill and gently being placed at the threshold. I wondered who had brought her to this spot to be found. Was it one or both of her parents, a relative, or a friend who had taken on this unbearable task? Did they hide and wait until someone found her? Was Ming cold and crying? Was the person who left her crying too? I was flooded with my own questions. Then Mr. Lu broke my concentration and pointed to a woman standing outside her small one-room home. He told us that this woman had worked in the orphanage when Ming was there. It wasn't until weeks later, when we were watching videos of this day, that Ming realized this woman was the caretaker who had traveled with her and the other babies from Xianning to Wuhan the day I adopted her. This was the woman who had actually handed Ming to me forever. I had taken a photo of her standing and holding Ming just before I stepped forward to receive her. I wish I had known it was her during our visit. I would have asked if she remembered Ming and tried to find out what, if anything, she could have told me about Ming's first few months.

We looked all around the building that had once been Ming's orphanage, but we could not go inside because several families now call it home. Then, suddenly and surprisingly, a sense of comfort overcame me. The questions stopped dancing in my head and I simply felt at peace. I think it was comforting to know there was a very short distance between Ming's finding spot and the orphanage. I was comforted by the fact that someone in China, Mr. Lu, who may not really remember Ming as a baby, could now delight in who she was and perhaps envision who she would grow up to be. But mostly I felt comforted by Ming's curiosity. I was moved by the way she explored these two spots, photographing them and acknowledging that these were her beginnings. At last she had a foundation from which to grow and a place to come back to. At least one of the missing pieces was now in place.

Formula for the Babies

Our next stop was to buy powdered milk with the donations Ming had collected at home. The store was a tiny variety store. While Mr. Lu was in the shop arranging the milk purchase with the clerk, Ming discovered a round display of colorful lollipops. When she started to take money out of her pocket to buy one, Mr. Lu stopped her and insisted on buying it. It was a lovely, tender moment.

We brought the cartons of powdered milk back to the orphanage and Mr. Lu insisted we come back upstairs to see his office and other parts of the orphanage. I was hoping we would see where the children slept, but we did not. Mr. Lu and others said most of the children were in school or in foster care. While I still wasn't quite satisfied with the answer, I chose not to pursue what may have been too uncomfortable for the staff. We had in fact stopped to see a child in foster care and visited the school, but at this point there were some unanswered questions: Why didn't the orphanage director want us to see the children's living quarters? Was it a matter of privacy or simply not allowed on the tour? I just didn't feel comfortable exploring these questions any further.

Mr. Lu proudly showed us his office and Ming giggled as she went around to sit in his chair behind the desk. They were being very playful with one another and in spite of the language barrier there was another unspoken language that they had developed through the day. It was clear that they had bonded. When it was time to say goodbye, Mr. Lu lifted Ming up and they gave each other a magnificent hug. Luckily I caught it on camera. That photo is framed and sits in a spot in our house that we both see at least once a day. There is sheer joy on both of their faces, and every time I take a moment to really examine the photo I think back to that day and I remember that peaceful and comforting feeling all over again.

"I Think I Love China"

After we said our goodbyes to Mr. Lu and his staff we got into our van and headed back to Wuhan, where we would stay overnight before our morning flight to Shanghai. It had been an extraordinary day. The anticipation had exhausted me and the moment we began our drive I shut my eyes and instantly fell asleep for just a few minutes. When I opened them I saw Ming, once again staring out the window, not wanting to miss a thing. "What are you thinking?" I asked. And without hesitation, Ming said, "I think I love China and I want to come back."

I gave her a kiss, smiled, and closed my eyes again. "Yes, it worked," I thought as I wiped a small tear from my cheek. There was no doubt in my mind that Ming not only saw China but now feels a real connection to it. I know that my daughter will someday return again to China, and I hope she will never stop being curious about her life's journey.

V

traveling with
CHILDREN
who face
EMOTIONAL CHALLENGES

Good Intentions, Difficult Consequences

23

Jane Samuel

"Would your family like to join us for a homeland tour to China in May 2007? Later, Meimei"

In the spring of 2006 I was sitting at my computer when that e-mail opened up on my screen. We were living with our three daughters in Singapore, where my husband was on assignment with his job. Meimei's invitation was tempting, although I had some very real concerns about how a return to her orphanage might affect our youngest daughter, Olivia.

After Olivia came home to us at the age of twelve months she seemed to never look back. She was a happy, outwardly healthy, and busy baby—but as the months, and then years, went by—I couldn't help wondering if she was busier and more outgoing than a toddler should be. She also seemed too wound up at times to sleep and would wake far too early in the morning, as if a switch had been flipped, though she was clearly still

Note: Some names in this chapter have been changed to protect privacy.

tired. Her switch would not flip off again until some fourteen hours later when she fell asleep, often in mid-sentence.

After our move to Asia, we realized Olivia needed help and so did we. An occupational therapy evaluation indicated Sensory Processing Disorder (SPD), a common result of having spent formative months in an institution. Olivia began weekly therapy and I began my second job: educating myself about Olivia. As I reached out online to other mothers, read enough to get a doctoral degree, and watched Olivia slowly come around, I realized there were more layers to her than an onion. Besides the SPD, she was also struggling with grief, attachment issues, and trauma. Most of the time Olivia was a happy and smart child, albeit a bit more controlling and on-the-go than most four-year-olds. But there were times when life seemed to overwhelm her and she became abnormally active or, even worse, collapsed into tantrums of grief over her birth mother.

How would this restless, lovable, grief-filled child of mine handle a ten-day trip "back in time?" Was she too young (she would be just shy of five at the time of the tour) to get anything out of it? Was she too fragile to endure the painful emotions it might trigger? Would the trip help or be a trigger that would set her back and close off even more of her heart and mind?

Like any good former lawyer, I began to research homeland tours. I turned to the Our Chinese Daughters Foundation (OCDF) website to read what its founder, Jane Liedtke, had to say. According to Liedtke, an expert on return trips, age four is young but theoretically not too young. Liedtke also highlights the benefits of traveling with other children of similar ages because of the shared experience. There would be several girls on our trip, ages six and seven, and their siblings. Definitely a plus, though Olivia's younger age would not make her a true peer.

But it was Liedtke's counsel on realistic expectations that gave me pause. Were we doing this trip for Olivia or for us? I began to wonder about our daughter's expectations. What would be her fears? Her desires? Was she even old enough to have desires? Would she understand why we were making the trip? What would she take home in her "toolbox?" Finally, would we be able to prepare her properly, to help her look at the trip realistically and not like some fantasy journey back to her birth mother?

Preparation

I remembered how my failure to realistically prepare our first daughters for Olivia's arrival had caused our middle daughter, Chloe, much heartache. I had let the excitement of the girls' giddy plans of sleeping with the baby and rocking and feeding her lull me into a false sense of optimism. When Olivia came home, Chloe struggled for months to make sense of her new, very big, and busy sibling who was certainly not going to let a petite kindergartner feed and rock her!

Similarly, our enthusiasm to do an overseas assignment had blunted our ability to see the downside of such a move for Olivia. By the time Olivia was four, she had lived in China, America, and then Singapore. I hadn't considered that she needed constancy and simplicity, rather than my well-intentioned efforts to immerse her in a Chinese society. Now, some two-and-a-half years later, Olivia has finally embraced Asian life, but her first year was certainly not the fantasy I had planned.

This time around, I was determined to think realistically and put myself in my child's shoes. I knew that just telling Olivia about our plans to go to her orphanage would not be enough. Younger children, especially those with Olivia's challenges, need concrete descriptions. Pictorial stories and role-playing can help in setting out an event that will take place, as well as showing feelings that might surface.

With this in mind, I put together a small book for Olivia. I illustrated it with photos I had of her, her travel mates, the city of Yiyang, and the orphanage. I pasted one or two photos on each page depicting what we would see, do, and experience. At the end of the book I created a few pages regarding feelings, using photos of Olivia with her sisters, as well as one of her taken during an especially pensive moment.

The story writing was more difficult. Adoption experts underscore the need to avoid sugar-coating the realities of an adoptive child's past life. While at times difficult to face, past events are still part of that child, and to gloss over them or relate them in an inaccurate or rosy manner can do more harm than good.

Similarly, as parents we might want to steer clear of discussing difficult feelings to avoid the pain and harm we feel these discussions cause. That's also a disservice to our children, who must know that we trust their feelings and love them in spite of those feelings and their intensity. Olivia's unexpected and unsolicited grief on her fourth birthday, when she broke into sobs, saying, "I miss my other parents," confirmed this. She will have her feelings whether I give voice to them or not.

Thus, in crafting the text for Olivia's book, I had to carefully consider the message I was sending about her orphanage experience, which we now believed to have been fair at best. I also had to think about what she might hope to gain from the visit, things that we might not be able to deliver. For example, we needed to be careful not to let Olivia think she could meet her birth mother or her caregiver—her *ayi*. Of course the identity of her birth mother is unknown, and we already knew that her last *ayi* was no longer at the orphanage. In addition, I wanted to make sure she knew she would be coming home with us when the trip was over, that there was no plan to return her to the orphanage.

I went through many drafts before I had the finished product: a small ten-page book which I hoped accurately set forth the story of this possible trip "home."

Preparing the book also allowed me to work through some of my own feelings regarding the trip. I needed to create a realistic plan, with contingencies depending on how Olivia reacted, for dealing with each phase of the tour. Once again, I reminded myself that the trip had to be about Olivia and what she needed, not what I wanted for myself or her siblings.

Given Olivia's weekly birth mother woes, it was not a difficult decision to put the orphanage visit in the "Plan B" column, something Liedtke specifically advises. If we were having a bad time at any point, we could always implement more of Plan B: Hang back at the hotel and play. Most importantly, I allowed myself the luxury of saying over and over again, "We can back out at any point and cancel." This was a necessary "Plan C."

Armed with Olivia's storybook and plans A, B, and C, I approached the next step with trepidation. Despite my own emotional preparation, I was afraid Olivia would not want to go and we would be done with the notion of a homeland tour, at least for now. It is not easy to put that kind of power in the hands of a four-year-old, but I felt, with the advice of the experts, that it was necessary.

Sitting on the couch in our sun-filled living room, I told Olivia that we were thinking about going on a trip to China to see where she had lived before she came to be our daughter. I reminded her that we had already been to China to see the Great Wall and explained how this trip would be different. Olivia looked at me in a somewhat ambivalent manner and said, "Okay."

With Olivia, ambivalence often meant she did not fully grasp the concept presented. I showed her the pictures in the book and used the story to give her a concrete idea of what I was talking about. During some of my previous attempts to read adoption-related picture books, she would close the book and tell me it was "stupid," but she did not do that now. Rather, she seemed genuinely interested in looking at the photos.

After e-mailing Meimei that we would be joining the group, I continued to read Olivia her book and ask her if she really did want to go to China. Each time her response was the same: "Yes, if I can hold the babies in the orphanage." Although not certain, I hoped this would be possible and told her so. We moved forward with booking flights and finalizing details, always keeping the possibility of a cancellation in the back of my mind.

A few months later, my husband, Terry, the girls, and I boarded a plane to Xi'an from Singapore. The adventure had begun.

In China

Once in China, Olivia seemed to do well at first. In Xi'an we effortlessly slipped into the group, which had already been together for a few days. We enjoyed touring this ancient city and seeing the famous terra-cotta warriors. From Xi'an we flew to Zhangjiajie National Park, a fairly remote forest area in northwestern Hunan province. Following an exhausting but beautiful day in the forest, everyone slept well in the mountain air and woke refreshed to board the bus for the drive to Yiyang. After waiting for a new tour bus when ours broke down, we made it to Yiyang some seven hours after leaving Zhangjiajie.

Our time in Yiyang was easily segregated into two rounds of activities: sightseeing and those involving the girls' first "home," the Yiyang Children's Welfare Institute. The side trips, to local sites like the park to feed the fish and the Buddhist temple, were perfect diversions before the more emotional orphanage trip, scheduled for later.

On the morning of the orphanage visit, I had to remind Olivia where we were going. Suddenly, she seemed to balk at the idea and I felt my heart pulled in two directions. I told her that if we didn't go that day there would not be another day to hold the babies; I also told her she did not have to go. She thought for a minute and again asked if she would be able to rock and feed them. After assurances that we would get to see them and we certainly would ask to rock them, she jumped up and said, "Let's go."

For me the visit was as emotional as my first trip there, while for Olivia it seemed to be less emotionally charged. She enjoyed playing with the babies and did get to hold and rock them. She also seemed pleased to show off her book to the orphanage director, and I wished I had made a copy for him to keep. She played with the fifteen or so children in the preschool, many of whom had special needs, and tried to help hold a four-year-old who clung to me, wanting to be carried to look out the window. If Olivia had any negative feelings they seemed to be locked away inside.

As the visit came to a close, we gathered outside in front of the famed gate where Olivia and several others in the group had been found. Olivia quietly shook hands with the man who had found her. Then, with the director behind them, the girls lined up for a special photo. Encouraged by her clowning siblings, Olivia laughed brightly for the camera, something she usually does not want to do. On the bus, a few of the older girls appeared pensive; Olivia, however, chattered on. Drained, I once again watched her first home disappear through the windows of a Chinese tour bus.

Impact of the Trip

I am still not so sure how this trip, both the sightseeing and the orphanage visit, affected Olivia. While she seemed to be generally fine during the trips out-and-about as well as the time spent de-stressing in the hotel room, she developed an unusual behavior only while in Yiyang. Olivia, our usually very busy child who never napped, chose the very hectic evening meals as a time to pull up a chair and fall sound asleep. Since she had never done this on any of our other Asian trips over the past year, I found it more than a bit odd and the term *dissociation* came to mind.

Dissociation, loosely defined, is a mental mechanism that allows one to disengage from the external world. This can involve distraction, avoidance, daydreaming, and, in the extreme, fainting or catatonia. Given that Olivia had never done this before and has not done it since (despite traveling many more times) it seems plausible that something about being in Yiyang caused it.

Perhaps for her it was a way of saying, "There are things here that remind my inner being of something and I need to take a break from the memories." All the smells, tastes, words, faces and even events may have spoken to Olivia in subconscious whispers, and the trip may have been more difficult for her than it outwardly appeared.

It was very hard to think that Olivia needed to "check out." It made me worry that I had not made the right choice. I was not sure if she was re-experiencing the traumas of her abandonment, her orphanage experience, or her transfer from everything she had known to our family. To a small child, any of these situations can be overwhelming, and the body has an amazing memory, even if we cannot speak about our earliest memories. As her mother, I certainly did not want to increase any trauma she may have suffered.

Olivia's behavior following the trip only increased this worry. At first I had been hopeful that our plans for after the trip, returning to our

Singapore home and then on to America for our six week home-leave, would give Olivia the closure that she needed to move on from China. This may not have been the best plan. For the entire time we were in America, Olivia was very emotional and out of control.

Unfortunately for her, and for us, her feelings about everything had to have an outlet and this outlet was tantrums. Every two to three days something set Olivia off, and she would spiral into an hour-long fit. Screaming and crying, legs kicking and body writhing, her sweet face turned dark as she let loose a litany of woes, from missing her birth-mother to being in the wrong family. And the most difficult of all to listen to was her argument to me that I had not allowed her to stay with her birth mother, but rather somehow had taken her away.

During these tirades she would not let me hold her; she spent most of her time on the bed beside me as I tried to use empathetic words to soothe her. At times she would scream for me to leave her alone. Instead, I prayed vehemently for her small heart to be healed.

Once back in Singapore for our next year of assignment, and back to weekly occupational therapy (OT) sessions and a better school, Olivia's tantrums began to subside. As the past year has gone by, she has learned more ways to keep herself regulated and has exploded developmentally, taking to writing, coloring, imaginative play, and even card games. And I have discovered more layers to this complex creature, some very happy and carefree—and some dark and brooding, waiting beneath a general sea of calm to rock our family boat.

Originally I felt that our home-leave—seeing grandparents, friends, and old teachers, and even re-experiencing Kentucky sounds and smells—was the driving force behind Olivia's emotional explosion that summer, and her subsequent developmental leap. Now, however, I find myself wondering what role our homeland trip played, whether it was a catalyst. If so, was it one that I would set in motion again?

From an emotional point of view, probably not. Olivia was too young. Her age made the trip more work for us and less meaningful to her. Yet there was more to her experience than just being too young.

Her strange behavior of using sleep to "sign off" while in Yiyang—and the subsequent summer of painful tantrums—were worrying. If I had known that these would occur, I might have left well enough alone for a few more years—years that might have given her more strength to draw on when the going got tough. At the time of our trip, Olivia had just begun a regime of OT (which we now know has worked wonders) and home attachment and trauma work, so waiting would have given her more time for healing and put more emotional tools at her fingertips—healing that might have made it easier for her to face the difficult memories; tools that would have enabled her to turn to me for support rather than fleeing into herself.

As a mother to three children, I know that life is not always as it seems, nor does it always turn out the way we intend. There are never any easy answers to the big decisions we make on behalf of these lives with which we are entrusted. However, I do know that proper preparation, planning, and—most importantly—patience and empathy go a long way in making even wrong decisions turn out for the best.

24

Traveling with a Traumatized Child

The author of this chapter wishes to remain anonymous to protect the privacy of her family.

When my husband and I adopted our daughter from China in 1996, I became passionately interested in international adoption and read everything I could on the subject. I very much wanted to do everything right in raising Lily, including taking her on a homeland trip. I wanted her to have real knowledge of her birth country, to see and experience her own cultural heritage, and to feel pride in being from China. I believed Lily would benefit from the experience of being in a place where everyone looks like her, and would gain an idea of what her life would have been like if she had not been abandoned or adopted abroad.

I also wanted to acknowledge that her life began in China, that she had lived with her birth family for a few months and then in a Social Welfare Institute. This is her own life history and she is absolutely entitled to ownership of it. I felt a strong obligation to reunite her with her past, and I believed that the experiences and memories gained on a homeland trip would equip Lily to deal better with adoption issues as she grows up.

Most experts recommend that families do a cultural tour first and then visit the orphanage on a second trip. This, they believe, gives the child a good impression of China before she confronts the more stressful experience of revisiting an orphanage. At the time, however, we did not have the money for two trips, so we wanted to visit my daughter's orphanage on this first, and perhaps only, visit.

The problem was, my child had reactive attachment disorder (RAD). Would it be advisable to take her to China? Would the trip trigger such trauma that all the hard work she and I had put into healing would be negated? Would she have meltdowns on the trip? How could we cope if she fell apart in China?

We did take her to China when she was eight years old, and she did not suffer any adverse long-term effects. In fact, I believe her experiences were another significant step in her healing. On looking back on our trip, I can identify several reasons why she did so well. These include the years of therapy and attachment work we had done prior to the trip, the ways we prepared Lily before traveling, and the ways we planned and carried out our trip.

Attachment Therapy

Lily was adopted from China as an infant. At age four, her controlling, hyperactive, and aggressive behavior led to a diagnosis of the anxious type of RAD. Evidently, her abandonment, and the institutional neglect inevitable in an orphanage, had led to her inability to form a loving attachment to me, her adoptive mother, and resulted in severe pervading anxiety about being abandoned again. I also know now that she had post-traumatic stress disorder (PTSD), which was not then officially part of her diagnosis.

Fortunately, I was able to stay home and become a therapeutic parent (as described in *Building the Bonds of Attachment*, by Daniel A. Hughes). I worked with two local attachment therapists who were well trained and experienced, with a high success rate. Their therapy emphasized

Holding Time, the practice of holding the child gently but firmly through resistance, crying and even rage, until parent and child reach a state of mutual attunement. (Holding Time was developed by Martha Welch and is described in detail in her book by the same name.) Holding Time is controversial; some consider it ineffective or even harmful, but it certainly worked for us. It was appropriate and effective for my preschool daughter's particular personality and needs.

I was taught to do holdings that helped Lily revisit and confront her infant trauma and learn to trust and rely on me, her mom. I also practiced highly nurturing and interactive attachment parenting. We two stayed home together as much as possible. I fed her, gave her drinks, dressed her, bathed and dried her, and brushed her teeth, just as if she were a toddler. I played endless board and card games with her, as well as imaginary games about abandonment and caring for babies in an orphanage. When she needed discipline, she got Time In, or Holding Time, never Time Out or spanking. I read all I could about RAD and joined the online support group Attach-China, where I got support and advice from other parents across the country.

Lily eventually responded well to the weekly therapy sessions and to my attachment parenting; she became very loving, drawing endless pictures of hearts and loving moms and daughters, and writing me little love notes. We reached the desired state of attunement in our relationship. She calmed down and became well-mannered, happy and sociable. By the time she was six, the therapist told us to stop coming regularly; she was healed.

No one today would know that she has had RAD; she is a well-behaved, loving child who makes friends easily and is a model student in school. However, she can expect her early trauma and neglect to affect her throughout life, especially in times of loss, separation, and the end of a relationship.

I believe we had an advantage planning a homeland visit, in having our child's difficult behavior correctly identified and officially diagnosed as RAD. Children adopted from abroad may have trauma-based misbehavior that is either tolerated by uninformed parents or misdiagnosed by therapists unfamiliar with the research on the impact of trauma on children's brains. A long-planned, much-anticipated homeland trip can turn into a disaster for both the adopted child and his or her parents. Shocked and bewildered parents might confront unanticipated tears, tantrums, and anger—or withdrawal, whining, and fear. Some children may become re-traumatized when they encounter once again the faces, sights, sounds, and smells of their first months and years of life, particularly in an orphanage.

I had learned to recognize what might be going on in our daughter's mind on the trip, and was trained to deal with any adverse reactions. I had learned the theories and studied the research that explained her triggers and her responses. I would know what to do if she became upset, and I had a whole toolbox of effective activities that we both already knew would help her calm down and recover. There would be no therapist to turn to in China, but I knew—and so did Lily—that I could cope with whatever happened.

My daughter had also done the work necessary to heal her heart and mind. She had already dealt with the major issues of abandonment, loss, neglect, and cultural loss. She was emotionally and mentally strong enough to cope with a homeland visit. I would not have taken my child to China if she had not come so far in healing from RAD.

Planning and Preparing for the Trip

After I gained our therapist's approval, I checked out two companies that organized homeland visits to China and discussed our situation with the tour operators. One of the tour companies, The Ties, sends a social worker along to help children deal with any issues that arise, but I felt that would not be ideal in our case. Both companies do group tours, which are a positive experience for most children, because they can share their experiences with the other adoptees on the tour.

But my child was very different. I chose to do a family-only tour with Our Chinese Daughters Foundation (OCDF), a tour in which I remained in control of every part of our itinerary. The travel group consisted of my husband and me, my teenage birth daughter (who had been left at home when we adopted), and eight-year-old Lily. I decided that traveling alone as a family would give us more flexibility and privacy to cope with Lily's reactions. I strongly recommend this option for families with a traumatized child.

Traveling alone puts Mom and Dad in control of the trip, which is necessary for children with trauma issues. Also, if a child misbehaves in a busload of other children, she will be humiliated and embarrassed, the other children may get scared, and Mom will feel constrained in her reactions. Therapeutic parenting can raise other parents' eyebrows and may lead to complaints, as it's not the way parents treat a normal child. For example, other parents may find the technique of babying a school-aged child weird. They might even consider other techniques—strict consequences for misbehavior, such as making the child stay right next to the parent all day or going straight back to the hotel, or physical restraint in the form of Holding Time—as abusive.

Also, when you travel with a group, you must conform to their schedule; on a family tour, you can adjust the schedule to deal with a child's needs. Another advantage is that your child spends all her time safely enclosed within the family: We all slept in the same room, traveled in our own mini-van, and ate some meals in a room with just the four of us. This strengthened Lily's sense of belonging primarily to her family.

OCDF provided extensive information about making the decision to go, preparing the child and the family for the trip, and handling issues that might arise on the trip. For instance, OCDF's founder, Jane Liedtke, strongly advises involving the child in "giving back" to the orphanage. Lily greatly enjoyed helping me choose school supplies and inexpensive toys to give to all the children at her orphanage. I also prepared a book about the trip, with lots of pictures of the wonderful, exciting places we would visit. We went over the book with Lily several times, so she knew exactly what to expect. I also prepared her for the poverty, beggars, and hagglers that might upset her, and I explained what the orphanage would look like. I even had her practice using a squat toilet (in our bathtub).

Visiting China

We went to Beijing to see the main tourist sites first, then to my daughter's home city, then on to Shanghai, where a dear friend lived, and then returned to Beijing on a night train. We included activities focused on children and families: visiting a *hutong* (a historic neighborhood of old courtyard houses along narrow alleys) and a school in Beijing, and the Children's Palace in Shanghai. Both our girls loved going to the markets and bargaining for trinkets. In Shanghai we spent time with our friend. Having someone they knew in China was very helpful for my girls; my little one happily went off with her at the market. It must have been an experience to pretend she was just another Chinese kid out shopping with her mom!

When we went to Lily's home city, we first paid a formal visit to the orphanage. In the reception room we met the new director and deputy director, and the very same pediatrician who had been there when we adopted Lily. We asked and answered many questions and learned precious new information about Lily's abandonment site, her condition on arrival at the orphanage, and who had named her and why. These new facts about her first days there explained so much of my daughter's post-traumatic stress reactions. Her fear of darkness likely comes from being left alone in the night, for instance.

It also meant a lot to me that her name had been carefully chosen in hopes of a good future for her. If we had not gone back in person, we would not have obtained the actual details of this crucial period in our child's life. So much is unknown about Chinese adoptees' beginnings; every fact you can get is priceless. For us, it gave me new insight into my daughter's challenges, and I was happy to realize that I had responded appropriately to her irrational fears over the years.

We gave the director a big photo album of our daughter's life since she was adopted. They were so thrilled to see her, and so appreciative that we had brought her back. The pediatrician remembered our girl well, gave her a big hug, and held her hand as we toured the orphanage. I am glad that our daughter met this doctor who had cared for her and cared about her as an abandoned infant.

My girls quietly amused themselves while the grown-ups tried to communicate with each other at our first meeting. Lily was quiet and shy, and very self-conscious with the pediatrician. She did not ask any questions or want to be involved in the discussion. Yet she was composed and did not shrink from the adults, or show any fear or act upset while we were with the officials. Nevertheless, it was a very emotional time for her.

We went upstairs to the baby floor, which had iron-mesh doors at the top of the stair that had to be unlocked. The rooms were bright and sunny, with shiny wood floors. The dozen or so babies there had serious medical conditions. The baby rooms were much nicer and better equipped than they had been in 1996, but I was saddened to witness a nurse feeding two infants by thrusting bottles into their mouths as they lay on their backs in their cribs; this was just the kind of detached care that had harmed my own child. Then we went up to the floor where they do rehabilitation, helping children with physical disabilities. We went into a classroom where several deaf youngsters were being given a drawing lesson. We did not see any rooms full of older babies or toddlers because they were mostly in foster care.

Finally, we toured the old building where Lily had lived as a baby. This is now the home of the children who are not available for adoption. We toured the third floor, which had once been the baby floor. Her room was now a dormitory, crammed with metal beds. All of each child's possessions were in a backpack placed on his or her bed. We saw the playroom, where the toys were stacked up on high shelves, including the dollhouse we had donated in 1996, and the classrooms—one was filled with computers, I was pleased to see. We gave the children a huge box of jelly beans and a pile of markers and pencils. Then we took the deputy director, the pediatrician, and an accountant out to lunch.

In the afternoon, we took five little girls and one boy to a department store to shop for outfits. We also bought an air conditioner for a children's room at the orphanage. The next morning, we took another six children to explore a park, then for lunch at McDonald's. These trips had been arranged ahead of time with a charity for orphanages in this province. The children were all very well-behaved and clearly enjoyed themselves. The older ones enjoyed trying out the English words they knew. I think it was very good for my daughter to see how normal these children were.

My teen had much more fun with these children than Lily did. While her sister played hand games and blew bubbles in the park, Lily held back and solemnly observed them all. She was, in fact, scared of a badly burned child because she thought her disfigurement was infectious. She may also have been uncomfortable with the attention I was paying to the other children. She did empathize with them when we went into a store to do the obligatory tourist shopping. The orphanage children and their nurse drank tea and ate peanuts while they waited for us, and my daughters both told us they thought it was insensitive to be buying more stuff for ourselves when these children had nothing. Later, on the way home, Lily asked a lot of questions about the children who were un-adoptable because they had hepatitis B. This really bothered her, and she told me she would like to grow up and do research to find a cure.

Reactions in China

When she was two and three years old, Lily had talked a lot about her birth mother and had been very upset about looking different from the rest of the family. In China, she had the experience of looking like everyone else, but also of being a bit of a curiosity because she was with a Caucasian family. She did grow irritated when Chinese people talked to her and expected her to know Mandarin. Unlike many children who go on homeland tours, she did not talk about the issue of race, nor did she talk about her birth family. Partly this is because it is not her nature to share her feelings, but I also believe that her years of intense therapy had resolved these issues for her.

Of course, things changed when we were in her home city. She was quiet and reserved during the orphanage visit and outings, just taking everything in. I did expect a reaction to such a momentous experience, and it came after we arrived in Shanghai. She became agitated and complained of a sore tummy. So she and I stayed in the hotel during the afternoon, playing games and having a nap together. She was able to go out to have dinner, but started complaining that her tummy hurt again when we were walking down crowded, brightly lit Nanjing Road with our friend. She started to cry and wanted to go back to the hotel. I immediately took her back, using the subway on our own. We did get a little bit lost when we went out the wrong exit, but soon found our hotel. She reminded me of that mistake for days! Once in our hotel room, I cuddled her and soothed her to sleep. That was the only time I really needed my therapeutic parenting skills. The next day, she was fine.

On the tenth day, Lily announced that she was tired of China and wanted to go home. I knew from the advice given in my OCDF notes that this is typical, so I did not worry about it. On the overnight train to Beijing, our cramped little compartment had very clean, comfortable beds with soft white quilts and a little table where we could eat the boxed meals provided, and we all settled down for a good night's sleep. We were happy to see our guide at the rail station and had breakfast and did a little more shopping before heading out to the airport, and the long flight home.

Returning Home and Traveling One More Time

Once home, our only big problem was getting over jet lag. Lily enjoyed giving out souvenirs to all her friends. I spent the rest of the summer making a splendid scrapbook of our trip, and she wanted to make her own little book, which she calls My Photos of China, with commentary like "Yucky Meal" and hearts drawn around the phrase "This is the summer palace from China!" She was clearly impressed with what she saw. "This is the Dragon Boat. It's a magnifisant place!" she wrote.

Over the next year, I saw some big changes in our daughter. She clearly felt firmly and securely part of our family. She had a stronger sense of self and more pride in being Chinese-American. She became a calmer, more centered person. She knows who she is, where she comes from, and where she belongs.

But that's not the end of the story. Last year, when Lily was eleven,

I was asked to take a group of students to China for service work in an orphanage. I was able to take Lily along. She and I shared a room, and I took care of her myself most of the time: We ate together, went on walks around the neighborhood of the hotel, went shopping together, and visited the tourist sights together. But we were also part of a larger group that included teenaged boys who acted as big brothers, teasing her and looking out for her, and older women who enjoyed taking her shopping when I was busy at an official luncheon.

On this trip, the focus was not on Lily, but on the children at the orphanage. It was a well-equipped orphanage, bright and sunny, and the older children had the run of the place. "This is much nicer than my orphanage," she commented. Even so, in the baby room, it was clear that the babies with mental or physical disabilities spent the entire day in their cribs, lying bare-bottomed on old towels (over thick plastic) that were changed when soiled. They were passive, under-stimulated, and physically weak. It was heartbreaking to see them perk up and become more alert and active as we all picked them up, carried them around, talked to them, and played with them.

Lily did not want to spend time in the baby room and stayed with the teenaged boys, who played with the older children. The days spent at the orphanage did not traumatize her at all, and I do think it was valuable to have another experience of what orphanage life is like.

When we got home and compared the photos of this trip with those from her homeland visit, I realized how emotionally demanding that first trip had been. In many of the pictures, especially during our time at the orphanage, Lily is somber and unsmiling, even worried-looking. She is clearly much happier and more relaxed in the second set of photographs. Her face is beaming, with big smiles. I am so glad we had an opportunity for her to enjoy China once again, without the emotional baggage of the homeland visit.

So that's my last piece of advice: Go to China again! Go as often as you can! My daughter is twelve now, and doing well in every way. She is learning Mandarin, and she and her best friend, also adopted from China, want to go back to Beijing when they are teenagers, to study Mandarin in a summer course.

VI

primary SOURCES

Adoptees' Own Experiences of Returning to China

Three on the Road in South China

25

Lorena GuiFeng Lyon

I'd wake at dawn, whenever the sun rises, wash up and maybe pull a jacket on, because it might be freezing. Then I'd have a breakfast of steamed bread or *congee*. Maybe before breakfast, I'd feed the chickens. During the day I might work, doing laundry on the big, flat rock near the stream or hauling water to the field, but probably there would be school, too. At night, in the dark, I'd be pulling up the sheets wishing for a heating system or air conditioner. This might have been my life if I had stayed a foster child in rural China. Instead, I was adopted by my mother and taken to the United States. That wasn't a bad thing, but I like the countryside, too. I might have been happy staying in China. Since I was a baby when I was adopted, I don't remember anything from my short experiences there, but I went back and saw some of that possible life.

In the spring of 2005, my mother wanted to visit China and see my sister's and my foster parents and our orphanages. I was a little excited, but it wasn't such a big thing for me, because I didn't care about my origins. I could go through my whole life without wanting to go back and unearth every secret. I know some books are written about kids going to find their birthparents, for example, *The Great Gilly Hopkins,* but I never feel emotion about trying to find my birth mother. I'm not angry at her for "abandoning" me, because for all I know I'm a crown-princess, hidden from the enemies of the throne.

I did want to see my foster mother. My mother told me she would be old, because she has a son in college. I expected a little, shrunken Chinese woman living in a small house with a straw ceiling, surrounded by acres of rice paddies or other crops.

Being in China wasn't a whole new experience. My mother and I had lived there when I was three (1999–2000), and we (my mother, sister, and I) were living in Singapore for the year when we visited China the second time. Singapore is a tiny island at the tip of Malaysia. Its people come from all over Asia, but mostly China. It is a developed society with good schools, parks, and shopping. I went to third grade at the Canadian International School. My sister, Coco, turned four in Singapore. She attended a bilingual daycare at my mother's work. We had fun traveling to Cambodia, Malaysia, and Thailand, but going to China was a special moment on our way home to the U.S.

If I hadn't been to China before, the trip would have been very difficult. The culture would have seemed very different and weird. It is crowded, but there are so many people to observe. The food is really good and cheap. I love *baozi* and *jiaozi*, soy milk, and sweet bean curd. My mother gave me money, and I got to buy things like I never do at home. We rode on trains, buses, and occasionally in cabs. Sometimes my mother had fights with cab drivers about their driving. I didn't like the squat toilets. They are smelly, and when I was little, I was afraid I would slip and fall. People in China really like children, though, and they like knowing kids are getting adopted from the orphanages.

The plane ride from Singapore to Beijing, China took six hours. We were already in Asia, but Asia is huge, covering almost a third of the world's land and containing sixty percent of the world's population. First, we visited friends in Beijing, a family we knew well. The children, Brian and Cynthia, and their mother, Xueting, usually lived near us in a big house in Buffalo, New York, where their father stayed and worked. In Buffalo, Xueting had been my Chinese teacher at Saturday school for years. They were in Beijing for a year so that the children could attend Chinese school and perfect their Chinese and so Xueting could develop her business.

When we visited, all six of us lived in a three-room apartment, now crowded with our luggage, their year of shopping, and endless rows of drying laundry. Brian was ten and Cynthia was nine. They both are fluent in Chinese and English, because they live in a Chinese household in America. I think school was really hard for them in Beijing because they went to a normal Chinese school and had to do everything in Chinese, including math class. I can't imagine doing that in Chinese! We liked going outside to play or sightsee. The apartment was in a complex of old concrete buildings, with convenience stores in the alley. For a quarter, we bought ice cream every night. My mother, my sister Coco, and I all slept together. The tiny washroom had a leaking washing machine, and since there were so many of us, the mothers did lots of wash. The floor was always wet, but Xueting cooked good meals most nights in her tiny kitchen. She showed us the old Beijing she remembered from her childhood and the new Beijing she had discovered in her year there.

My sister and I come from Southeast China. I come from Guixi, a small town in the province of Jiangxi. My sister came from Guilin, Guangxi. We took a twenty-four-hour train ride down to Guilin. My mother speaks enough Chinese to get us on the right bus or to the right train, so we didn't have an interpreter for much of the trip. We just hired them for the visits with the foster families and trips to the orphanage. During the train ride, I played the card game War with Coco many, many times. We stayed in a room with four beds. There were two on the bottom and two bunks on the top. A small table jutted out from beneath the wall, below the window. The countryside sped by and it changed from fields to craggy mountains or karsts.

Visiting Guilin and seeing my sister meet her foster family first helped me think about my beginnings. Coco had been a toddler when she was adopted, and even though she hadn't seen them since she was seventeen months old, she still must have recognized them. She smiled so hard when her foster mother got into the van and scooped her up. Her foster mother was middle-aged and had more curves than my foster mother; she probably got better food in the city. The foster father was more serious, but obviously happy, too. He gave us gum.

I think my sister's foster mother adored Coco. We took a lot of pictures and went in their apartment, which was bigger and nicer than our apartment in Beijing. They had candy and lots of other food. They also insisted on carrying my sister around. She was pleased with all the attention. We treated them to lunch at a restaurant they liked. When we left on the train, sitting inside with the foster parents looking in, my sister, her foster mother, and my mother were about to cry, but then the foster mother pounded on the window, laughing and waving goodbye. She made us remember the fun of meeting and not the pain of another parting.

I interviewed my sister about what she remembered. She's seven years old now. It is still hard for her to talk about the trip in a clear way. She has too many ideas that don't go together. She says that she was "happy" to see her foster parents, but didn't think she remembered them. I asked how she felt when we left and if she missed them. Coco said, "I felt sad to leave. I cried 'cause I was going to miss them. I still remember them from when I was a little kid and from looking at pictures of going back." I asked if she belonged there more than with Mummy. She said, "No, I felt like I belonged to Mummy." She is happy to have a sister and dog and live in America, but also says she would have been happy to stay with her foster family if she hadn't met our mother and me.

After an overnight train ride, we got to Nanchang, capital of my province, Jiangxi. We stayed at the Lakeview Hotel where my mother and grandma had stayed when they came for me. The hotel was near a park and a lake. We walked around the lake, and my mother told me about how we had spent our first week together. In the dining room, I sat on her lap again and she fed me with chopsticks. Another family took a picture, and later we compared it to old pictures of baby me being fed on her lap.

The next day we drove four hours to the small city of Guixi. We had been there when I was three, but I didn't remember the city. Last time the orphanage, Guixi Social Welfare Institute, wouldn't see us, but this time they were accustomed to returning families and they welcomed us, showed us the building, introduced my foster family, and treated us to dinner. In Singapore I had written a letter to my foster mother. I read it to her and all the officials. I was happy my Chinese was good enough for that, but I really couldn't have a conversation. I told them my age and how long I had studied Chinese, a few little things, but mostly I looked. The orphanage where I was found had been torn down. There were now two buildings, a blue one and a pink one. We saw a nursery with many new furnishings, and there were beautiful babies that were about to have their new parents pick them up (after the parents did all their paperwork, of course!). There were playground sets in vivid colors, but more vivid was the gigantic natural stone arch towering red-gold above us all. Obviously we asked to climb to the top. It was a steep climb with loose rocks, but my four-year-old sister did it, too. All the orphanage directors helped her and fussed over her.

Finally at the top, wow, it looks so much better than when you look up at it. I saw the pink and blue buildings of the orphanage. Across a river there was industrialization. Nuclear energy towers stuck out like a sore thumb. A bridge reached across to both banks. On this side of the river, rice paddies spread out like a Japanese lunchbox, in layers. Some clusters of supervised children from the town were playing on the rock. They would shout across the gaps, measuring from five decimeters to five meters. There were wild azalea bushes on the part of the rock farthest from the bridge part and covered with soil. My foster brother, now college-aged, picked some branches of the pink blossoms for me. In the photo, I hold the branches covered in flowers, looking like a visiting queen.

Later, we drove out to some farmland. My foster mother came out to greet me. She was short, a bit taller than me, and she looked as old as my grandmother. My foster father had died a couple years before. My foster mother lived in a stone house with swallows in the rafters. A quite dreamy place, but probably cold in the winter. Diversely colored chickens bobbed around, jabbing the ground whenever they spied a loose bug or corn kernel. In the middle of them a rooster strutted, oblivious to the fact that he was smaller than most things. Twenty-five feet from the house a small stream ran. A big, flat, horizontal rock sat on the riverbank, and on it some women were doing the laundry. There was a thin bamboo forest nearby and the random haystack gated a well-used path. The azaleas were in bloom everywhere. Two cows grazed and picked at the hay. They were brown and as small as a large Great Dane. I saw one small, tan dog on the path in the bamboo forest, walking with his people. I could live here, possibly enjoy it.

It's not like I don't like her, my foster mother, but I wouldn't go back again, because it wasn't personal. When I visited her, she had another baby in a cradle, so I think she has just taken care of babies for years. If it was my birth mother, then it would be really personal, but even then I'm not sure I want to meet her. It would be cool to see how I might look when I grow up; on the other hand, what if she is a mean or ugly person? It is safer not to meet her at all.

My sister's visit was more personal, because she was their baby for a year, and her foster family remembered her, greeted her warmly, and missed her a lot. They laughed and were good company. Still, I was happy to see how I might have lived if my mother didn't adopt me, and I always like to travel.

Returning Home

Step by Step

Jenna Cook

In June of 1992, at the age of four months, I was adopted from Wuhan, China. I grew up on the East coast of Massachusetts in a small town, in which I was one of very few Asians. I have returned to my homeland, China, three times—the first two trips with my adoptive family, and the third trip without them. These are the stories of the journeys to my birthplace.

Trip 1: Age 10

My adoptive parents have always loved China, and even now that I am older, we sometimes joke that they are like Chinese souls with Caucasian outsides. No, they cannot speak Mandarin or Cantonese, and they certainly don't know every facet and fact about the country, but I have always felt the presence of my parents' enthusiasm and love for my native culture. I will always remember the Chinese artifacts in houses I grew up in: the cherry blossom scrolls and paper lanterns, little teapots and

Buddhas. To this day, our collection of Chinese books is ever growing, including picture books, cookbooks, and novels. As a little girl, my mother read me stories by Demi and Laurence Yep, and then I began reading works by Adeline Yen Mah and Amy Tan as I began to grow into a young adult.

Every year for ten years, my parents would come into my classroom during Chinese New Year and teach my classmates how to fold dumplings, use chopsticks, or make Chinese paper lanterns. Each year the activities were unique, but the outcome was always the same: My peers ooh-ed and aah-ed at the tasty foods and interesting stories. I was able to prance around in a silk dress all day and help teach my friends how to write their names in Chinese. On those days, I always felt so proud.

But none of it was forced; it all felt so natural. All were manifestations of my parents' thirst to learn more about my place of origin. It wasn't the material things—the teapots or bound paper—that helped me to realize that being one of the only Chinese people in town was nothing to be ashamed of; it was my Caucasian parents who taught me to love my Chinese culture.

And so I feel it was only natural that I would desire to return to this place I couldn't remember living in but had read so much about. It was years from the moment that I said, "Yes, I would like to go back," to the time we stepped foot on the plane. During this time we saved up money to fly to the other side of the world and live there for one month. All of our spare change went into the big glass "China jar" to go towards our trip. There were four of us—my parents and I, and my six-year-old sister, who was adopted from Yiwu, China.

I remember feeling very nervous and excited on the plane to China, but at the time I would never have been able to turn to you and say, "Gee, I'm nervous!" China was unknown and I could sense that this trip was not the same as any other family vacation before. I knew I would never be able to change the fact that China held my family history or the fact that I held China in my almond eyes and black hair. It was like being stuck to someone I had never met face to face, and more than anything I just wanted to end up liking this person, this place, to which I was forever glued.

My parents were sensitive to my feelings and took everything very slowly. Instead of trying to cram everything into one trip—the orphanage, the finding site, all of China's great monuments—we just did a little at a time. On this first trip, we visited the orphanage for one day but did not go to the finding site. For me this was just right, because for the first trip back to my homeland, going to visit the orphanage was enough emotionally.

I cried when I visited the orphanage because I was in awe that I was finally back to the place where my journey had begun, because I was thankful to have grown up in America with my family, because my heart yearned to meet my birth family . . . so many feelings.

I wasn't able to see my file or meet my foster mother, which although I wished I could have at the time, I think it's just as well now. Just standing in the place where I used to live and watching the orphanage workers smiling at us as they bounced and fed the babies—this was enough of a comfort. Hearing my adoptive mother's footsteps beside mine the whole time was enough of a message.

Throughout that one month, my family traveled in a tour group to five places: Beijing, Xi'an, Guilin, Guangzhou, Hong Kong, and Wuhan. What struck me the most was neither the magnitude of The Great Wall nor the scenic views of the Guilin mountains, but that every person walking down the street looked just like me, with black hair and yellow skin. I had never before seen this many Asians. It was a physical sense of belonging that I had never experienced before.

Looking back on that very first trip, I know that most of what I experienced wasn't the "real China," and what I mean by this is that I didn't visit any of the places that locals would visit. We saw all of the traditional tourist sights, such as the Yellow Crane Tower and the terracotta soldiers. I basically rode around in an air-conditioned bus from a five-star hotel to the Summer Palace. But at the same time, it was just what I needed. I couldn't have had a more positive experience. The trip showed me that China could be fun, safe, and comfortable, and that my adoptive family was beside me the whole time. I was now able to match the word *China* with memories of tasty food and beautiful sights. China no longer existed only in books, but as a real place that I knew and that I had begun to love.

Trip 2: Age 14

When we returned home from the first trip, we immediately began saving for a second one. This time we wanted the trip to be different; my parents, especially, were tired of chasing after a tour guide with a yellow flag, and so we opted to go alone as a family and not as part of a tour. On this trip we ate authentic Chinese food from street vendors and explored many hidden streets. We visited three new cities: Shanghai, Hangzhou, and Yiwu, and we also revisited Wuhan.

It was on this second visit to Wuhan that I asked the orphanage director about volunteering at the orphanage. She said for the moment I was too young, but maybe in a few years. It was from this inquiry that my third trip to China was born.

Visiting my finding site was such an emotionally complex experience, that even years later I find I am still contemplating it and pulling back more layers to uncover deeper understanding. My family was supportive walking beside me to the police station, but even so I felt such loneliness and grief for my first family which I had lost. A year after seeing my finding site I wrote the following words, which I now believe describe my feelings in that moment, when I was standing at the place where the past and the present seemed to meld into one:

Mother. Do you know how my heart calls for you? When the harmonies of guitar strings reverberate in my ears, I wonder, do you hear their vibrations? Looking back on my childhood, how would YOU have raised me? Would the language I am now struggling with, flow easily from my lips—rapid sentences, fluid phrases? Is it English that would instead hover awkwardly? I wonder. When I see the full moon, emanating golden light, I think of all the ones I love. And you. Do you remember me? Your lost daughter. Do you remember that night that changed our lives forever? Did you cry for me, Mother, when you walked back to your house empty-handed? I wonder so much. My mind overflows with questions, but my heart . . . My heart knows. Knows that I was always loved. My heart knows that when you gave me up, it was to give me a better chance. Another chance. My heart knows that I am meant to be where I am standing today. But Mother, I miss you.

Trip 3: Age 16

Returning for the third trip was really the first time China began to feel genuinely like home to me, not only a homeland but a place where I might want to live for a while when I am an adult. Flying home alone from Hong Kong to Chicago, I felt so relieved when I found out the people sitting next to me spoke Chinese, not English. Even after being immersed in Chinese for only a month, speaking English felt foreign and uncomfortable. When the customs officer addressed me in the Chicago airport, I couldn't recognize that English voice that was coming out of my mouth. Why was the officer referring to me as "Jenna" when my friends in China always called me "Huasi"? The culture shock was only beginning to settle in.

I think my "feeling Chinese"—in a way I hadn't felt after returning to America before—was closely connected with my staying with local families. It was the first time I had the opportunity to experience what life is like for the local people who live in Wuhan. I treasured simple tasks: going to the market with Auntie to catch a fresh fish, walking to the local park with sweat rolling down my upper lip, tutoring my host brother or sister in English, making dumplings for dinner, hanging my underpants outside the window to dry like everyone else in the apartment building did, watching my host mom clean the floor with a bamboo mop . . . all of the real living. I loved it. "This could have been my alternate life," I thought. "Maybe my birth mother folds dumplings like this? Maybe my dad smokes these Yellow Crane Tower brand cigarettes?"

Even though I am now an ocean away, I still dream at night of those incredibly kind and welcoming families who invited me into their home. I can still hear their voices calling my Chinese name, their laughter resonating with the pulsations of my heart. I wish I had had the skills in Chinese at the time to ask more people what they thought about me—a girl adopted from China. Did they know any families who had given up children? Were they aware that the orphanage was just around the corner? Did they see me as Chinese or American?

Returning to volunteer in the same orphanage where I once lay as a baby was such a gift. The days were long: 9–5 p.m., six days a week. But it was more than worth it; I wouldn't have given it up for anything. The children were incredible. I felt pride in my growing familiarity with the halls and layout of the orphanage buildings. I loved watching the reactions of workers when I told them I used to be one of the babies under that same roof sixteen years ago. "Really?!" they would exclaim. "You came back home!" I think many of the orphanage workers I met believed that once they had said their good-byes to the children who were internationally adopted, they would never see them again. I felt that to many of the orphanage workers the thread is cut, the ties are lost, when the child embarks on his or her "new life." But it felt so gratifying for my presence, my story, to illustrate that we do come back. Our families abroad extend that thread of our history, a thread that will always trace us back to China. The workers were amazed at how healthy I had become, commenting on my shiny hair, the muscles in my legs and arms—which showed I had been fed well—and also commenting on my smile and laughter—which showed I had been loved well. They share their hope with me: "Maybe more will come back."

I know I cannot speak for every child who has an adoption story like mine. We, sisters mostly, are alike in our history, but incredibly diverse in our personalities, upbringings, and interests. I know not all of us will return home, and that's okay; everyone is different.

If I could only send one message to adoptive parents on the topic of returning to China, I would say, "Listen to your child." Offer them the opportunity to travel to their home country if they have the desire to, and trust and respect them if they say they are not ready. To me, there is no one magic number, no single perfect age to bring a child back. I had a great first experience at age ten, but who's to say I couldn't have had another great experience if I had been five or fifteen or even thirty-five years old? If I someday adopt my own daughter or son from China, I would wait until my child feels ready. Regardless of how much information my future child and I find out about his or her past, my priority will be for our trip to be a positive experience. I hope that, after our first trip, my child will want to go back again someday.

For me, returning to China was truly a gradual journey: I explored a little at a time, first on a tour, then just with my family, and later independently as an individual. There are so many adventures I still hope to experience in China, and I have to remind myself that there is no rush. There is no limit on the number of times I can go back. Each time, I can have a unique experience and deepen my understanding of my country of birth. My plan is to take it slowly, step by step.

27

Coming Full Circle

Stephanie W.

It all started when my husband and I officially began the adoption "paper chase" for our second child. (At that point, we already had a four-year-old daughter, our biological child.) Who would have thought that in my forties I would have all these unexpected feelings about my own adoption? As I come full circle during this amazing adoption journey, my emotions have come out in ways that I did not anticipate and for which I did not prepare.

I always knew I wanted to adopt, as early as I can remember. You see, I too was adopted over forty years ago, from Hong Kong, by a family of Chinese descent. I wanted to give a child the same wonderful experiences and opportunities I had growing up. I was raised in San Francisco, a culturally rich and diverse city, yet I was still teased about my ethnicity by people of other racial groups. Within my family, however, I didn't have any problems fitting in. The fact that I was adopted was never an issue in my immediate family or with our friends and relatives. I always felt like there wasn't any difference, since we all looked the same. I never felt left out; both my brother and I were always treated equally, irrespective of how we entered our family.

Growing up, I was curious about my birthparents. I thought, "Wouldn't it be great to find them and be able to ask them all the questions that are locked away in my mind?" My parents fully supported me in every way and would have helped me search in Hong Kong if that were possible. That fantasy was short-lived, however; when I was sixteen years old I realized that it would be virtually impossible to find my birthparents due to poor family record keeping. Thinking it wouldn't be important to me, my parents did not keep all of my adoption paperwork. I did not know what orphanage I came from nor my finding date or location. Prior to adopting my second daughter, I was curious but never consumed by a sense of loss over not knowing every detail of my birth and early life. What was important was that my parents loved me, and I have always believed that my biological parents loved me as well, even if they had to make the very hard choice not to raise me.

However, as I waited for a referral for our second daughter, deep emotions bubbled up and poured out at unexpected times. I couldn't watch a "Gotcha Day" video without tears; there's just such a deep connection for me that never, ever goes away. I thought I was very calm and rational about the process of adopting my daughter, but when I attended a workshop for waiting parents, my feelings erupted as I listened to other parents talk about their experiences of adopting children from all over the world. When it came to my turn, I talked about being adopted myself and coming full circle. People had questions about how I, as an adult adoptee, would address birth history questions with my daughter. I expressed my hope that although children adopted from China have very limited access to information about birth families, my daughter would at least have more detailed records than I had so she could have a sense of connection to her past. I will support her in every way (making a heritage trip to China, searching for her birth family if that's what she chooses). As an international adoptee myself, I will understand the importance of finding those connections to her past.

Seeking Information About My Own Adoption

As I progressed through my adoption journey to my second daughter I began to ask questions about my own adoption, wanting to know more about my birth country and especially my orphanage, including such basic information as its name. I thought, "How will my daughter be able to tell her story if I can't even tell my own?" Anticipating questions my daughter may have about her past, I started to seek answers about my own. The quest to know more about my origins has never before been as prominent in my life as it is now.

I did have the name of the social worker who helped my parents adopt me. I found her phone number but I was afraid to call. I didn't know how she'd receive me, over forty years later. She had just finished graduate school at the time of my adoption; I didn't even know whether she was still in the business after all these years. Finally, my husband called her and she warmly welcomed me, inviting us to visit her in Hawaii. She was very kind, but she didn't have a great deal of information to share. And meeting her changed one picture in my mind about the people connected to my adoption: I'd had the idea that she did international adoption work out of her love for children, but no, she said, she simply wanted to travel.

I continued to search for information, and I was able to find the Hong Kong Welfare Institute, the governing agency that handles all the adoption agencies in Hong Kong. I could contact them to try to find my orphanage, but I had conflicting feelings. What if I was opening up a Pandora's box? Thinking about my daughter-to-be, however, and the questions she may have about her own birth country and the circumstances of her early life, I wanted to establish a connection with my homeland and find out more about myself and my origins.

My Father's Heritage Trip

When my father made a heritage trip a decade ago, he found it so exciting to get in touch with his roots that he then returned every few years.

My father is from Canton, China, which is now Guangzhou. He left China when he was twelve years old to come to the United States for a better life. He landed in San Francisco with only a few dollars in his pocket, but he worked hard and eventually owned his own wholesale meat company. He married my mother, and after several miscarriages they decided to adopt a little girl—me—from Hong Kong.

My father, like many immigrant parents, was a very hard worker. He worked six days a week, ten- or twelve-hour days. After many years without any vacation, he finally took the time to visit China. He returned to his village in the countryside and reconnected with relatives he hadn't seen in many years. He had fond memories of growing up in his village. He said that while the people there didn't have the same modern amenities that we have here in the States, they were still very content with their lives. There continues to be a close-knit community in the village because everyone knows everyone else.

I never thought much about taking a heritage trip myself—until my adoption agency put one together for prospective adoptive parents to learn more about the culture and history of their future daughters' birth country. We jumped at the opportunity to show our four-year-old the place of her family's origins, to see China ourselves, to gain a concrete idea of our second daughter's homeland, and, for me, to return to Hong Kong for the first time.

Going to China

Growing up in America, I was never much interested in exploring my Chinese heritage. Many of my peers, who were also raised in immigrant families, have no desire to return to the country of their ancestors. They're trying to be so Westernized and think, "I'm already Chinese; I don't have to go to China to learn about who I am." I used to think the same way.

Yet once I found myself in China, I was awed by its history and beauty, and I felt a very strong emotional pull towards and appreciation of my heritage. I fell in love with China. We visited four cities in ten days: Beijing, Xi'an, Hangzhou, and Hong Kong. The images I had only seen in postcards now became real to me; they were breathtakingly beautiful, and it felt almost surreal to find myself a part of those pictures. I wondered why I had waited so long to go back to visit.

We traveled with four other prospective adoptive families, and we were the only family of Chinese descent in the group. Some members of the group relied on me for help with translation once we arrived in Hong Kong, where people speak Cantonese. It was fun to brush up on my language skills and learn some new words, but some words were difficult for me to understand. I had stopped speaking Chinese once I entered kindergarten, since English was the main language at that time in the San Francisco Unified School District. I am so thrilled to see Mandarin-immersion and two-way immersion school programs grow in popularity recently—due to increasing demand from Chinese-American families, economic trade with China, and adoptive parents with children from China who want their children to be bicultural and bilingual.

On our tour we saw all the main tourist attractions, including the Great Wall, Tiananmen Square, the Forbidden City, the terra-cotta warriors of Xi'an, and more. We climbed four towers of the Great Wall and could see for miles as we reached each tower. My four-year-old was one of the youngest climbers. There was a slight fog overhead, and The Great Wall looked just like it did in the postcards. As we climbed each step, we met local people and others from countries around the world. It felt as if our climb on this incredible structure made us all connected.

In Xi'an, our visit to the terra-cotta warriors stirred me to tears because of the history behind the development and building of the warriors and horses. I couldn't imagine how hard labor was back then and the many years it must have taken to build them. The amount of detail on each one and the fact that there are thousands of them—and none are exactly the same—is extraordinary.

In Beijing, we had a chance to take a rickshaw ride through a *hutong*, an old, historic neighborhood where some elderly people live in government-run, subsidized housing. Most *hutong* dwellers are now being moved out of their homes, which are being razed to make way for new high-rises, but the few *hutong* that remain house a rapidly vanishing but close-knit community. A seventy-two-year-old couple invited us into their home to share family photos, drink tea, watch a tai chi demonstration, and give us a tour around their home. I saw many similarities to our older generation of relatives here in the United States. When the husband demonstrated tai chi and I saw how flexible he was, I thought, "Oh my gosh, that's just like my uncle." Passing around the tea, making sure everyone had something to eat, seeing similar photographs and hearing similar stories: We could have been in Chinatown with my own family members.

We had the opportunity to visit CCAA (China Center of Adoption Affairs), which was a special treat. We had a personal tour with the director and saw the famous review and matching room, where dossiers are logged in and forever families matched with their children. Seeing the matching room and hearing about how they make the matches made the process so concrete. Our review and child match would be done in those very same rooms. I felt a strong sense of connection.

Things had been done so differently when I was adopted. My parents received one photo of me, which I still have, and they had only one chance to accept me or not. If they had not accepted me, the social worker would have presented them with a photo of another child. When my father saw my picture, he knew I was "the one" and chose me immediately. Instead of traveling to Hong Kong to pick me up, they met me at the airport. My father told me that when I first met him, I embraced him immediately. He told me it was such an incredible memory that he will never forget it.

Our agency also planned a day of volunteer work at an orphanage in Hangzhou. We donated diapers and helped to paint the new orphanage. It was a very emotional day for me because some of those kids will never be adopted. I wanted to take every one of them home with me, adoptable or not. It was also emotional because it brought home the fact that I, too, came from an orphanage. Was my orphanage like this one? I wondered. Was I taken care of by similar caregivers? What would have happened to me if I hadn't been adopted? Would I be alive? Would I be living in government housing? What would my life be like?

When we arrived in Hong Kong on our last stop, I felt ambivalent.

I kept thinking that my birth mother was around every corner, and I kept looking at all the faces in the crowd, wondering if one of them was her. At times, I felt like the baby bird in the children's book *Are You My Mother?* by P. D. Eastman, who was continuously searching for his mother who had left the nest. At other times, I completely forgot that I was born in Hong Kong and simply enjoyed visiting Stanley Market, Aberdeen Fishing Village, Victoria Peak, and some of the famous night markets. I realized that I wasn't ready to visit the Hong Kong Welfare Institute, with which I had made contact earlier in my orphanage search. I haven't had information about my origins for over forty years; why would it make any difference now? How would it add value to my life? Perhaps, I thought, I will pursue the search sometime in the future; for now, just being in Hong Kong was enough.

Back to China: Adopting Our Second Daughter

When we finally received our referral call for my younger daughter, I was both scared and excited—scared to be parenting for the second time and wondering whether she would bond with our family, and excited that she would finally be home with us. Within a few days of getting the referral, though, a sense of sadness hit me hard and unexpectedly. While most of the families in our travel group felt elated and were counting down the minutes to "Gotcha Day," I grieved for my daughter's loss, and for her birthparents and mine. I imagined everything she must have gone through—and was still experiencing—and realized that I may have gone through the same thing when I was adopted as a toddler.

When the time came to travel to China, I was excited that the very long wait was over and our new life with my second daughter would soon begin. Still, throughout the adoption trip, I remained emotionally fragile. I cried when our travel guides talked about the finding ads because they were a concrete reminder that my daughter was abandoned. I cried when we were taken to the Buddhist temple to pray for our children. I saw a young Chinese woman in the same temple praying and sobbing, and my husband and I had the same thought—this woman could very well have been one of the birthmothers praying for the child she gave up, perhaps even our daughter. It was such a profound and deeply personal experience for me.

When we received our daughter, we were so elated. She is the sweetest and most beautiful child, and she bonded to us almost immediately. My grief lifted once I had her in my arms. We so look forward to building happy memories with our new family of four.

Since adopting my daughter, I decided to pursue a search for more information from the Hong Kong Social Welfare Institute. I now know the facts about my finding information, caregiver background, and the orphanage in which I was placed. I found out that the adoption story my father told me has some inaccuracies, and I now have a revised version. Learning that the story I had always taken as fact was not entirely true was difficult to face, but I have come to terms with it and I'm glad I now have the correct information.

Coming Full Circle

As I come full circle through the process of adopting my second daughter, I often think how lucky I am that my parents adopted me and that we share such beautiful memories. I often ponder where I would be if my parents hadn't adopted me. Would I still be alive, living impoverished in China, adopted by a local family, living the rest of my adult life as an orphan? These thoughts run through my mind. Will my daughter have similar experiences and feel the same as I do? I don't know. I realize that while these questions will probably follow me for the rest of my life, I can't look back because I have no control over the past. All I can do is look forward and act on what I do have control over.

My first trip back to China affected me in many ways. It gave me, as a Chinese American, a fuller understanding of who I am and of my culture and history. I gained an appreciation of my ancestral homeland and realized how grateful I am to have the life that I do and to be able to travel back to my birth country. Traveling the world opens up your eyes and heart in many unexpected ways. I'm so glad I was able to visit China with my first daughter, rather than later in my life. And I plan to make another heritage trip with my second daughter when she's old enough to remember it.

Going back again to adopt my second daughter brought questions and emotions to the surface that surprised me with their intensity. I needed to grieve in order to end one journey and embark on another. I know that pieces of my early life will always be missing, and I can accept that and have come to terms with it. I will fully support, listen to, and validate my second daughter when she begins to ask questions and search for her information.

As an international adoptee just now experiencing this full cycle of emotions, in my forties, I have learned that it is okay to grieve and grieve some more. I know that when my daughter gets older, I must allow her to go through what she needs to go through in order to come to terms with her past. As parents we instinctively try to resolve problems for our children, but the sense of loss associated with adoption is one thing we cannot fix. No matter what we parents do or say, it will not change the way our children feel. The best we can do is validate their feelings and be their pillars of emotional support. Grief, questioning and searching—as well as acceptance and even joy—are all part of our life-long adoption journey. The experience of adoption will touch me deeply for the rest of my life.

Goodnight Moon, Goodnight Mom

28

Jennifer Bao Yu *"Precious Jade" Jue-Steuck*

We stand
all of us drawn here
by an invisible cord eons long
awaiting the start of a ritual
removed from its womb
by distance and by hope . . .

—**Janet Jue**

Writing is an act of hope.

—**Isabel Allende**

She is four years old. Mom reads her all-time favorite picture book, *Goodnight Moon*. Nestled under her Winnie-the-Pooh covers, her small head is sandwiched between Mom's outstretched arms, the book directly in front of her brown eyes. The green-and-red-colored pictures leap out, filling her with wonder and appreciation.

"Goodnight moon," coos Mom, softly petting her long brown hair. Goodnight Mom. Goodnight stars.

"Goodnight kittens," continues Mom, kissing the shiny wisps on her small head. She is nearly asleep. Her small fingers on her mother's firm arm detach. Her eyes wilting shut like a flower folding from too much sun.

"Goodnight stars. Goodnight air." Mom's voice is softer now. Quiet.

"Goodnight, Mommy," says a half-asleep four-year-old as she yawns and Mom slips out of the covers, carefully and lovingly tucking them round her little frame. Bending down to kiss her forehead. Strings of dark brown hair stick fuzzily above her head, defying gravity, on her faded Winnie-the-Pooh pillow.

Her miniature stomach rises and falls slowly with warm puffs of air. The light fades. The door creaks to its nearly closed position. A soft glow from the hallway falls into her room, warning monsters to stay far, far away. The light leads to safety—like runway lights that guide airplanes back to earth in pitch-black, stormy nights. Straight to the 24/7 haven of Mom's protective embrace.

Goodnight, Jen. See you in the morning.

Goodnight, Mommy. Goodbye.

Mom tiptoes away, her figure a small blip in the dark.

/// \\\

Then one morning, a hospice care worker arrives at the house just before dawn, just before two strange, scary men in black suits roll Mom out our front door, down our driveway, down the majestic mountain where our home kisses the California sky, down the long stretch of Highway 1 that cradles the coast and nearly dips into the deep blue of the Pacific, down and away . . . until nothing is left but the smell of Mom's perfume, a fog of memories, and the whisper of her voice reverberating in my heart.

My name is Jennifer *Bao Yu* "Precious Jade" Jue-Steuck. I am thirty years old. My birth mother is from Jiangsu province, China. In 1979, when I was nearly two years old, I was adopted privately by an American couple from California, at a time when adoption of Chinese children was almost unheard of. It was a complex affair. Paperwork for my adoption was issued through Hong Kong and Taiwan, where birth mother lived when I was born. My first tongue was Mandarin, followed by English (post-adoption), Cantonese (at Chinese school in California), French (from age seven at school), and a sprinkling of Californian Spanish.

During my childhood, I never gave much thought to being adopted—I was far too busy with homework, cross-country running, dance team, cello, and piano. But when my American mother died from the "silent cancer" (ovarian) in 1999, I felt a *double loss* and experienced a *double mourning*: the loss of my mom, to whom I was very close and, to my astonishment, a second loss that sprang out of the blue, lurking in a place so deep and layered I didn't even know of its existence—the loss of my birth mother, the mother I never knew, yet whose breath, blood, and spirit make these words possible.

I think of both mothers now, listening to the roar of engines as our plane takes off from Hong Kong, China, bound for London's Heathrow Airport. I am returning West from my first trip to China since my adoption twenty-eight years ago. . . .

The momentous occasion for my inaugural return to China is Hong Kong's First Adoption Festival. The three-week-long series of educational talks, interviews, workshops, film screenings, and press meetings—hosted by the nonprofit organization Mother's Choice (Hong Kong) in November 2008—includes fellow guest speakers Dr. Amanda Baden, Jessica Emmett, Adam Pertman, and Nancy Thomas.

During the festival, we meet hundreds of adoptive families in Hong Kong. It seems that at least half of them belong to expat communities. As a co-founder of Chinese Adoptee Links (CAL) International—an all-volunteer group with the mission of creating a multigenerational social network for the 150,000+ Chinese adoptees living in twenty-six countries—I've had the privilege of meeting adoption communities in eight countries. This is by far the most diverse group of parents I've met in a single locale. One night, after the festival screening of the newly released feature film, *The Ticket* (based on a true-life Chinese adoption tale), a parent raises her hand and asks, "Jennifer, why did you set up Chinese Adoptee Links (CAL) International?"

"Well . . ." I pause, wondering how to explain the serendipitous series of events and "chance encounters" spread over thirty years. "You see," I say, as my mind travels back, "it all started with a pen pal."

"A pen pal?"

"Yes, a pen pal. In Paris."

We were nine years old. Her name was Valérie, and we only exchanged three letters. But ten years later—at the age of nineteen—I was a sophomore university student studying abroad in Paris.

I didn't know a soul in France.

But I had something special in my pocket from America: Valérie's letters. The letters she had mailed ten years before (when I was the new kid in fourth grade) to my house in Laguna Beach (Orange County), California. Valérie loved to draw, and I remember a large envelope included one of her creations—a fantastic cartoon caricature on the back flap. How I loved looking at the soft brown envelope with its peculiar French stamps. It was large and luminous, and unlike anything I had ever seen before. The cartoon etched into its silky soft skin looked so beautiful—indeed, to my eyes, *magical*—especially since I couldn't draw at all!

I remember receiving the letter one day after school. It was my first year as a new student at Laguna Beach's Top of the World Elementary School, and I was having a hard time adjusting to my very Euro-American school. For the first time in my life, America's deep-seated racial tensions were being thrust into my face right on the playground. I felt sad. Confused. And, at its worst, humiliated and ashamed. But of what? Of being Chinese? Of being adopted? Of being different? Probably all of these. I begged my mom to send me back to my old school. How comforting it was to know that I had a friend halfway across the world, a friend who seemed to appreciate, and actually delight in, my difference.

As I nervously clutched an enormous encyclopedia-sized telephone book in Paris (they still had telephone books in 1999), I sucked in a deep breath and watched its pages fly. *Don't worry,* I chatted to the butterflies in my stomach, *she's probably moved.*

But as I flipped through, my eyes fell on her very name and number! My heart skipped a beat.

I dialed and said, "Bonjour."

It turned out we were neighbors! We met in person for the first time and Valérie showed me her apartment, and even treated me to a delicious meal at her parents' gorgeous restaurant in the Sixième district. She lent me some much-needed student supplies (like a Walkman, a radio, some fun books), and shared a bit of *her* City of Light, as only a lifetime resident of Paris could.

Nearly a decade later—at the age of twenty-eight—I found myself wandering the streets of Barcelona, Spain. I was there for dissertation research as a Ph.D. student at the University of California, Berkeley. To my surprise, I continually bumped into Chinese adoptees. In the grocery store. At the library. Strolling down streets arm-in-arm with their Spanish parents. My heart warmed at the sight of so many adopted girls, and fond thoughts of my own childhood surfaced from shadows of memories long forgotten.

But there was one little girl in particular I will never forget. It was a beautiful afternoon, and as I turned a corner onto a busy Barcelona side street, two little brown eyes bored a hole into mine.

The intense eyes belonged to an adopted Asian girl, walking towards me on the street with her mother. She kept staring at me in such a haunted way that her gaze sent chills down my spine. As we passed one another, it was as if our spirits touched, awakened in a flash of mutual recognition. Her eyes, flushed with longing, held onto mine until she could no longer see me and the cord was cut. *What was that all about?* I wondered as I shook a ghostly shadow from my shoulders. *She looked at me as if . . . as if I could be . . . her birth mom.* I fought back tears.

I couldn't believe how many Chinese adoptees there were in Europe. In Cork, Dublin, London, Paris, Barcelona. It seemed like they were everywhere. Later that summer, I was privileged to meet Chinese adoptees in Ireland. We were excited to connect. One little girl in particular, named Maeve, reached for my hand as we crossed a street in southern Ireland and wouldn't let go. Her mom, Mary D. Healy, looked surprised. "Maeve normally doesn't take to new people." Another little girl embraced me and asked if she could go home with me.

As I spoke with several families in the Emerald Isle, we wondered how we might be able to create a global community. There was just one obstacle: the Atlantic Ocean. How could we possibly bridge the "pond"? On the plane ride home to California, I thought of little Maeve, and the girl with haunting eyes in the streets of Barcelona. They tugged at my heart. What could I do for them? Was it possible that there might be a special connection between adoptees that I had never—in my entire life—known? Or was it merely coincidence that we seemed to share a special bond?

Back in California, I had a thought. I remembered Valérie, my pen pal in Paris. I asked Mary D. Healy of the Irish Chinese Contact Group (a Families with Children from China branch of Ireland) if we might be able to start a transatlantic pen pal program. If I could find participants in the U.S., I thought, the pen pal program could connect Chinese adoptees in America to Chinese adoptees in Ireland.

As Siobhan Hegarty, a volunteer parent in Dublin, matched Irish Chinese adoptee pen pals to teens in the FCC Northern California chapter, I began to wonder, Why haven't I ever met a Chinese adoptee *my own age*? Were there others like me? If so, where were they? And what were their perspectives on life as adopted people?

I went online and searched. *Nada*.

I couldn't find a single group that I—a young adult Chinese adoptee—could join. My heart sank. From DESIS United (for adoptees from India) to VAN (Vietnamese Adoptee Network) to FAN (Filipino Adoptee Network), I didn't seem to "belong" anywhere. Families with Children from China seemed a tad closer (at least I was Chinese!), but I wasn't yet a "family" and I certainly didn't have any children, let alone children from China. What could I do?

Since I didn't know any other adult Chinese adoptees, I decided to find them by starting my own organization: Chinese Adoptee Links (CAL) International. First, I wrote to Ruthanne Lum McCunn, author of *Thousand Pieces of Gold*, one of my favorite childhood books, who had kindly responded years before to a letter I had sent to her for a sixth-grade English project. I asked if she might be willing to serve on the CAL Board of Advisors, and she said yes.

That encouragement led to a series of letters sent round the world and the ensuing discovery of fellow adult Chinese adoptees who called places like Israel, England, Italy, New Zealand, New York City, and Hong Kong home. Slowly, one letter at a time, CAL International—the first global group created by and for the more than 150,000 Chinese adoptees and friends in twenty-six countries—was formed. Our website, *Book of Dreams*, launched on Valentine's Day 2006.

This summer we returned from our second all-volunteer CAL G2 "Global Girls" Ambassadors Teen Trip to Europe, and Maeve (the girl who held my hand in Ireland two years ago and wouldn't let go) hugged me at the end and said, "Jennifer, I'll miss you until I see you again." My heart melted. And I thought, *I'll miss you, too, Maeve.*

When Mom was first diagnosed with ovarian cancer (stage IIIC), she went in for emergency surgery on Christmas Eve. I was nineteen. A fighter to the end, she baffled all her doctors and beat the odds (of living only three to six months longer). She slipped away quietly two years later, sometime between skylight and twilight, sleeping beside me under our living room Christmas tree. The holiday lights blinked on and off as I whispered in her ear, endlessly repeating the names of people who loved her: "Popo (grandmother) loves you. Dad loves you. I love you. Chris loves you. Auntie Suzie loves you. Di Yee (first aunt) loves you. Mitsuye loves you. *I love you, Mom. . . .*"

When two men in black suits came to our house, the younger one stole a glance at me and whispered, "Is that your mom?" staring at the lifeless body beside me.

My voice wouldn't come. Couldn't come.

All I could do was nod. Just once. Just in time to bury my face and swallow an ocean of tears. "Yes," I had wanted to say, "that's my mom. That . . . *was* . . . my mom. My hero."

But the words evaporated on my tongue as my heart quietly shattered into a million pieces. We had had so many dreams together. *How am I supposed to do this without you, Mom? This was our dream together. How am I supposed to go on without you?*

The death of a parent is symbolically a closing of one's adoption story, since our adoption narratives, or origin stories, often begin with them and their heroic journeys to travel halfway around the world to connect with us. To find us. It is difficult to describe what it feels like to lose a parent when you are adopted, and how many feelings—often deeply layered—this can trigger about one's adoption. There are no instruction manuals, and often few (if any) mentors to offer guidance when parents die. How can anyone be prepared for death, adopted or not?

The first trip back can also be a symbolic closing and re-opening of one's adoption story. (In my case, it is the story of twenty-eight years. The story of my lifetime "abroad" and the events that helped shape my search for identity.) But it is a route we know by heart. For we have traveled it before. Just in the opposite direction. For some, it can unearth a host of questions and memories. For others, it might not.

On the flight home from Hong Kong's First Adoption Festival, I feel a deep sense of gratitude to Mother's Choice for hosting this historic event. I thank Mother's Choice for the opportunity to return to China, to meet the adoption communities in Hong Kong, to exchange stories, to share CAL's story, and most importantly, to listen and to learn from one another with compassion, dignity, and grace.

Two festival events, in particular, comprise "firsts" for me. One, meeting a group of prospective birth mothers at the Mother's Choice Pregnant Girl's Home, is a special gift. With the help of Cantonese translators, the pregnant girls (ages thirteen to twenty-four) ask their most pressing questions: "Do you miss your birth mother? Are you angry at her? Have you had a good life with your adoptive family?" Dr. Amanda Baden, Jessica Emmett, and I share our adoption stories, our feelings about our birth mothers. I'm the last person to speak: "I have to be honest," I say. "There have been times in my life when I felt angry towards my birth mom." A few of the girls recoil, holding their swollen bellies. "But I understand that she did the best she could and I am grateful to her." Their eyes soften. "Even if I never meet her in my entire life, she will always be a part of me. I will always be extremely proud of her."

Suddenly, we all burst into tears—the circle of young birth moms-to-be, the adult adoptees, the translators, and the organizers. One pregnant girl wipes away a tear and says, "Before meeting you today, I thought that I would place my baby for adoption. But now," she adds, tears streaming down her cheeks, "now I'm not so sure." She hugs her baby by wrapping her arms around her tummy.

My heart beams a ray of compassion to this young girl, no more than sixteen years old, who faces such a tough decision. *She's just a girl,* I think to myself. *Practically a child herself. I am nearly twice her age, and yet . . . I have no concept of her experience, except that she is the same age my birth mother was when I was born. This girl, this young woman,* the realization sinks in, *could be my birth mom.* I look into her eyes softly. At that moment, an interior clap of thunder sends my eyes scanning the horizon, *Where are you, birth mom? Where are you today? Could you be here in Hong Kong even, your spirit roaming this very mountain?*

Little did I know that a few days later, I would actually bump into *another* birth mom—Dr. Amanda Baden's birth mother. In the flesh! Dr. Baden gently nudges me after one of her talks and says, "Jennifer, I want you to meet my birth mom." My gaze follows hers and—lo and behold—I see the most radiant, gorgeous fifty-something woman standing at a distance in one of Hong Kong's most elegant shopping malls, chatting in Cantonese to a friend. Seeing someone's birth mom is like seeing a film celebrity you've admired—for years—for the very first time in real life. Suddenly, they don't seem so *super-human*, so mysterious, anymore. And yet their magical aura is very real. "Does she speak English?" I ask.

"No. Not really." Amanda smiles, waving to her birth mom.

"Do *you* speak Cantonese?"

"No. Not really." Amanda smiles again, this time looking at me. "But somehow," her eyes sparkle, "we manage."

I keep staring at them (I know I shouldn't, but they both look so beautiful), going down the escalators of the mall with the festival organizers. And then I realize why I keep staring. *I've never seen a birth mother and daughter* together *before. It looks so ordinary and so extraordinary at the same time.*

My last glimpse of them—Amanda and her birth mom—is in that chic mall, standing side by side, chatting like old friends.

Without the warm welcoming embrace of Mary Child, David Youtz, the wonderful Mother's Choice family, and fellow guest speakers

Dr. Amanda Baden, Jessica Emmett, Adam Pertman, and Nancy Thomas, I think the "return" trip would have hardly been a return at all. For what is a *home*land trip? What does it really mean to go home? To me, home is neither a place nor a country (for nations' appellations and borders can and *do* change over time), nor even necessarily the land that rests beneath our feet. Today, China may be my "home." Tomorrow it might not. Today, America *and* China may be my home. Tomorrow, they might not.

To go home, "to return," is—at its core—more about people (including the ghosts of our pasts, presents, and futures), community, and a sense of continuity, belonging, legacy, and pride: *adoption pride.* As adopted people and global citizens, we may find ourselves cloaked in several identities during the course of our lives. To have a community of role models, friends, peers, and families who support us throughout our lives as we travel back, sway East, sway West, lose our parents, travel forward, raise our own children, forge unique paths, and continue to remember and to re-remember, to explore, to mourn our loss, to appreciate our gifts, to embrace our challenges, to connect and reconnect with our birth countries, our passions, and perhaps—one day—our birth families, is the home that may have no particular name or distinguished slot in Greenwich Mean Time or identifiable plot on the crisscrossed lines of latitude and longitude. Rather, the *home*land trip is—in essence—a lifetime journey, one that varies as much as the vicissitudes and veracities of each individual human spirit.

What I know for sure is this: There is no such thing as perfect parents. Losing a parent ultimately makes you appreciate what you have *all the more.* No one can ever replace your parents, *adopted or not.* My mind drifts to a dream as our plane turns, casts a shadow over Hong Kong, and veers towards London. Returning once more to the memories of the person whose heart will always be my home. *Home*, as they say, *is where the heart is. . . .*

A little girl, Jennifer Precious Jade, and her adoptive mom, Janet Jue, descend from the plane.

"This is *Bao Yu* (Precious Jade)," beams Janet proudly, "my daughter," to a crowd of aunties and uncles—and then under her breath she whispers, "My baby, my Precious Jade, this is your new home now. In America all of the dreams of your teen-aged mom and all of the dreams of the mothers before will be realized. I will love you forever. I will protect you forever."

Precious Jade sinks deeper into her mother's arms, and hides her dark brown eyes behind her mother's shoulders, safe from the onslaught of curious eyes. . . .

"Mommy, did you know that there are thousands of us now?"

She could not have known. She could not have known when she picked the little girl up all by herself, when she flew to Hong Kong and the Republic of China all by herself, speaking Spanish sprinkled with perfect American English and creative Cantonese—"Canglish" to Mandarin translators—that twenty years later there would be so many Chinese girls adopted throughout the world.

"I am not lost, Mommy. Not in any sense of the word that English can express. There may be some things that I do not know, like my first words and the first day I learned to walk and to speak in Mandarin, but these things are lost *to* me; it is *not me* who is lost. The word *lost* implies having a ghostly owner, and I am no possession," Precious Jade says to the sky, who nods and winks.

Mommy nods, relief flooding her face. Her voice travels across ghostly lands and ghostly galaxies and seven high seas, soaring over tall mountains that tickle the blue belly of the sky with their rounded tips.

I forgot to give you this. I come from ghostly lands to bring you this gift—the gift of my living words. It may come in memories of dreams of sleepless nights and salty tears, but in it lies all of my hopes that you will write every day of your life as your truest self. You are capable of things that I could only dream of, because you are overcoming challenges that I could not. Inside of you is not just my courage and strength, but also an alchemy of authenticity and ability from your birth mother, and from her mother and from me, from my mother, and from all our great grandmothers before us, an endless cord eons long . . . awaiting the start of a ritual—that ritual is the gift of you. With every breath you take, our collective hope herein lies. You are authentic, powerful, lovable, beautiful, kind, worthy, creative, and capable. Both of our families—by birth and by love—are so proud of you. Go forth with these gifts, removed from our wombs by distance—and by hope—but connected by our words, our breath stitched onto this very sheet of paper by ink, sewed to an invisible live cord eons long, by the geometry of our greatest gifts, our collective sorrows, and the mystical mana of our mothers' enduring love. Remember—

We stand
all of us drawn here
by an invisible cord eons long
awaiting the start of a ritual
removed from its womb
by distance and by hope . . .*

This ritual is the *Gift of You.*

"Goodnight moon," coos Mom, softly petting her daughter's long brown hair. "Goodnight stars. Goodnight air." Mom's voice is softer now. Quiet.

"Goodnight, Mommy," says a half-asleep four-year-old. Her miniature stomach rises and falls slowly with warm puffs of air. A soft glow from the hallway falls into her room, warning monsters to stay far, far away. The light leads to safety—like runway lights that guide airplanes back to earth in pitch-black, stormy nights. Straight to the 24/7 haven of Mom's protective embrace.

Goodnight, Jen. See you in the morning.

Goodnight, Mommy. Goodbye.

Mom tiptoes away, her figure a small blip in the dark.

I love you, Mom.

**This passage is an excerpt from "Poon," a poem by Janet Jue (1941–1999), published in Sowing Ti Leaves: Writings by Multicultural Women, edited by Sarie Sachie Hylkema and Mitsuye Yamada, 2nd edition (Irvine, Calif.: MCWW Press, 1990).*

VII

extending the **TRIP**

Living in China Temporarily

Making the Homeland "Home" 29

Dawn Faulkner Schmokel

I was a stay-at-home mom with two daughters adopted from China. My husband of twenty-two years and I were waiting for the referral of our third daughter. I was living the life I had always wanted.

Our oldest, Anna, was about to start kindergarten the next day. That night at bedtime, my husband, Mark, collapsed from the effects of a massive bleed in his brain. Sixteen days later, on what would have been his forty-fifth birthday, the girls and I buried their daddy.

I held on to the idea that I would still adopt the third baby, until I realized that I was doing about all that I could do already: raising two little girls alone. With a heavy heart, I let go of that third adoption.

Here I was: no husband, no job, and no new baby. Although I was sad at the enormous losses in our lives, I also recognized the opportunity. I had always wanted to give my girls an authentic Chinese experience, and I knew that if I did not do it now I never would. I had always felt badly about taking my children away from their language, their culture, and their people. I wanted them to understand and value what it meant to be Chinese, to be proud of their ancient and rich heritage, and

I wanted to gain insight and understanding into Chinese culture and people for myself as well.

I started researching opportunities to go to China to live and teach, but doors were closing at every turn. Some places wanted a two-year commitment. Some wanted *me* to pay *them* (an option I could not afford). Most suggested that I either not bring my children or have someone with me to home-school them and provide childcare for the times I would be teaching. With these kinds of limitations I knew we could not go, and I put the idea aside.

Only days later, I received an e-mail from a friend. She was forwarding a notice she had received about an organization that was recruiting English teachers for the very town that Anna was from: Changzhou. To my surprise, they offered a six-month teaching option. The liaison with whom I spoke made it clear that not only were they thrilled that I would be bringing my Chinese children with me, but they were also offering whatever support services I needed: help finding living arrangements, childcare, schools, training for my job, teaching resources, and more. A week later I had a signed contract and three round-trip airline tickets to China.

Settling In

We spent a few days in Hong Kong acclimating ourselves to the time change and seeing the sights. Then we were off to Nanjing, which was to be our home for the next six months. For the first month we lived in the home of a local family, during which time I was trained, along with the other new teachers, to teach English to Chinese primary school children. Our "home-stay" family graciously fed us, housed us, and taught us many things about Chinese lifestyle and culture that we would never have learned any other way.

For example, we learned that children rarely, if ever, drink cold beverages; even their milk is warmed, and they often drink hot water as well. In fact, many people in China believe that cold beverages shock the system and are unhealthy for children. We also learned that most Chinese meals include a soup rather than a beverage. Living with our homestay family also allowed us a glimpse into Chinese family structure and relationships; we learned that although the parents work and earn the income, the grandparents make nearly all decisions related to raising the children. I had a conversation with our family's mom about this issue; she said it made her sad to not be able to make decisions about her own child and that she liked the "American way" better. The members of this family became our friends in the city, the people who could help us find what we needed, and we felt connected—a little, at least.

When it was time for us to find an apartment of our own, the organization I worked for helped line up places for us to look at and choose from. I decided, with endorsement from the program staff, that the girls and I should live in Nanjing rather than in Changzhou as originally planned. Nanjing offered better support for us than did cities farther away from the office of my employer.

Looking for a reasonable place to live turned out to be rather daunting, however. The apartments were not in an international community, and the standard of living in the Chinese neighborhoods we saw was very different from what I was used to in the U.S. We saw apartment after apartment and it was difficult for me to imagine that I could live in any of those places, especially with my children. They were mostly very small, dark, and dirty. After several days of looking we finally found an apartment that I thought would work. It was on the eleventh floor of a thirty-five-story building in the old downtown area of Nanjing. Although the building was dingy and dirty and the neighborhood rundown, the apartment was charming. It was bathed in golden afternoon light, had etched-glass sliding doors to the bathroom, kitchen, and laundry porch, and had beautiful black-and-white ceramic tiles lining the entire tiny bathroom.

I especially liked the laundry porch, with its solid white tiles, windows on three sides, and little washing machine that required washing the clothes on one side, then moving them to the other to spin the excess moisture out. (They call this part the "dryer," although all laundry is hung to dry.) The process of doing the laundry in this way was charming—until the weather got cold and damp and things took days to dry, and ended up strung all over the inside of the apartment. My Maytags were the one thing I looked forward to seeing most upon returning home.

My job turned out to be different than I had expected. The two classes I taught, each of which met twice a week, were part of an after-school program. So my work schedule ran from 3:30–5:30, Mondays through Thursdays, and I also tutored a pair of children in their home on Friday afternoons. This was considered full-time work, although I was aware that special considerations were given to me because of my status as a single mom. The work was challenging (keeping a room full of children engaged after a full day of school was tough) and fun. The children were bright and adorable, and I loved this work.

During my time with the children, I was able to see firsthand the effects of the one-child policy. Most children had difficulty sharing and taking turns. There also seemed to be a lot of pressure on these children to do well; they were highly competitive, and many had a hard time accepting the loss of a game or a contest. I saw parents and grandparents scolding their children after class for what they thought was poor performance. I guess when two parents and four grandparents have just one child on whom to focus, they understandably consider the child's success important. In my interactions with the children, I also learned some Chinese words (they thought my pronunciation was hilarious) and that most Chinese children have collections, such as coins or special toys. In addition, nearly all Chinese children carry a jump rope in their pocket and use it at every opportunity.

Language

You are probably wondering if I speak Chinese. The answer is no, not enough to make a difference, anyway. And in the places we were, most people did not speak English. So how did we manage? First, my English-speaking teaching assistants did whatever translating needed to be done in the classroom. In rare situations outside of the classroom, when I needed to speak to someone and could not make myself understood (like the time I was in the supermarket trying to find bug spray for our apartment and just could not find it, nor could I make myself understood by the clerk), I would use my cell phone to call one of my teaching assistants or one of the people in the office where I worked, and they would translate for me. But, for the most part, people really did work hard at helping us and trying to understand what we were trying to say. We got pretty good at negotiating prices, communicating with taxi drivers, and finding things at the stores. In train stations we could almost always find an English-speaking college student who gladly helped us out.

The only time language was really an issue was when we were on our own, ordering in restaurants. For the first month in our own apartment, we mostly lived on fruit and peanut butter sandwiches. We became very familiar with the fruit seller in our neighborhood, as fruit was comfortable and safe for us to eat. We could buy it on our own just by picking it up and handing it to the seller, and she would show us on her calculator how much we owed her. When we got brave enough to try the neighborhood restaurants (just little places that were partly enclosed, partly on the street), we discovered that although the menus were all in Chinese, the people were friendly and wanted to accommodate us. I ended up going into the kitchen part of the restaurant and just pointing to what I wanted the cook to prepare for us. When he got to know our tastes, he started suggesting things—holding up a particular vegetable, for example, to ask if we wanted to try that dish.

The food was amazing; we have never eaten better food than during those months in China. We did not experience a single episode of food- or water-borne illness, either. We got so comfortable with eating "on the streets" that we would buy the fabulous baked sweet potatoes from the street vendors or the amazing variety of steamed or fried dumplings available for breakfast on the street-level near our building. I still miss those dumplings.

Language was an issue in one other situation: school for the girls. I really did want us to be immersed in Chinese language and culture, and to send my girls to an international school seemed counter to that goal. So, to start, we set up my six-year-old in the primary school in our neighborhood, one of the schools where I would be teaching. In some ways, it seemed okay; she was starting school at the same time as all the other children, who were entering their first days and first year of primary school. Those children, too, would be learning to write Chinese characters for the first time and learning to read. But for those children, Chinese was their first language, and it became clear within minutes that this was not going to work.

I took Anna out of that classroom and put the two girls together into what was called "kindergarten." In China, kindergarten is more like preschool or daycare in the U.S. The school was warm, bright, clean, and nurturing. The food they served there was beautiful and wholesome; many days I wanted to stay to try the steamed and fruited pumpkin bread, or the bowls of steaming vegetable soup. The children took naps on real beds, with thick, warm comforters. My girls were able to participate in the games, songs, dancing, and other activities without too much difficulty with language. And they had each other so they did not feel too terribly isolated, although this is also the reason why they did not have to try too hard to communicate with anyone else and did not learn much Chinese.

Traveling and Visiting the Orphanages

When I had holidays from teaching, the girls and I traveled. In addition to the trips we took to each of their orphanages, we were invited to the hometown of one of my teaching assistants. That visit was one of the most memorable things we experienced in China. We had been guests in other homes, but this time it was different; we were with a family with whom we felt very closely connected through my work. The family lived in the country, and that was so different from being in the city. And we experienced daily life in the Chinese countryside in a way that no tourist could experience.

We noticed that the practice of Buddhism was much more obvious and prevalent in the countryside than in the city. The homes were different, too. We were guests in a single-family farmhouse. In one of the rooms, there was an ornate and elaborate bed, draped with beautiful fabric hangings, set atop a hard-packed dirt floor; this was another of the many contrasts and ironies we experienced in China. There was no heating in this home and although it was cold enough for the puddles outside to freeze, the doors and windows were left wide open to admit the fresh air. We saw old-fashioned cookstoves still in use—the kind that have two built-in cooking pots (one for stir-frying, and one for soup making) and are heated by burning wood, which is fed through an opening in the rear of the stove. What a gift that visit was for my girls, and for me. We feel so connected to this family that we plan to return next year for the Spring Festival, one of the main family times in China's year.

When we visited the girls' orphanages, I learned something about the difference between visiting China and living there. Early on in our time in China we went to Changzhou, where my first daughter was adopted. Although we were not allowed to visit the orphanage where the children were currently living, we were able to see the facility where my daughter had lived as a baby. I experienced deep, aching, and overwhelming emotion at being in that same place where my husband and I had met our first daughter. I relived the sadness I had experienced during our adoption trip: sadness at the unfairness of it all, sadness regarding the living conditions of these beautiful, precious babies and children, sadness at the thought that some of these children will grow up without ever being part of a family. I was exhausted by the emotion of that trip.

At the end of our time in China we visited Hunan, where my second daughter was from. I fully expected to have similar feelings to those I experienced during the first orphanage visit. Surprisingly, I did not. I felt so at peace, so good about the orphanage, the care the children were getting, their sense of being loved and having a place to belong. I was confused by this reaction that was so different from the earlier one. I spent a lot of time reflecting on this experience. I concluded that, after having lived with Chinese people, rather than just visiting as a tourist, I had come to an understanding and appreciation of Chinese life and culture that allowed me to see the orphanage experience in a different way. I was able to compare the living circumstances of the children in the orphanage to what their lives would be like if they grew up in China, rather than viewing their circumstances through the filter of how we Americans think things ought to be. Not in a "better than/worse than" way, but rather in a "this-is-how-things-are-in-China" way. I was so grateful for the sense of peace I had gained by living among Chinese people, and in China. The difference in my reaction to the two orphanage visits was not due to a difference in the orphanages, but rather because of a change in me.

How did my girls react to the orphanage visits? In their beautiful and naive way, my girls were curious and intrigued, but they seemed to be more interested in *my* reactions than aware of any emotional response of their own. In reflecting on this, it occurs to me that many of us put much thought into the best age to take our children back for homeland visits. Often we conclude that we should go when our children can understand and remember the significance of it all. Although I did not plan the timing of our trip, I think the advantage I had was that my girls were young enough (ages four and six) to learn about and appreciate China, without being old enough to recognize the emotional magnitude of their origins. It gave my girls an opportunity to accept and appreciate Chinese culture and people *before* they have to wrestle with the tougher issues of abandonment and adoption.

Thinking About Next Time

Sometimes I think about what we would do the same—or differently—if we have the opportunity to live abroad again (something my girls and I would like to do, by the way). Things I would do the same include teaching, or doing some kind of work. It gives you a sense of purpose and belonging that you don't get by being a visitor. I would still live in regular neighborhoods, not international communities. I would again stay for six months—any longer and we would have missed too much at home, and any shorter we would not have experienced real life and work in China.

I would do some things differently, though. I would avoid Western foods and just eat local fare. I think we missed out on some fabulous eating every time we ate at McDonald's or KFC. I would be more selective about the things I brought with me and the things I brought home. In other words, I would travel lightly. I would send my children to the international schools next time, where they would have the opportunity to learn Chinese as a second language. And I would not be afraid—I would just dive in and enjoy the experience.

Writing this piece was hard for me because finding extra time, as a single mom, is difficult. But I wrote it in the hope that other people will read about what we did and think, "If they could do it, then so could we." Yes, it was out of my comfort level, for sure. But it was very do-able. Once we started down the path, the momentum just carried us on.

Going to China to teach for six months was one of the best things I have done in my life, and I am so glad, and grateful, to have had the opportunity. My girls and I have been forever altered by our experience. We see China, Chinese people, and ourselves differently, and all for the better. I will never again see China through the lens of American egocentrism. I will never again think that what we have in the U.S. is superior to what others have. Now I know that things are neither better than, nor worse than, but just different. Americans have a lot to offer others, and others have a lot to offer us. It is my fervent wish that more people take this kind of trip: It is good for our kids, good for us as parents, good for China, and good for the world.

30 Six Months in China

The Good, the Bad, and the Ugly

Anne Donohue

I never asked my daughter if she wanted to live in China. In fact, I never asked my husband, my teenaged sons, or my aging parents. I just sat in my air-conditioned office at Boston University one hot summer day and filled out the application to be a Fulbright Scholar in China, thinking my chances of getting the coveted award were slim to none. Six months later, I got a cryptic letter from the Fulbright bureaucracy indicating I had made it over the first hurdle, and a few months after that, another letter saying that I was in. Only then did I share my plan with my family.

We agreed to go to Shanghai for the spring semester of 2004. However, three weeks before our departure, after our boxes had been shipped and tuition payments made to international schools, my father was diagnosed with an advanced stage of terminal cancer. We made the difficult but correct decision to forgo our trip, and I am grateful to have been home with my dad for the last three months of his life.

Four years later, I decided to apply again. And again, I never told anyone of my plan. I didn't want to jinx it or get my hopes up only to have them shattered once more. But this time, we finally got off the ground. On Valentine's Day of 2008, we left Boston for six months in Beijing, where I would teach journalism at Renmin (People's) University. Both of my sons were in college, so they were not part of the contingent. And my husband was only coming for short visits, so most of the time my daughter and I would be on our own.

In the months leading up the trip, my ten-year-old daughter, Katie (adopted from Yiyang, Hunan), was both excited and a little apprehensive. She didn't want to leave her friends, her bunk bed, or her stuffed animal collection, but she was thrilled to miss out on MCAS, the dreaded Massachusetts statewide assessment tests given each spring.

In contrast to what my more psychologically attuned friends would have done, I did very little to prepare Katie for this trip. We had visited China, her orphanage, and her abandonment site three summers before, and she had handled all that in stride. Katie doesn't dwell on things or worry much about anything. She just goes with the flow most of the time, and I figured she would on this adventure as well. I think any discussion of what we might expect would have been greeted with disdain: *Do we really need to talk about all this stuff right now?* And deep down I had the constant fear that this trip too would be aborted before take off, so I didn't want to invest a lot of energy into preparing for what might-not-be.

Adjusting to Life in China

Our first few days in China were hectic, jet-lagged and not very kid-friendly. But once Katie enrolled in an international school, all was well, more or less. Katie makes friends easily, and within her first few days at school she had already been invited to a pizza party to celebrate the "gotcha day" of another Chinese adoptee in her class. Most of the children in her school were Asian, mainly from Korea or India, and only two were Caucasian.

Katie had taken very, very basic "playgroup" Chinese at home: colors, numbers, and *ni hao,* but not much more. Initially, she was put into an intermediate Chinese language class (all of her regular classes were taught in English), but quickly the school realized she hadn't had much exposure to Mandarin. She was then placed in the beginner level and given more challenging lessons to get her back up to the intermediate class within a few weeks.

Routinely, Chinese people would assume she spoke the language. Taxi drivers, people on the elevator, and shopkeepers would talk to her in Chinese, expecting that she understood. Initially this bothered her because, she explained, she didn't want people to "rely" on her, but quickly she learned to ignore them or say *ting bu dong*—I don't understand. But before long, she was picking up the language, especially those tricky four tones. She was a much better student than I was, routinely correcting my botched pronunciations. Within a few weeks she was able to order *xue bi* (Sprite) and *han bao bao* (hamburger) with aplomb. Quickly, though, her diet turned to *jiaozi* (dumplings) and *mian* (noodles). Katie was willing to try almost every food put in front of her, except perhaps duck heads and whole fish, which we were often served.

My adjustment to China did not go as well as Katie's. I was bothered by the noise, the smells, the smog, the traffic, and the hassles of living in a very big city. Our apartment was in a university dorm and it was plagued with plumbing, electrical, and heating issues, and was very noisy at night. The beds were as hard as rocks, there was no hot water in the kitchen, no heat at all after March 1, and dust, dust, dust everywhere. (After I spent a week plunging the toilet and sleeping in my down parka, one friend suggested I should write a sequel to Elizabeth Gilbert's *Eat, Love, Pray* entitled *Freeze, Plunge, Gasp*.)

I was concerned that all my ranting about the physical plant would be construed by Katie as anger at China or the Chinese. I had to be very careful to separate the problems from the people. Without exception, every Chinese person we dealt with was unfailingly nice and helpful, even if they couldn't always fix the overflowing toilet.

My husband had the easiest time adjusting, perhaps because he wasn't staying for the whole megillah. He loved every aspect of life in China, including, thankfully, the insane grocery store scene where you had to shove your way through the throngs for every item of food, much of which is being hawked by young girls in Britney Spears-style headset microphones. The sensory overload, the smells, the noise, and the complete absence of any sense of personal space were things I never got accustomed to.

Despite the less than perfect living arrangements, I loved waking up to tai chi outside my window every morning, and watching the old folks dance in the park until late at night. And without a car, I walked many miles a week, which is a habit I am trying to continue now that I am back in auto-centered America.

Reactions to Our Family

One day early in our tenure in China, we were taking a Sunday afternoon walk when an older man, maybe in his late sixties, pulled off the road on his bike and with a big smile said in English, "Adopted?" My husband replied, "Yes, from Hunan." "*Hen hao,*" (very good), he replied, and pedaled away, beaming. Other people were equally direct and indiscreet, but not always as kind. Katie's advice to adoptees coming to China: Be prepared to be stared at. Many Chinese people would stop, do a double take at the Asian kid holding my Caucasian hand, and then move on. One man at a restaurant turned his chair completely around so that he could gawk at us without craning his neck uncomfortably. I just glared back at him until he returned to his meal. Usually, older women would give me a knowing nod or smile when they saw Katie and me together. But young people were less friendly, like the two male students riding across campus together on a bike, who both turned around to gawk at us as they drove past. It was a funny moment when Katie and I both looked at them, then looked at each other, and simultaneously said, "I hope they fall off."

I found that most Chinese people did not have a good understanding of international adoption. When I told my students that my daughter was from China, some were ashamed that their country could not take care of its own, while others were just surprised that this (Westerners adopting Chinese children) happened at all. In May, I gave a lecture on adoption to a group of students at Nanjing Normal University. None of the fifty or so students in the audience knew of anyone who had been adopted domestically in China. Few of them knew the scale of the numbers of Chinese children being adopted by Americans and other Westerners. Later that summer I gave another lecture on adoption at an English-language summer school, and one student told me her sister was adopted. Her father had found the baby lying on the side of the road and brought her home. They raised her for five years and then gave her to a relative who wanted a daughter. I had read about stories like this hundreds of times before, but the idea of this type of adoption had seemed so abstract; now, in front of me, was living proof that this kind of arrangement really does happen.

While we were in China, one of my BU graduate students, a twenty-four-year-old Chinese woman nicknamed Celine, was back in Beijing doing an internship with NBC News for the Olympics. She and Katie hit it off immediately, constantly sending text messages and e-mails back and forth. Katie told me she preferred to go out with Celine, because people assumed they belonged together, two Asian "sisters," and fewer people stared. She says it made her more comfortable goofing around without "eyes on her everywhere she went." Katie clearly saw me as a magnet for unwanted attention. One time, when we were forced by construction debris to walk out onto an incredibly busy street, I tried to hold Katie's hand, but she refused. She insisted on walking several feet behind me, apparently so no one would see us together. This might have been the beginnings of "tween" separation, but I think it was also a desire to not be part of that odd Anglo-Asian duo.

Limited After-School and Play-Date Opportunities

Katie told me it didn't really matter to her one way or the other that she was living in a mostly Chinese environment. Her personal radar consisted largely of her classmates; the bigger picture, of actually living in China, only occasionally filtered in. Her biggest complaint while we were there was boredom. In the States, we lived two houses away from her school, her friends were all within walking distance from our house, and she could easily find kids in the neighborhood to play with. She was also involved in a slew of after-school and weekend activities.

But in Beijing, none of that was possible. We lived in the northwestern corner of the city on the campus of Renmin University, devoid of any kids her age. Her classmates all lived on the eastern side of town, an hour by cab on a good day and ninety minutes with killer traffic. So after-school play-dates were out of the question, and weekend play-dates were often a logistical headache. The only soccer league practiced about ninety minutes from our house, and I was told it was impossible to grab a taxi out there, so we never pursued a soccer team. And many of her school's after-school activities were full by the time we arrived in February. She did take one after-school art class on Thursdays, but every other afternoon it was fun-with-mom, which often meant schlepping to the grocery store and facing the chaotic scene there.

I was a single mom most of the time—my husband visited three times for two or three weeks at a stretch. I was busy preparing for classes that I had never taught before, following as best I could the Chinese media, and writing in my blog (www.chinajourn.blogspot.com). So I really needed Katie to amuse herself much of the time. We had no access to English language TV, except for the state-run CCTV news channel, so Katie did a lot of reading, playing Game Boy, and working on arts and crafts projects. It is amazing what you can do with duct tape! When we first arrived, she would watch Saturday morning cartoons on YouTube, but after Tibet erupted in pre-Olympics violence, the Chinese government blocked the YouTube site. Forget democracy and human rights; Katie's beef with the Chinese government consisted of "give me back my cartoons on YouTube."

I think it was good for her to get off her go-go-go schedule for a while and learn to be happy without a three-ring circus, but I am sorry she could not find any Chinese children her age in our neighborhood. When I asked faculty members if they had kids, most did not, and those who did said their children were busy every day, all day, including weekends, doing school work. This was not a polite brush-off—I quickly learned that this was the case all over China, and I am glad we did not put Katie in a Chinese public school (which we had seriously considered).

As a journalist, I could not have asked for a more news-filled six months: the uprising in Tibet, the disruption of the Olympic Torch relay, the Sichuan earthquake, and the Olympics. Without friends, family, or husband around, it often got lonely, but the upside was that I had much more time to devote to work. I found the almost monk-like existence refreshing and productive. I have made lifelong friendships with some of my students and I was intellectually stimulated every day trying to get my head around this amazingly vibrant country.

The Gift of Eve

One of the gifts that came out of this trip was my student Eve. A few weeks into the semester, Katie had no school, but I did. Our babysitter, Celine, was running late and I needed to get to my office for a meeting, so Katie tagged along to wait for the sitter there. A few minutes later, Eve (her Chinese name is Zeng Yi) arrived for our meeting to discuss Thoreau, her favorite author. She was in awe that I actually swim in Walden Pond.

When Eve saw Katie in my office, she asked if this Asian child was my daughter. "Yes, adopted, from Hunan." Eve replied that she was from Hunan. I said, "Katie is from Yiyang" . . . and you can guess how the story ends: Eve is from Yiyang. All three of us gasped. What are the odds in a country of 1.3 billion people and a class of only ten students that one would be from the small city of Yiyang? I had goose bumps. Katie got quiet. I am not sure what was going through her mind, but I sensed that this was a turning point in her understanding of Yiyang: It suddenly changed from a poor city where women had to abandon their children to a city that could spawn this bright, sophisticated young student named Eve. And although she never said it, I think Katie found this somewhat disconcerting.

Later, Eve told me that she had called her mother back in Yiyang and that they both felt sadness that this child could not be raised in her city of birth. Eve spent that afternoon taking a dozen city buses all over traffic-clogged Beijing to find Yiyang-made food to share with Katie later that day. I was moved to tears, but Katie was blasé. This new person had somehow changed the framework of her understanding of her identity as an adopted Chinese girl. Initially, Katie did not warm up to Eve as she has with every other college girl she has met. There was a reticence there that she has never verbalized.

A few days later, Eve told me she had written a letter to Katie in Chinese and would translate it for her some day. A few weeks later, the translation came: a poetic, heartfelt meditation on the loss and love of Katie's circumstance. Whether it was Eve's letter or other experiences in China that provided the trigger, Katie eventually spoke about her adoption in ways she never had before.

An Opening

Whenever I have asked Katie about her adoption she doesn't really want to talk about it and says she doesn't really know how to express the way she feels. When I told her I would be writing this chapter and wanted her input, she asked me to write the questions on a piece of paper and she replied in writing. She has a lot of the same questions that any adoptee has: *Who are my birthparents? Do I have siblings? What is my exact birth date?* I reassured her that these were perfectly normal questions and concerns and that she shouldn't feel uncomfortable talking about them. But in reality, I know, at least for now, she just wants to be a normal, everyday American kid, not "the adopted kid" or "the Chinese kid." At home, near Boston, Katie's "story" is old news. No longer do friends and strangers ask *Is she adopted? Is she Chinese?* And no one speaks to her in Chinese or stares awkwardly at this Anglo-Asian family. Ironically, the biggest difference between home and China is that Katie feels like she fits in at home in the U.S., belongs there, but does not fit in so well in China.

But being in China eventually brought the issues of her origins front and center, and the armor that Katie had been wearing all these years began to crack. In June, I was invited to give a lecture in Guangzhou and

I agreed, provided the host university would allow us to stay at the White Swan Hotel, where we had stayed ten years earlier when we adopted Katie. Most of the guests at the White Swan are Americans proudly toting Chinese babies, awaiting a visa from the U.S. consulate next door. Katie and I spent our first night there at the restaurant overlooking the river. We watched as several first-time Caucasian parents struggled through a meal with their new Chinese children. Katie, almost nonchalantly, said she wanted to know all there was to know about why she was adopted. She revealed that as long ago as the first grade she had cried herself to sleep wondering why she had been abandoned. I was taken aback. All this time, despite my efforts to raise these issues, she had kept them buried. But now, an opening.

In July, we returned to Yiyang with Eve. Ever since our first trip there to adopt Katie in January of 1998, I have wanted to walk around the rice paddies surrounding the city and talk to the people there. If most adoptees come from rural families, I wanted to get a clearer picture of these folks and what their lives were like. Eve arranged for us to go out to a village north of the city, where we visited a small pig farm. About a dozen villagers were inside the room attached to the pigsty, staying out of the midday sun. The women were curious about whether Katie wanted to know her birthparents, and I said yes, and then started to well up. The women looked at me sympathetically.

When Katie and my husband, Stephen, went out for a walk, I asked a lot of questions about adoption and the one-child policy. I seemed to get a different story from everyone I spoke with: *The one-child policy is strictly enforced. The one-child policy is not enforced.* We spent several hours in this village. Katie loved walking around the farm, playing with new puppies, watching farm women rake the drying rice, and feeding the chickens and baby piglets. I couldn't help but think that her lifelong love of animals and the outdoors may be hard-wired from her rural Chinese roots.

One well-to-do man, a friend of Eve's, looked Katie over intently, checking out all her birthmarks and moles, noticing that she was left-handed, and asking about her medical history. He offered to search for Katie's biological family if we were interested. For her part, Katie is eager to learn everything there is to know: Who are her birthparents? Does she have bio-siblings? Why was she relinquished? My husband and I are wrestling with whether to pursue a search, what might it mean to the birth family, whether they would want to revisit this chapter in their lives. We worry they could face punishment or humiliation. We also are uncertain about what would it mean to us: How would we incorporate Katie's blood relations into the family that we have created? And the bottom line: It is a one-in-a-billion chance that we would find them.

Returning Home

On July 13, Katie and my husband packed up to return to the United States. (I was staying on for another month to do some freelance journalism during the Olympics, moving into an ex-pat enclave in the center of the city for my last month in Beijing.) I am usually an overly sentimental person, but packing up this apartment was an unemotional event for me. I was *really* ready to leave the dorm—especially the plumbing and the noise—and move to better accommodations. But previously unsentimental Katie waved a tearful goodbye to her bed, her favorite pink plastic chopsticks, and all the things that "had made it a second home" to her. And she bid farewell to her friends, whom she promised she would never forget.

Katie says she's glad she went to China, and she is happy for the friends she made and the school she attended. But the *Chinese-ness* of it all hasn't had an overt lasting effect. She had to choose a foreign language to take in sixth grade, and although Chinese was one of the offerings, she's taking Spanish. She is happy to be home where the toilet flushes, the clothes dryer leaves her clothes soft (unlike the stiff air-dried jeans she had to wear in China), and where her stuffed animals surround her. Mostly she's glad to be home "where everybody knows me."

Many people have asked me why I wanted to go on this adventure—many of the same people who asked me why we adopted Katie in the first place. I have never had a good answer to either question. I just did it. It seemed like the right thing to do, and despite the ups and downs, both decisions have made my life richer in ways that are impossible to measure. I have had an interest in China for more than twenty years, in some ways a very romantic notion of the Chinese people, colored by my antipathy for much of the Chinese government's undemocratic and often callous behavior toward its people. This extended stay has helped to round out my images and deepen my understanding of China.

Ambassador Nicholas Platt, one of the first U.S. diplomats to live in China in the 1970s, offered this piece of advice during a talk he gave at the U.S. embassy in Beijing last spring: Don't assess your experience in China until you have been home for six months. I am beginning to understand why that is good advice. Quickly, the toilets and smog recede into the background; now, when I look back at my photographs and my blog, I am overwhelmed by how much I have learned about China, about myself, and about my daughter. We are all wiser for the experience. I am convinced that in the months and years ahead, Katie will have a deeper understanding of her place of birth and—with luck—she will be able to make better sense of the circumstances that have brought us all together.

Living Behind the Great Wall

31

Marion Radin

It's just about 6 p.m. on a week night in early spring, and I'm standing in front of the gate of my daughters' school. Parents and grandparents are milling around, waiting for the guards to come and string up the yellow "limit line" tape and then open the gates to let us in. The weather had been pleasant today but now the wind has picked up, carrying stinging particles of dust, and I pull my scarf up from around my neck to cover my face and head. The woman next to me comments about the wind. I reply the best I can, thankful that my Chinese language teacher has been devoting a portion of each class to conversation about the weather.

The school is a private Chinese school in a quiet suburb of northwest Beijing, China; I am the only Westerner in the crowd, yet my daughters look like all the other students. Our twin daughters were born in the Guangxi Zhuang Autonomous region, and my husband and I adopted them when they were eleven months old. We are an American family living temporarily in Beijing.

Fast forward to September; it's a beautiful autumn day in the northeastern United States, and I'm sitting at my desk. Our daughters have returned to their school and activities here in the U.S., and life is back to normal. Sometimes, it doesn't seem possible that we lived in China for six months, and then I hear my daughters talking to one another—in Chinese! Then I smile to myself. We did it.

How did we come to be living in Beijing? My husband works for a software company in upstate New York, and the company decided to open an office in China to add development staff. My husband's manager had worked on a similar assignment in China, with another firm, so we had contacts and a network already in place. During a few exciting weeks in the summer of 2007, the idea of living in China went from a dream to a possibility to a reality with breathtaking speed.

Culture and Identity

Even before adopting our daughters, my husband and I tried to make their birth culture accessible in our home, to help our children feel pride in their cultural heritage. We bought the books, the language videos, the dolls, the home decorations. All of this is great, but it felt superficial, not enough to give the girls a real appreciation of China. As soon as they were old enough we started going to Chinese School, we attended Chinese culture camps, and we are very active in our local Families with Children from Asia adoption group. Through these activities, we had more hands-on experiences and became friendly with many Chinese and Chinese-American families living in our area, but there's no substitute for actually living in China.

My husband and I were confident that spending six months in China would provide a lifetime of benefit to our daughters. I had been reading a lot about adoption parenting and homeland visits in books and online. Two books in particular, *Adoption Parenting: Creating a Toolbox, Building Connections* and *A Passage to the Heart: Writings from Families with Children from China,* were helpful in reassuring us that we were on the right track. Dr. Jane Liedtke's OCDF (Our Chinese Daughters Foundation) website had a great deal of helpful suggestions and advice for handling a return to our daughters' homeland.

Several contributors to these books, including Dr. Liedtke, affirmed that visiting the birth country gives adopted children the opportunity to "see, touch, and taste" their birth culture and helps them form positive connections to that culture. Social worker Jane Brown, writing in *A Passage to the Heart*, states that a homeland visit gives the child the chance to learn a "balance of good and bad, beautiful and ugly, joy and sorrow, ancient ways and new, in the land of her birth."

Rallying the Troops

At the time that we were discussing the move, our daughters, who are identical twins, were seven years old and about to enter second grade in the U.S. They were not very happy about the plans at first, and had many suggestions for how to avoid six months of living in China: Maybe Daddy could go alone and we could visit. Maybe we could cut the time to two or three months. Maybe someone else from the office could go. The list went on and on, but the theme remained constant. They did not want to leave the comfort of their home, their school, their friends, and their hobbies for the unknown. The prospect of attending a new school, not understanding the language, and not knowing anyone were almost overwhelming to them.

Their reluctance came as somewhat of a surprise to me. For several years, our daughters had talked about China openly; how they wanted to go back and see where they were from. We had always reassured them that we would go back one day and had even started reading brochures from various homeland reunion tour companies that specialize in China. However, a two-week sightseeing sprint around China is much different from living there, even for just six months, and the girls understood that.

To help the girls accept this move, we started a low-key campaign to reassure them. We commiserated with them over the pain of separating from family and friends, even though the separation was temporary. We reminded them of how easily they had switched schools from preschool to kindergarten and how quickly they had made new friends. We also shared some of our own fears and anxieties about the move: What will the apartment be like? What kind of food will I cook? Where will we shop? Will we be able to communicate with anyone?

We also went as a family to talk to an adoption social worker whom we know and admire. She had some great suggestions for us and the girls to prepare for the move and also to keep us on an even keel while we were in China. Her enthusiasm and practical advice helped us convince ourselves that we were doing the right thing. If you are considering a temporary move to your child's birth country, I strongly recommend that you talk to a professional.

We were fortunate that, before our trip, the new director of the Beijing office, Jenny, was able to travel to the U.S. to meet her new American associates. During her week-long stay, we had her over to our house for dinner and conversation. Using Google Earth, she showed us where her apartment is and where the office would be, and we talked about where we should live while we were there. It was exciting to be able to see the area where we'd be spending time and to begin to think more concretely about what it was going to be like.

Also, about one month before our move, my husband traveled to China to help conduct interviews and to scope out the school and apartment possibilities. While we missed him terribly during this trip, it was very helpful to hear his reports and to see the photographs. His excitement was contagious, and soon we were all looking forward to our big family adventure. Finally, while still not overjoyed at the prospect of the move, the girls felt ready to embark on the journey, both physically and emotionally.

Language

When we moved to Beijing, we already knew a smattering of Mandarin because we had been going to Chinese language school as a family for a few years. Since the girls' classes meet just once a week for two hours, progress was slow. They did make steady improvement in character writing and recognition, but their ability to converse in Chinese was practically nonexistent. We hired a tutor to help improve their conversational

Chinese and vocabulary (which I also benefited from) during the spring and summer before our move.

The language barrier was the one area that the girls feared most. They were very nervous about having to speak and understand Chinese, and they really wanted to go to an international school, where English was the primary language. And a part of me wished we could go that route as well. How comfortable it would be with other English-speaking parents! How easy to cocoon in an English-speaking world where our neighbors were Westerners, the stores offered familiar groceries, and *ayi*'s and drivers were available to cook and clean and even get the kids to and from school.

Back to reality—our relocation package did not reimburse for those types of expenses. This turned out to be for the best for us. Since we were planning such a short stay, we wanted to truly experience life in China for the Chinese. We didn't want to replicate our American lifestyle in China; we'd be returning to that soon enough.

As it turned out, our Beijing lifestyle was hardly comparable to that of the average Chinese citizen. Our apartment complex was expensive and catered to middle-class Chinese and foreigners (mostly Japanese and Korean). The neighborhood was close to several famous universities, so students and professors from all over China and the world converged in this area. It was pretty easy to get by with English only—even the local restaurants had English on the menu.

And yet, we all did see remarkable improvement in our Chinese language skills. My husband can direct a taxi driver with ease, I can order a custom cake at a bakery, and my daughters can speak and understand most Chinese conversations now. We are so proud of their achievements and are working hard to help them maintain their level of fluency.

The First Few Weeks

We spent the next several days scrubbing our furnished apartment from top to bottom and taking breaks to explore the neighborhood. Associates from the office took us sightseeing around Beijing, and we ended our second week with a trip to Harbin to experience the famous ice and snow festival. During this long weekend, one of our daughters turned to us and said, "I can't wait to get back to our apartment in Beijing!" Music to our ears!

Part of adjusting to life in China involved adjusting to constant attention. Twins are relatively rare in China, so the girls were subject to a lot of comments and questions. The fact that my husband and I are white Westerners with Asian daughters meant that our family as a whole received a lot of attention wherever we went. Taxi drivers, grandmothers on the playground, even waitresses and maids in hotels wanted to know our family's story, especially if only one of us was with the girls. The girls wearily translated for us, "Mom, he wants to know why we have yellow skin." "Mom, he wants to know if Dad is Chinese." We would giggle about that, and I would always ask the girls' permission before telling a stranger that they had been adopted as infants and were now U.S. citizens.

Staying in Touch with Home

Thanks to modern technology, staying in touch was not difficult at all. We made sure that our families and even the girls' classroom in New York had computer cameras and access to Skype or MSN Messenger. We set up a Vonage account before we left and took the necessary hardware with us. Using Vonage, I could call friends back home using their seven-digit phone numbers. People could leave us voice mail messages and we used e-mail extensively. My husband and I downloaded our favorite TV show each week, and we also downloaded a movie each week for entertainment.

I decided to start blogging, and set up an account before we left. The blog served two functions: While we were in China, it allowed us to keep our friends and families up to date on our activities and to share photographs. Now it serves as a journal/scrapbook of our adventure.

During our stay, the things we missed the most were our families, our friends, and our dogs. Fortunately, we received many visitors from home. It was wonderful to see these visitors, to get caught up on goings-on back home, and to show them "our" China. We allowed the girls to take some time off from school each time a family member or friend visited, for travel or for some down-time at home.

Otherwise, we did not miss much about home. Knowing that we would be in China for only six months and would be returning to our home and other possessions soon enough, we felt great freedom during our stay and made the most of every minute.

Since the girls had a long school day (they left the house at 7 a.m., and I left the house at 5:15 p.m. to pick them up), I had a lot of free time during the week. I took a Chinese language class at a local school and made some friends while greatly improving my language skills. I also helped out at my husband's office by leading an English language practice class twice a week. Through this class, I learned so much from my students about life in China today and about growing up in China during the 1960s and 1970s. This was a wonderful learning experience for my husband and me as well.

School in China

We arrived in Beijing in mid-January, but school didn't start up until late February due to the extended New Year's holiday. Before school started I was able to meet the girls' teacher, who spoke English well. We exchanged cell phone numbers and e-mail addresses. She also told me that there were a few other children from the United States in her classroom, and that these children would be able to help our girls with the language and classroom culture. What a relief!

The first day of school was difficult for all of us. We had to get up an hour earlier than usual, and we weren't sure how long it would take to go by subway. We arrived at the classroom just in time; the teacher greeted the girls and brought them to their desks. We stood in the doorway watching, waiting to wave goodbye. The girls looked as though they were made of stone, their faces frozen in panic. They looked at the doorway, but did not appear to see us standing there and didn't react when we waved and smiled. We stood in the hall, wondering what to do, and decided to head out. I was so worried about what the day would bring for them.

That evening, my husband and I went together to pick them up. What a relief to see their two smiling faces! They ran over to us and gave us big hugs and told us that school was fun. They chattered all the way to the subway station about the food that had been served at lunch and at dinner, and how they had been too excited to sleep during nap time. Of course, there were some tears later that evening, but each day got better and better until soon they were looking forward to school each morning.

That first day of school describes their entire experience at this school. At first, it was hard. They had to make new friends, they didn't understand many of the directions, and the teaching style in China is very different from that in the U.S., but each day got easier and easier. They quickly learned the language. They were paired with the other children from the U.S., who were bilingual. They made friends, they were popular with their classmates and teachers alike, and they did well in school despite the language issues.

The school day was enjoyable for them. They had art class three times a week, music class and Go class each once a week, and English class twice a day. They befriended their young English teacher from Chicago who was so surprised to hear them speak flawless English on their first day in class. Each day at noon they had a two-hour break for lunch and a nap. Just before dismissal, they had a delicious, filling dinner. I was so envious!

They learned more Chinese in four weeks at school in Beijing than they had in four years of weekly Chinese School here at home. That in itself was worth the trip. And they became good friends with several of their classmates, which has fueled a desire to return to Beijing some day soon. This is exactly what we had hoped would happen for them.

Travel in China

We'd been saving for an adoption homeland tour and decided to use this money to do some travel within China during our stay. In addition to our trip to Harbin, we also traveled to Datong, Suzhou, and Hangzhou. We also took a cruise on the Yangtze River.

However, the most important and meaningful trip was the visit to our daughters' orphanage and foster parents, and we decided to make this visit within a couple of months of arriving in China. The social worker back home had suggested this so that we would have time to make a return visit if it turned out to be necessary or desired. We made our arrangements through OCDF and joined one of their "No Frills" tours which had started in Beijing. Their driver picked us up on the way to the train station, and we got to know the three other families on the way to Xi'an.

Our daughters had a wonderful time on this trip. As it turned out, there were two other eight-year-old girls in the group, so the four girls banded together and taught one another new hand games, played make-believe, and sat in the back of the bus, chatting up a storm. There were several other children in the group, and our daughters enjoyed spending time with all of them. All of the kids except one were Asian and adopted, but I think the most important factor for our daughters was that they all spoke English. At this point in our adventure, they really missed speaking English with other kids.

This trip took us to Xi'an by overnight train, which was a lot of fun. Seeing the terra-cotta soldiers was one of the top must-sees on our family list, and it did not disappoint. Our hotel in Xi'an turned out to be the hotel where we had stayed eight years earlier, during the sightseeing portion of our adoption trip. As we walked into the building, I turned to the girls and told them that the last time I'd walked through that lobby was on the day that we met them and became a family.

The next stop was Guilin and Yangshuo, which was very important for our family, not just for the gorgeous scenery, but mostly because our daughters were born in Guilin. During our stay in Yangshuo, we enjoyed a cruise down the Li River and took in a phenomenal show that was performed on the Li River, with the beautiful karst peaks as a natural backdrop. The girls were thrilled with the performance, and I felt a rush of emotion realizing that our daughters were really happy as they experienced some of the culture of their birthplace.

Visiting the Social Welfare Institute and Foster Family

At the end of the organized tour, we stayed on in Guilin for the Social Welfare Institute (SWI) and foster family visit. Early on the morning of our visit, one of our daughters came in complaining of not feeling well. She got sick five times that morning but insisted that we continue with our plans—she knew that it was nerves and not illness. We were all a little nervous about this part of the trip. The SWI visit went fine; we met the new director and his English-speaking assistant. We also met one of the girls' former caretakers. We took a tour of the facility and gave our gifts and donations. The OCDF guide also made a donation of clothing and money to the SWI, which I found very touching.

Our daughters' foster mother finally arrived at the SWI and guided us back to her home, which is very close. We had visited them during our adoption trip, and we noticed many improvements to their home. Since our last visit, their son had married, and there was a grandbaby to take care of. We were happy to see the foster father (the primary caregiver in this family), along with their daughter-in-law. Foster mom had prepared a "snack" for our visit—this "snack" covered the table and then some!

We came away from this visit with more than just memories; we also obtained e-mail addresses from both the SWI and the foster family, which will make it much easier to share news and photographs over time. We also learned some additional information about our daughters' time at the SWI, but no information about their birth family (which we did not expect anyway).

This visit, while very positive for my husband and me, was very difficult for our daughters. They are naturally quiet and reserved and did not know how to react to the many "strangers" who claimed them at the SWI and at the foster family's home. They hardly smiled and looked like they were made of stone when people wanted to hold them. We quickly stepped in and picked them up so that all hugs could be experienced from the comfort and security of a parent's arms. Later that day, when we were back in the privacy of our hotel room, one of our daughters told us that, "we only need one set of parents, and you're it." While I'm disappointed that the girls did not enjoy this reunion more, I'm gratified to have my position as "Mom" validated so emphatically.

Was It Too Short or Too Long?

Many people have asked us some variation on this question, and our answer has been that it was just right. From a practical standpoint, six months was a perfect length of stay for our family. We had decided to leave our house vacant, so we drained the water lines, set the heat to low, and arranged with some friends to make weekly visits to make sure that everything was okay. We had our mail forwarded to one set of parents and our dogs and cars went to the other set of parents. When we left for China, we felt like we had covered all of the bases and that we had a support network back home to handle whatever we had missed.

Since we weren't sure how school in China would work out, we had made preparations to home school our daughters, if necessary, during our stay. The girls' teacher in New York gave us all the spelling, math, and English books that they would need to keep pace with the class. He explained to us that our daughters were already performing at the next grade level, which was reassuring. The girls enjoyed working on these books during their spare time—it was so much easier than their Chinese homework that it felt like play. It was also a great way to keep them occupied during long flights and free time in hotels during our trips.

It was an interesting six months to be in China. During the first month, unusually severe winter weather hit regions of China that are not accustomed to ice and snow. The subsequent power outages, transportation problems, and food shortages made the headlines around the world. Many people back home contacted us to find out if we were all right. Also, on May 12, the devastating earthquake hit Sichuan province, with far-reaching impact. Again, friends and family flooded our voice mail and e-mail to make sure we were okay. All the while, preparations for the 2008 Olympic Games were going on at a frantic pace. The torch relay with its disruptions was another blow to the national psyche, as were the many complaints about China's lack of civil liberties.

And yet, throughout the ups and downs, our family was treated with nothing but kindness, respect, and civility. At worst, people were indifferent to us. We did receive more than our share of lectures about how certain regions of the country had prospered and improved under Chinese authority—information that contradicted the reports we received from Western news sources. We turned these experiences into learning opportunities for our children and had many interesting discussions about politics, the media, and how different styles of government work.

By the time the six months were up, we were ready to go home, yet we were also sad to leave. The word *bittersweet* captured our emotions perfectly. The girls told us that they weren't ready yet; they didn't want to leave their friends at school. And yet, it was time. A new family from the home office was arriving, and we needed to return to our family, our old friends, and our own home. We packed up our belongings, said good-bye to our new friends, our apartment, our neighborhood, and Beijing, and left for home with full hearts and a promise to return.

Celebrating the Return

When they were babies, our daughters were given unusual names by the director of their Social Welfare Institute. One daughter's Chinese given name is Qing (pronounced "ching"), which means "celebrate." The other daughter's Chinese name is Gui (pronounced "gwey"), which means "return." They were named to celebrate the return of Macau to Chinese rule, which happened about the time they came to the SWI. Today, however, I like to think that their Chinese names capture precisely the nature of our Chinese adventure. We celebrated our daughters' return to their homeland, to their birthplace, and we celebrated our return to the place where we became parents, where we became a family so many years ago.

To return is both a journey from home to the homeland and a rite of passage in the life of the family.

—**Sheena Macrae**, "Returning: The Journey of the Soul," in *Adoption Parenting: Creating a Toolbox, Building Connections* (Warren, N.J.: EMK Press, 2006), 475.

Additional Resources We Used When Planning Our Trip to China

Yahoo Groups: "Ask Jane in China," "Beijing Café," and "Homeland Travel—China"

Our Chinese Daughters Foundation (www.ocdf.org), a nonprofit organization committed to supporting families who have adopted children from China

Books: *Living Abroad in China*, by Stuart and Barbara Strother; *Chinese Business Etiquette: A Guide to Protocol, Manners, and Culture in the People's Republic of China*, by Scott D. Seligman; and *The China Executive: Marrying Western and Chinese Strengths to Generate Profitability from Your Investment in China*, by Wei Wang

VIII

HOME *again*

Lasting Impact of the Trip

What the Children Have Taught Me

32

Jane A. Brown, M.S.W.

Living as I do in the southwestern part of the United States, I have long been fascinated by Native American Storyteller figurines—endearing Pueblo clay figures whose mouths form an "o" as though speaking, recounting the ways of The People and the colorful origin stories of their particular tribe. These Storytellers symbolize the power and universality of human storytelling—in particular, the power of the Wise Ones, who pass their tales and wisdom down through the generations. The stories of the Wise Ones are important because they bind the people of the tribal nation together, providing a cohesive framework for explaining why they are one people and how they can navigate their way together. My own treasured collection started because the beautiful clay figures remind me of the Storytellers within our adoption community—those who share with us their adoption-related stories, some of which are about return trips to where their families originated or expanded via adoption.

In my work as an adoption social worker, I have the privilege of listening to one very special group of Storytellers: thousands of adopted youngsters, many of whom were born in China and have returned one or more times. Many eagerly take the opportunity during our sessions together to share their thoughts, feelings, questions, and fantasies about a great many things that they do or observe on those trips. It has proven to be a very normalizing and therapeutic experience for them, whether they are telling or listening to the stories.

In the China adoption community we have plenty of other Wisdom Keepers, too, including adoptive parents, who tell tales about homeland tours during which they retraced their route to their beginnings as adoptive families. Their fascinating stories often possess many common elements to those the youngsters tell. As parents, we love to tell our stories. We especially enjoy telling these stories when we have an audience of other adoptive parents who can relate very personally to the tales we share.

Hearing and Telling Stories at Adoption Playshops

Parents and youngsters tell many of these stories during Adoption Playshop weekends, where adopted children and their non-adopted siblings participate in workshops designed to help them explore what it means to be growing up adopted and how to build or expand strategies for living in a mostly non-adopted world. The parents and children have separate groups in which to meet and talk with others just like themselves, without the distraction of being surrounded by people who little understand the uniqueness of being members of adoptive families.

Facilitating the Adoption Playshops program has taken me all over the United States, Canada, and Australia to work with adopted youngsters and their parents. I see thousands of youngsters each year, and work with many of the same ones year after year. I engage them in interactive lessons that help them explore loss and gain in adoption, their thoughts, questions and feelings about birthparents, their racial-ethnic identity, their shared experience in school and community, and how to develop and practice strategies for standing up to racism or stereotyping. Stories about their trips to China—and how these trips have shaped their beliefs and assumptions about themselves—are woven into the tapestry of activities that adopted youngsters engage in during these Playshop sessions.

As they tell their stories, many of the youngsters ask questions or reveal thoughts or beliefs that they admit they have never before given voice to—or would not be willing to reveal or discuss with others who are not adopted, including their parents. In this way, they have the opportunity to really explore, face, and express their thoughts and feelings about what their homeland trips mean.

Telling their own stories, they can sometimes begin to heal themselves after challenging or painful experiences. They see reflected in the faces surrounding them that their stories matter, or in some cases, are shared territory. The young participants of these groups often express how comforting and thrilling it is to talk about or ask questions about these homeland trips with their adopted peers. This experience enhances their pride in themselves, their homelands, and their connectedness with one another in ways that cannot be replicated through other means.

Differing Points of View

It is through storytelling—the constructing of their own stories and the imbuing of their stories with meaning—that our adopted youngsters make sense of their unremembered and often undocumented past. They can use these insights to know and appreciate themselves, to heal from the sorrows and losses buried in the past, and to build a satisfying future. It is the children and youth whose stories matter the most, and to whom we must give the privilege of being the Storytellers, the Wise Ones. Doing so is the best way for parents and professionals to understand these youngsters, so that we can really see their needs, their vulnerabilities, their strengths, and their possibilities for the future.

Yet parents do not always allow their children to have ownership of their own stories. Through my work of facilitating parent workshops and Playshops for children, I have compared the parents' versions and the children's versions of the same stories. Hearing the same stories from different points of view is very illuminating: Sometimes the stories are so different that the children and their adoptive parents seem to be speaking a different language and do not understand one another. Often, parents do not truly hear, heed, or understand the meaning of their children's stories because they cannot help but hear them through the filter of their own experiences. Or, perhaps, parents get only the sentimental "*Readers' Digest*" version because their children do not feel comfortable revealing the authentic version of their adoption stories.

Then, too, parents sometimes fail to pause in their own eagerness to be storytellers, to give the youngsters permission and encouragement to tell their own stories. Parents may not recognize that their children may view the same experiences very differently from the way they do. Many parents tend to assume that they know how their adopted children view the events that unfold, that they know how their children feel about the places and people they visit. As parents, we aren't always cognizant of the fact that we tend to overshadow our children in our eagerness to spin our tales of wonder—and that in doing so we are completely overlooking our children's differing interpretation of the people, places, and events encountered. Yet it is fundamentally important that parents recognize that the point of view from which their children see every detail of the trip matters, and matters quite a lot.

One of the most important outcomes of bringing youngsters together to discuss growing up adopted is that we learn a great deal about how different their point of view about adoption is from that of their parents. We have learned that allowing youngsters to discover firsthand that others think and feel as they do empowers them to be more open and honest with their parents about their life journey. We have also learned that—while we may be doing a good job of talking with children as parents or as therapists—adopted youngsters benefit, in ways that cannot be duplicated, through having guided opportunities to talk with their adopted peers about what usually lies below the surface, unspoken.

What the Children Say

What do they talk about? What do the Storytellers reveal to themselves? How do their stories differ from those of their parents? What do the other youngsters wish to know about? What unspoken assumptions, beliefs, or self-theories lie beneath the surface—ideas that they do not usually admit to themselves, to their parents, or to others? Let's take a look at what these youngsters share about their homeland visits.

"Mostly, I loved visiting China, but sometimes I felt so bad because the places we stayed in were like beautiful, glamorous palaces, but when I looked out the windows, I could see lots of poverty that left me feeling terribly upset and sad so that I got a tummy ache. I didn't want my parents to know because it would have spoiled things for them, and they were trying so hard to make it a perfect trip for me. I kept wishing that we could have spent some of our money on people who don't have enough, instead of staying in such fancy places and buying so many beautiful things that we didn't really need." These were the thoughts of one Midwestern teen about the homeland trip she'd made with her parents two years previously.

Another (age nine), when asked by other young adopted kids about her recent visit to China, said, "The very *best* thing about my trip to China was . . . well, I hope its okay to say this . . . at the end of the trip, we *all* came home *together. No* one got left there. That was what I was afraid of, but didn't want to tell, from the time my mom told me that we were going to go." Her words are similar to those of many others, amongst the thousands of youngsters I have worked with in the Adoption Playshops program over the last decade.

Many describe having noticed and been drawn to small details that the grown-ups didn't notice—or at least didn't "see" in quite the same way until the children pointed them out. One child said, "There was a window right over the crib I slept in when I was in the baby room of the orphanage. Maybe that is why I like the sky and windows through which I can see the sky, now, when I am lying in my bed. I think that that may be why I have bad dreams of being closed in and scared when I have a sleepover away from home and there is no window."

Another spoke of an orphanage visit: "My mom and the other parents tell people that they saw lots of babies and that they were all cute and cuddly and happy. I just saw how scared and worried the babies looked. I saw that some of them wouldn't look at me or anyone else, like they just wanted to be left alone—maybe because they didn't want anyone to get close to them, but I don't think the parents noticed that. They don't know what that feels like, because they've never really been that alone in their whole lives. But all the kids saw that, and understood it."

One ten-year-old described seeing toddlers who pushed themselves away from the caregivers, as though they didn't really like them, and wondered out loud whether they "even knew them," or instead, were being held by strangers or people they didn't see often. She, too, told of how she was struck by the parents' seeming lack of awareness of how the babies were reacting to the people who were holding them. "But after we got home, every time my parents tell somebody about our trip, sometimes I think I must not be remembering the right way. My parents are grown, but I am still young, so maybe I am wrong about how I saw and remember about those babies. But I am pretty sure—most of the time—that that is how those babies were acting."

The theme of safety, within the context of racial identity, emerges regularly: "When I was in China, I didn't have to count how many people were in the places we went who are brown, like me, so I didn't feel nervous like I usually do. Here, most people are the regular kind of people. They aren't brown."

Or, they noticed people enjoying seemingly satisfactory lives—smiling, playing, working, chatting, cuddling their children, enjoying mealtimes together—even if they were living quite modestly: "The kids and their parents were happy. Even if they didn't have fancy clothes, or lived in small houses or were working in their villages. I thought to myself, 'Maybe I would have been happy, even if I had stayed there instead of getting adopted.' It didn't look scary like I thought it would. But I really *do* love my *now*-parents!"

Others have shared that they felt scared while they were visiting with their foster families, wondering whether, if their foster parents asked to keep them, they would be returned and wouldn't be allowed to go home with their parents. They describe having felt scared, but having tried to put on a brave face because their parents thought it was so very important to meet and visit their foster families.

A girl who had been adopted as a preschooler shared that she was angry at her parents for taking her to visit the orphanage, but hadn't said so. She had not felt safe in the orphanage and instead remembered that the caregivers often frowned, scolded, and pinched her when she had lived there. She was relieved, however, upon returning, to see that the current staff lovingly tends the children in their care, and that the children appear to be happy and fond of their caregivers.

Sometimes, the youngsters reveal how their preconceived notions were corrected by having made these very special journeys, surrounded by the comfort and safety of having their loving and supportive parents beside them as they ventured into the unknown, but imagined, places that inhabit the early chapters of their lives. One youngster told his fellow adopted peers that prior to his trip with his parents to the social welfare institute in which he'd been cared for as an infant, he'd believed that a single birth mother lived there and kept producing lots of babies, so that people who wanted to adopt could have them. He was surprised, and relieved, to learn that birth parents do *not* live in the social welfare institutes, do not make babies just to satisfy the desire of prospective adoptive applicants to become parents, and more than likely lead normal lives that are similar to those of the people he saw in the city in which he'd been cared for, so that they are not readily identifiable at all.

Another told of having thought she would see a line of birth mothers at the orphanage door, waiting to hand over their children and walking away without looking back. She'd dreaded visiting the orphanage and had pleaded with her parents not to take her there. The experience of going to the orphanage, seeing her file so that she knew for certain that she had not been casually dropped off, and being enthusiastically welcomed "home" by people who remembered her as a baby, was a liberating experience so that she is now more willing to think about and talk about her birth parents.

Seeing the Country of Birth Before It Changes Irrevocably

Longevity as a member of the greater-adoption community has also yielded, for me, the view that internationally adopted individuals who leave their country of birth as infants or toddlers and do not return until they are adults lose the opportunity to see and experience firsthand something of what that place was like at the time that they were available to be adopted. In the intervening years, their country of birth is, of course, greatly changed from the place it once was. Globalization, economic growth, contributions from technology, and the expansion of the population change their birthplaces more than some can envision.

Korea, for example, is today unrecognizable from the country I visited more than twenty-five years ago, which is when I first started to go there for the purpose of escorting babies and children to their waiting adoptive families in the United States. Some adult adoptees have directed great anger towards Korea and its people because they cannot envision the poor and disorganized country it was following the Korean War, and the conditions that led their birth families to be unable to keep and parent them. They also can't understand why the Korean government couldn't have provided funding, job counseling, and housing so that unmarried mothers might have had a choice as to whether to raise or relinquish them for adoption.

Hopefully, the adopted Chinese children who return and get to see at least a slice of China will have a more realistic understanding of why their original families might not have been able to pay the fines that would have enabled them to keep and raise the children they abandoned. Already, adoptees discuss among themselves the conditions they observed while traveling to the villages or countryside in the locale in which they were found and cared for. They are able to speculate about the conditions their birth families may have been contending with at the time that they were abandoned.

Secret Hopes and Fantasies

Many of the children share that they had carried secret hopes or fantasies with them, but had never revealed these to anyone. The opportunity to trade stories about homeland visits in a group—especially because there were no adoptive parents listening and watching—seems to give them the courage to share these fantasies with other kids like themselves.

Some of these secret hopes and fears include being recognized by their birthparents, being able to find out if they have a brother or sister in their original families, and being remembered by someone in the village in which they were found. Or discovering that their birthparents had left a note, after all, even though none was mentioned in the original documents their parents were given at the time that they were adopted. They share their longing to have found and been able to bring home photographs of themselves as young infants, and their almost unendurable disappointment at learning that none were taken. They sometimes reveal their disappointment, hurt, or even anger and resentment that no one thought to take photographs, write down details about what they looked like or did in early infancy, who cared for them, what they were wearing when they were found, or (in the early years of adoption from China) where they were found and in what condition they were left.

Emotional Fallout

Many children describe bravely holding back their emotions during the trip to China, but crying buckets of tears upon their return over what they had hoped to recover, but did not. They are relieved to learn that they are not alone and that others, too, have had similar experiences—and a wide array of reactions to what they found or didn't find on these orphanage visits. Most say that they did not talk about this aspect of their experience with other adopted youngsters during the homeland tours, but saw, or thought they saw, the same set of emotions reflected in the eyes and faces of others, which they describe as having been comforting.

For some adopted children, a return trip to China and the location of the traumatizing experiences they had, but cannot remember clearly or at all, is a very challenging one. Some tell of having had nightmares afterward, of never wanting to return to China again, of having felt exposed and vulnerable because people stared, pointed, and shouted at them in a language they could not understand—but with facial expressions they could—and which caused them to feel very self-conscious. One girl described returning to her finding location as "returning to scene of the crime, with my mother excited about being able to see it and take photos," while she felt angry and betrayed because no one recognized how upset she was at seeing that place, and having been "dragged there without anyone asking me whether I wanted to go or not or even telling where we were going before we got there."

Many of these youngsters, if they have sensitive, empathetic parents and/or therapists who can help them process the emotional content of the homeland trips, are far better able to develop personal narratives about the past. Processing these homeland experiences can help them to better understand themselves, especially their emotional reactivity to subsequent separations and losses, to transitions, and to their parents' absences or illnesses. It can help them to formulate answers to questions asked by their peers at school—and to decide whether they want to try to give answers or not. It can help them to feel comfortable with individuals, families, or groups of people with whom they share ethnicity. Children who have successfully processed the effects of their homeland trips appear to have derived considerable and lasting benefit, so that they are more able to handle separations from their parents, to make and keep friendships with other youngsters of Asian heritage, to develop pride in their cultural heritage, and to build confidence in themselves.

Forging Special Friendships

Friendships with other adopted youngsters are often forged or strengthened during the course of homeland trips. Sometimes new friendships form among children who were originally cared for in the same orphanage, who came from the same province, or who had quite different beginnings but share common interests now. Many of these friendships continue long after the families return home, because the shared experiences were so life-altering and emotionally powerful. Many children describe having revisited China with other youngsters whose parents traveled together to adopt them and who had been cared for in the same orphanage. Sometimes children who had been crib-mates in their social welfare institute travel together. Experiencing the trip with a sibling can also make it more significant, because each child plays a significant role in supporting the other while seeing the orphanage or meeting a foster family and feeling quite anxious or excited. Perhaps the greatest value of traveling together is that it makes the process of uncovering the past—and discovering how that past informs both who they are now and who they can be in the future—far less lonely and daunting.

In 2004, my own daughter (of Chinese birth)—the youngest of our eight children—traveled with me and an international group of families with children born and adopted from the same province. She was eight years old at the time of our trip. Members of our group came from San Francisco, Phoenix, Belgium, Canada, and the U.K. to meet in Beijing and spend a few weeks traveling together in China. We parents forged wonderful friendships that have lasted, but it is the friendships that our children have developed and sustained that are the best gifts from our trip. The girls, thanks to the wonder of the Internet, regularly communicate with one another and are especially thrilled when they can arrange a face-to-face chat via webcams. Their excitement over one another's achievements, academic successes, and post-high school goals—and their support for these friends when one has a difficult challenge or sorrow—is very touching to witness. Their concern for one another is at a whole different level than their feelings for most of their other friends—perhaps due to some of the very personal experiences they shared while visiting their orphanages, walking through the countryside in their province, and fantasizing about their birthparents' lives and the lives they might have lived.

My daughter also corresponds with an older girl she met in one of the shops in her Chinese hometown, when that girl and her classmate shyly approached us because they wanted to try out their new English language skills. Later that evening, they knocked on the door to our hotel room and came in to visit, bringing their young, delightful mothers along to meet us. Through her friend in China, my daughter is able to get a tiny glimpse into the life she might have led had she remained in that city, and she will continue to be able to get updated photos of her hometown as it changes and grows.

My daughter counts herself fortunate to have these very special friendships, and she intends to keep them. I hope that she does, for they seem to fill in some of the missing pieces of her history for her. These girls, and their life stories, are linked with her own, past history.

Listening and Responding

We parents and adoption professionals need to do a far better job of listening and responding to the words our children are saying—and not saying—and the underlying feelings and meanings of the messages they convey to us, intentionally or unintentionally.

It makes me sad when I hear the parents of a child who has been in a Playshop session describe what they believe was their child's experience on their return trip to China very discordantly from the way the child herself told her story—as though they had been on two completely unrelated trips. It's sad to realize that the parents have no idea how their child was impacted by particular people or incidents—and that they seem unwilling to consider that their understanding might be off-target. They don't know how to put aside their own assumptions and interpretations in order to be able to genuinely see and hear their child.

As adoptive parents and adoption professionals, we must try to shed our own preconceived notions of what these homeland visits are about for our adopted youngsters. We need the wisdom to realize that our children do not see, feel, or interpret events, conversations, or experiences through the same lens of experience and beliefs that we do. If we want to understand how these important experiences influence our children and their future lives, we need to transform ourselves into better interviewers and listeners.

One way to better prepare ourselves and our children for homeland visits—and to have more meaningful, honest discussions about their after-effects—is to listen to and read the accounts of adults who were internationally adopted, as they describe their return visits to their countries of origin. These adult adoptees have the maturity to be analytical and reflective about the effects of their return visits. Their accounts are a more parallel representation of our children's experiences than are those written by adoptive parents, for they were lived by those who also had to process the meaning of what occurred in their lives prior to adoption. Most adult adoptees do not remember the events of their early lives, but those events remain highly emotionally-loaded and foundational to how they live their lives and see themselves. Their perspective is very different from the "Walk Down Memory Lane" that these trips tend to represent to us as parents. It is these narratives that can help us understand that point of view makes all the difference, in experiencing and in weaving stories about these homeland visits.

I can hardly wait for the day when the first few waves of Chinese-born adoptees return to China as adults, and grant us the occasional insider-glimpses of what those homeland visits they made during their childhood were all about for them—and how they've utilized those experiences to develop their personal life narratives. I anticipate that they will have impressions of and experiences within China and with the Chinese people that we cannot now imagine, as they return on their own—as individuals and in groups with their adopted peers. I expect that they will transform themselves as they pursue those quests for information about their shared past, their origins, and their identity development by returning to China, in ways we will hardly be able to fathom. I am looking forward to the young women and men they will someday be, and to what their written and spoken stories about future homeland visits will reveal about who they've become.

33 "Owning" a Little Piece of China

Phyllis Pincus

When we decided to make a heritage trip to China, our twins were two months shy of six years old. I had initially thought they might be too young for a visit to their birth country and orphanage, but a friend whose daughter is from the same orphanage, and is about the same age as ours, was putting together a small group of families for a return trip and asked us to join them. I liked the dynamics—all the girls were rising first graders, from the same or nearby orphanages, and every family already knew at least one other family in the group. Indeed, it worked out well. The five girls instantly found it easy to interact with each other on the same level. They lined the back seat of the tour bus, exchanging Leapster cartridges on long rides, singing funny clapping songs and staring out the windows together. We all enjoyed traveling in this small group.

To prepare for the trip, our daughters, Lucy and Emma, took a few months of Mandarin classes. My husband Gary and I also studied for several months with the same teacher. We reread books we like about China and watched our favorite videos, including *Big Bird in China*,

One Day in Ping Wei, and our adoption video. We showed our daughters photos from the Internet of the hotels where we'd be staying in each city, and they found reassurance in those kinds of details. They know their adoption story inside-out, and knew we weren't going to China expecting to see birthparents or relatives. We just planned to see some of the beauty of China, and visit their small-town orphanage. The orphanage and "hometown" visit were sandwiched in the middle of an otherwise fun-filled trip.

We did make an extra effort to explain about the changes at the orphanage since our adoption trip. Five years ago when we adopted, the CWI had 180 babies, mostly healthy; now they have perhaps twenty babies, twenty preschoolers, and thirty school-age children. Many of these seventy children have special needs, and there are a few older kids who will never be able to leave the orphanage. Judging by my daughters' retelling of the orphanage visit (see below), I think we adequately prepared them for that part of the trip.

When we'd been home from our trip for two months, a friend who writes the neighborhood column for a local paper asked if I would give him an article and pictures about our trip. I decided to ask Lucy and Emma if they wanted to write the article instead. In those two months, they had only occasionally expressed remembrances of the trip, mostly good and interesting stuff, and sometimes they asked a question. So I was a little surprised when they were *very* excited to write the article.

We decided to have some fun and expedite the process by taping them on the camcorder like a TV show, as they pulled up photos on their side-by-side computers. Our 2,800 (yikes!) best photos had been on their computers since we returned home. They were arranged chronologically, into subfolders for each place on the trip, and our daughters had been browsing through these photos for two months. They knew where their favorite pictures were and enjoyed zooming in on funny or fascinating things.

As the camcorder rolled, Emma and Lucy talked for *one hour*, politely taking turns, skipping some photo folders altogether, and telling about their trip to China. I did very little talking or prodding during the hour; these were their own thoughts and remembrances. I was amazed at the detail they provided and what they had absorbed and found interesting about our trip. They intentionally skipped over some of the things they had actually enjoyed on the trip (gondola ride, kite-flying, silk factory, noodles restaurant) and talked about things that I had no idea had made such an impact. In that one hour of talking, two months after returning home, I knew the trip had been well worth it. They "owned" a little piece of China, in their minds. They would not be intimidated to go back at a more mature age with more mature questions, if they wanted to. But even if they never go back, they at least could say they'd been there and seen some of China.

Now it's been fourteen months since our trip, and my daughters have just turned seven. Every time they see something about China on TV, they say, "We saw that! We were there! I remember that!" Even around our town, they will see a pretty red sunset and remark that it reminds them of one they saw in China. Or they will catch a whiff of something that reminds them of some specific place in China. Our daughters will pull our China books off the shelves and pore through them from time to time. And sometimes I see them trying to write Chinese characters, using the stroke chart we brought home from our trip.

They aren't interested in continuing Mandarin (yet they still remember everything they learned prior to the trip) or in joining the local Chinese Girls Dance Troupe. They just want to hang out with their friends, read books, play soccer, swim, climb trees, ride bikes and ponies, go fishing, play the piano—be the little American girls that they are. But that's okay. We just want them to be comfortable with where they came from, and to be happy with who they are. I think that's happening. Last spring, when their Brownie troop needed a foreign country exhibit for Thinking Day, they quickly volunteered China, and all the troop had a good time with it. For two years now, our daughters have volunteered us to set up the China exhibit at the school's International Night, and to arrange for the Lion Dance (the kids' favorite). China is not as strange and mysterious to them now as it would have been without our return visit.

In the last year, Emma and Lucy have become less enthusiastic about going back to China again (been there, done that), but the Olympics may also have played a part in diminishing their interest. Kids in school would say things to them like, "I think the China girls' gymnastics team lied about their ages." This left Emma and Lucy wondering, "Why are you telling *me* this?" So sometimes, now, they resent being categorized as Chinese. "We're just American," they say. Yet when I fear that they want to totally deny their Chinese heritage, they decide to be lion dancers for Halloween, or use some of their Chinese words in the middle of a conversation, or volunteer us again for the Chinese exhibit at their International Night. So I think that deep down they accept their Chinese heritage, and the trip helped them develop a sense of affinity for China and all things Chinese.

I also think it was good to go back at a young age, especially since the trip included visits to some of the usual fun and fascinating tourist sites, filled in with non-tourist experiences like visiting the orphanage. China will likely be quite different in another ten years, and by then it might be hard for our daughters to understand the struggling, changing China that their abandoning parents knew. The orphanage might not even be there, and their town might be thriving. On our trip, in their home province of Hunan, they saw a struggling economy, people working hard, people waiting in their small businesses for customers, countryside homes with no utilities, and lone workers in a rice field. The trip definitely made for lasting impressions and memories, and I'm very glad we went.

Our Trip to China

(Told by Emma and Lucy Pincus, six-year-old twins, on video to Mom, for a local newspaper article)

MOM: Emma and Lucy, tell the readers about our trip to China.

LUCY: We were gone two weeks [in June of 2007]. We went with Jamie and Alana and Emma Joy who are also starting the first grade, and Emma S. who's a little younger. And their families. We had a good time and learned a lot.

EMMA: We carried little backpacks, with our cameras, Leapsters for long bus rides, journal notebooks, tissues, everything we needed.

Our Flight

EMMA: Our flight to China was very, very nice. We got bumped to business class and every chair had a TV. But we put them down at night to sleep.

LUCY: It took us one night and one day to fly to China [fifteen hours]. I saw big mountains out the window that had snow on them [Alaska].

EMMA: You see, when they are eating breakfast in China, we are eating dinner; when we go to bed, they are just waking up; because they are on the opposite side of Earth from us, and the sun only shines on one side at a time as Earth turns.

LUCY: We were really sleepy those first days in China.

Beijing

EMMA: First we went to the Great Wall of China [at Mutianyu, north of Beijing]. It's the widest building on the earth. It's really, really long, and we had to walk for a long time and we got hot. There were a lot of steps to climb. We saw a donkey and a camel there. The donkey was carrying a person to the Wall. We took a gondola down from the wall to our bus. Lucy, what do you have to say?

LUCY: We went to the Beijing Zoo, too, and saw pandas. They were much bigger than me. They eat bamboo mostly, but carrots too; people don't really know that about them. We also looked at birds, bears, lions and tigers, and foxes. The lions were eating big pieces of raw meat.

EMMA: We got to see the emperor's palace in Beijing [Forbidden City], and the big chair he sat on to greet people, and the bedrooms in the back buildings of the palace. They had beautiful rugs and beds and desks. It was nice of him to leave it all for us to see. There were big lion statues too, and the daddy lion always has a ball under his foot, and the mommy lion has a baby under her foot.

LUCY: One night we saw the famous Beijing student acrobats, both boys and girls. They could juggle umbrellas, and toss yo-yos and spin plates. And the boys did a lot of tumbling and climbing and jumping rope.

Xi'an

EMMA: We slept on a train [from Beijing to Xi'an] that had bunk beds. Was that cool or what?! We even ate noodles for breakfast, on the train, in our room.

LUCY: We rented bicycles for two, and rode around the top of the old town wall. Daddy fixed a chain that came off a bike and we kept riding. And we went to the bell tower and hit the big bell, and we went to the drum tower and hit the drums too. I don't really like the loud stuff though, and the air was pretty foggy there [farmers were burning fields]. Your turn, Emma.

EMMA: Next we went to see the terra-cotta warriors. They are made of clay, not real people. They were found when someone was digging for a water fountain. First they found a head, then they found the rest of the pieces and they are still putting them back together. They all had different kinds of faces. Some are missing heads because there are so many pieces to put together. The first emperor thought that these clay warriors could take care of him when he died. But a general broke up as many as he could after the emperor died.

Zhangjiajie (Hunan Province)

LUCY: We went to a stone mountain forest [Zhangjiajie, in northwest Hunan, awesome!], and the sidewalks along the stream were really pretty, with fancy rocks to walk on. We walked along this stream, then took an elevator to the top of the mountains, then took a gondola ride back down. Some of the others were a little afraid of how high it was, but not us.

EMMA: I saw the monkeys first, coming down from the trees. One jumped on a man eating his lunch, but the man pushed him off. The monkeys got very close, but we didn't pet them. One baby monkey was hanging on underneath his mother. It was really neat.

Orphanage City (Hunan Province)

EMMA: Our adoption group went to our old orphanage and saw all the babies and the nannies. They were all in the playroom having fun, and we got to play with them too. We helped them get more things from a nearby store. They need lots of things, like love, care, but most of all love. The nannies are really, really gentle with the babies because some are hurt [special needs, actually] and one had a patch on his eye. Some need a little surgery. Then we moved on to the toddler playroom where the little kids were playing at tables with their nannies. [The older kids were in school that day, so we didn't meet them.]

LUCY: In the lake park, we drove a little motor boat around, and got to feed the really big fish in the lake. They were orange and yellow and red and white, and we fed them long noodles. They acted hungry, but they were very fat.

EMMA: We also saw the bamboo market. They make beautiful sleeping mats and rugs there, the best in China. In this town we had to use a different kind of toilet, called a squat potty. It's really, really hard to use and I didn't like it.

Changsha (Hunan Province)

LUCY: We stayed at the same hotel [in Changsha, Hunan] where we got Mom and Dad [in 2002]. We played with our group in the same play area in front of the elevators where we played when we were just babies. I learned to walk in those hallways. It was a really pretty hotel with a fancy lobby with a gold tower in the middle that had a story on it.

Shanghai

EMMA: Shanghai is really pretty along the river at night, and the restaurant near our hotel was great. We ate fish and chicken, and some other animals I think, maybe pigs.

LUCY: We went on a really, really fast train, just before our plane ride home. I liked it a lot of course. It goes 100 million and 50 miles. [actually 268 mph. It's the maglev train from Shanghai to the international airport—eighteen urban miles in seven minutes!] When it comes into the station, it slows down a lot though, so people can get off.

Wrap-Up

Mom: So, was there anything you didn't like about China?

Lucy: We didn't like the old, not-too-colorful parts [especially the poor areas of the Hunan countryside and towns].

Mom: Anything else you want to say?

Emma: Some people in China have pets. They have dogs and cats and turtles and lots of birds hanging in cages. Lots of mynah birds that talk and sing.

Mom: Would you want to go there again on vacation?

Emma: Of course.

Lucy: Next year I think!

THOUGHTS *for further* INQUIRY

What the Research Tells Us

Chinese Views on International Adoption

34

Tony Xing Tan, Ed.D.,
and Xaiohui Fan, Ph.D.

For over a decade now, Chinese children have been adopted internationally by families in countries such as the United States, Canada, Australia, Spain, the United Kingdom, Norway, the Netherlands, Ireland, and Finland. The vast majority of these children's adoptive parents are keen on instilling in their children a sense of pride in their Chinese heritage. In addition to exposing their children to various cultural activities, many adoptive parents also travel (or plan to travel) to China with their children. These trips are deemed to play an important role in adopted children's ethnic identity development and may help foster a better understanding of the meaning of adoption.

As more parents visit China with their adopted children, the trend of international infant adoption—especially by Americans—is becoming more familiar to local Chinese residents. Due to the racial and ethnic differences between adoptive parents and their children, these families often draw a great deal of attention in China. In this essay we examine how Chinese people feel about Americans adopting Chinese children, an important but relatively under-explored topic, and we look at some of the reactions families may encounter from people living in both urban and rural areas.

Background on the Domestic Context of China

Before delving into the findings of our study, we will first provide some background on the domestic circumstances in China that have led to international adoption. Since transitioning from a centrally planned to a market economy in 1978, Chinese society has undergone dramatic transformations that have led to increasing social disparity between rural and urban areas. These regional differences have greatly contributed to the trend of infant abandonment in the current period.

In its constitution, China defines itself as a state "under the people's democratic dictatorship led by the working class." The working class, referred to as *chengli ren* (urban residents) or *gongren* (workers), has historically consisted of urban residents who typically worked in state-run factories. However, less than one-third of Chinese residents actually live in cities. The vast majority of the population are rural residents, called *nongcun ren* (rural residents) or *nongmin* (peasants). Since the founding of the People's Republic of China in 1949, these two classes of people have been separated according to their area of residence. Citizens' official residence permits, known as *hukou*, determine access to a wide variety of state-provided resources, with urban permit-holders entitled to far more advantages than their rural counterparts.

An urban *hukou* is still a prerequisite for receiving many government-provided educational opportunities and medical and occupational benefits. In comparison, people with rural *hukou* are often denied access to many of these resources. Consequently, Chinese rural residents lag considerably behind their urban counterparts in terms of income, education, and overall living conditions. Rural women also suffer further political victimization because of the Chinese culture of male preference; they are more likely to have a lower level of education and a higher level of emotional stress than rural men. Moreover, rural Chinese women tragically have the highest suicide rate in the world. When rural parents relinquish female infants, they do so mainly because of a combination of factors, including a cultural preference for boys, poverty, male-dominance in rural family decision-making, educational deprivation, and the one-child policy.

In recent years, despite the prosperity that many urban residents have experienced, life in many agricultural areas of China remains unbearably difficult, and child abandonment continues to be a painful reality for some rural families. According to Professor Xiaoyuan Shang of Beijing Normal University, among the estimated 400,000–600,000 orphans in China (not including children recently orphaned by the Sichuan earthquake), about 50,000–60,000 have been abandoned by their parents (see "Welfare Provision for Vulnerable Children: The Missing Role of the State," by Xiaoyuan Shang, Xiaoming Wu and Yue Wu, published in *The China Quarterly,* 2005, pp. 122–136). These abandoned children are usually cared for in state-run orphanages and are the major source of children for international adoption.

Current Inquiry

For this study, we decided to ask people in both urban and rural settings for their opinions on the adoption of Chinese children by families in the U.S. It was important to include both viewpoints because infant abandonment, as a social phenomenon, results not only from cultural values, but also from the poverty that has followed the unequal distribution of resources between urban and rural settings. Our interviews included roughly thirty urban residents in Xi'an City, where Professor Fan lives and works. We also interviewed a group of rural women in Sichuan Province, where Professor Tan was born and raised. As the topic was so sensitive and emotionally tense and painful for many rural women, they were only informally interviewed during one of their early afternoon gatherings under the shade of a large tree (usually called a time for "nonsense gossip" by the women). This type of gathering occurs daily among the women from the same village. The women use this gathering to chat about all sorts of things (e.g., childrearing, farm work, family issues). The women felt that a group setting like this was more comfortable and supportive than answering questions alone. We hoped that their responses would offer some insights to adoptive parents.

Summary of Findings

The urban respondents to our survey included college students, administrators, teachers, police officers, lawyers, public servants, businessmen, and judges, some of whom have their own children. In general, most of the urban respondents did not disapprove of foreigners adopting Chinese children. The majority of the urban respondents focused on the benefits that adoption brings to these children, though a few questioned whether international adoption truly serves the best interests of the children.

Of the sixteen male respondents, twelve approved of Chinese children being adopted into the U.S. As for the fifteen female respondents, the picture was more complex: Six were completely in support of international adoption, eight had mixed feelings towards it, and one was against it. The major themes that emerged from the urban respondents are described below.

International Adoption Is Beneficial

Overall, urban respondents tended to perceive international adoption of Chinese children as a positive trend. A mother and teacher said, "Of course this [adoption] is better for the children than staying in an orphanage." A college sophomore also mentioned that as there are so many Chinese children available for adoption, it is fortunate that Americans are willing to adopt them. Another student felt that adoption is good for both parents and children.

Some respondents viewed adoption as a good thing because it "shows universal human love and a reflection of the human spirit to help one another" (male Ph.D. candidate). Interestingly, a thirty-two-year-old male teacher believed that international adoption helps resolve some of China's issues with overpopulation, saying that this "population relocation is beneficial to both China and the U.S." Most likely, he was unaware that most of these "relocated" children are girls.

Some also focused on the bonds between parents and child as being the most important thing, as a male Ph.D. candidate commented:

> If the adoptive parents are patient, and give the children encouragement and support, things will be fine. Human beings, especially children, are receptive and reciprocal to love. Love and time will help wash off all differences. Family is about love and trust, not blood.

Adopted Children Are Lucky

> Adopted Chinese children are lucky because they leave the orphanage and have someone who really cares about them. Whoever the parents may be, as long as they show love for the children, the children will live a better life than before.

These comments by a thirty-year-old female teacher nicely summarize how eleven of the more than thirty urban respondents (four male and seven female) felt about Chinese children being adopted by American parents. Many emphasized the importance of family in children's growth, as parents can provide essential financial resources and emotional support. Many respondents regarded adopted Chinese children as fortunate because their families will give them the opportunity to receive a good education, especially better English-language education, and many other benefits offered in the United States. Finally, the respondents felt that these adopted children are lucky because the United States is more advanced than China socially, culturally, and economically.

This belief in the educational and developmental benefits of being adopted by American parents is further illustrated by the comments of three mothers with school-age children.

All three women expressed a noticeable degree of envy towards internationally adopted Chinese children, comparing their more relaxed upbringing with the constant educational pressure children growing up in China receive. These mothers felt that adopted children must have a much happier childhood and far easier school experience in the U.S.—because American students do not have to study for the entrance exams that Chinese students must pass in order to progress to the next level of education. It was clear from their comments that these mothers were quite knowledgeable about the American educational system and were aware that American primary-school and middle-school students have far less homework than their Chinese counterparts, who must spend most of their time studying.

In urban areas, families traveling with their adopted children may hear comments about how lucky the children are. Many respondents felt that adopted children are lucky because they will have a family, solid financial resources, and emotional support, while living in a more advanced society where children enjoy a better experience growing up. They feel that these children will have a brighter future in the United States than in China, and that their overall quality of life will also be significantly better.

Adoption Is a Rescue Act

Several respondents also tended to view adoption as an act of rescuing an abandoned child, for which adoptive parents should be lauded. For instance, a forty-year-old police officer said: "Charitable American parents must feel that they are doing something merciful." Another male public servant actually used the term "humanitarian rescue" to describe adoption. And finally, a thirty-year-old lawyer described being "grateful" to American parents.

Many respondents described being touched by the fact that the bonds of love in adoption are able to transcend national and racial boundaries. They trusted that American parents are loving and responsible and that their adopted children are lucky because their life is forever improved. For example, according to one thirty-five-year-old female teacher:

> American parents show great internationalism by adopting Chinese children. They have to take the trouble to go through strict procedures to adopt children in China. Most of them show unselfish love to

Chinese children, who seem to have their fate changed for the better overnight.

Two female respondents reflected on their own observations of a few American couples who have adopted Chinese children. They noted that the parents adored the children and treated them as if they were their own biological children, which is an important criterion by which Chinese people evaluate adoptive parents. In other words, our respondents felt that good adoptive parents see no difference between adopted and biological children, while bad adoptive parents treat adopted children as if they were inferior to biological children.

Interestingly, no respondents (except for one who felt that adoption was good for both parents and child) viewed adoption as an opportunity for the parents to fulfill their dreams of having a family, as well as an opportunity to give an abandoned child a "second-chance." The respondents' lack of recognition that parents also benefit from adoption indicated that adoption is viewed by many to be an act of rescue by unselfish parents. This point of view, however, does not seem to be unique to Chinese people. Adoptive parents in the United States have frequently reported that strangers in the U.S. sometimes applaud them for adopting a child from an orphanage.

Racial Difference Matters

Four male respondents had concerns about adoption, although they generally approved of the practice. They were mostly concerned about issues of race and wondered how children would fit into American society. For instance, a Ph.D. candidate wondered if racial difference might create additional challenges to children's learning or cause adopted children to become particularly rebellious in adolescence. A twenty-seven-year-old lawyer said that while he did not question the love that American parents have for their adopted children, he was also somewhat skeptical about their motivation in adopting a racially different child in a nation where skin color still matters greatly.

Continuing along these lines, a forty-year-old police officer argued that because racial differences might affect the child's entire life, it would be best if Chinese children were adopted by other Chinese. Finally, a judge felt that while a good social and educational system does benefit children's development, their futures are largely determined by their own individual efforts and talents. Implying that it would be unlikely that the child would benefit much from adoption, he thus encouraged foreign couples to adopt children from their own countries.

Eight female respondents also held mixed views. While they praised Americans for adopting Chinese children, they were not as certain about the children's fate in their new country. They questioned whether American parents would really take good care of the children and whether the children could happily live in a country with such major cultural differences with China. These respondents also expressed concerns regarding discrimination against Chinese and other Asian people. They pointed out that it should be ensured that adopted children are well protected and have a fair environment in which to grow. A twenty-eight-year-old teacher provided a very interesting observation. She said:

> If this child is raised in America, I think it should be a fortunate thing, but if she lives in China with an American couple, it won't be good for her because the Chinese will talk about her behind her back.

During the follow-up interview, she commented that Chinese people were usually very curious about people who are different from themselves. Because the child was adopted by white parents, Chinese people would speculate about the child's background: Where was she from? Was she abandoned by a couple in the rural area because they only wanted a baby boy, or was she abandoned by a unmarried teenager? Why did the American couple adopt the child? Was it because they were infertile or for some other reason? Why did they choose to live in China instead of America? These people may also wonder about the child's future.

Cultural Heritage Is Important

One female respondent held a completely negative attitude towards international adoption. She disapproved of the practice because the child can easily find herself different from her parents, which will have a negative impact on herself and her family. Three female respondents with mixed feelings about adoption were concerned about adopted children's sense of cultural identity. They expressed feeling a bit perplexed by international adoption, and even, deep inside, looked down on adopted Chinese children who physically look Chinese, but are American in the inside. This Americanization includes speaking fluent English and having little knowledge about Chinese culture, even though China is their native country. As one respondent put it,

> They speak native English, but they can't pronounce their Chinese names clearly. They use chopsticks to eat Western food and black eyes to read English books. I feel both sorry and happy for them. They were unfortunate to be abandoned in infancy, while they were lucky to have an integrated family. I feel sorry for them because they are American kids in my eyes.

The respondents worried that some adopted children may find themselves without roots when they grow up. Because of racial and cultural differences, they were concerned that adoption might have negative effects on the children's futures. One of them even doubted whether adoption truly gives children a better living environment and is beneficial to their growth.

In sum, the respondents felt that it is crucial for adoptive parents to encourage their children to learn about Chinese culture and not to forget their Chinese roots.

Comments from Rural Women

We also had an opportunity to interview a group of rural women from Professor Tan's home village about their views of international adoption. They offered a rather different perspective from that of the urban residents. When they were asked how they felt about Americans adopting Chinese children, they responded that they were not aware that this was actually happening. After they were told that some of the abandoned children were eventually adopted from the orphanages by "*waiguo ren*" (foreign nationals), they still responded by focusing on the tremendous pain that the birth mothers who gave up their children must have gone through. They believed that if the birth mothers had any say in their family decision-making, they would not give up their children, even if they knew that their children would end up being adopted by families with financial means. One woman announced, "No matter how better off the American families were, children would much rather be with their birthparents, even if their birthparents are dirt poor."

Overall, the rural women focused on the birth mothers' psychological state (e.g., anguish, shame, helplessness) and the challenges such women faced in handling pressures from other family members. Due to the sensitivity of this topic among these rural women and the ethical concerns from us about their well-being in answering questions individually, we did not probe into deeper discussions.

Conclusion and Recommendations

As a group, urban respondents viewed international adoption as an acceptable solution to the pressing social problems that China faces. Most responses from urban residents regarding international adoption reflect Chinese social values. Respondents appeared to evaluate international adoption by weighing whether the child will have a good family who will provide financial stability, love, and educational opportunities. Additionally, they also tended to value the overall living standards in the United States. Respondents felt that adoption needs to serve the best interests of the child (i.e., that children are happy and healthy under the care of American parents), and also that adoptive parents need to ensure that their children do not forget their cultural heritage. Rural women, however, were more likely to focus on the difficulties that Chinese women experienced in giving up their children. As rural women were less familiar with international adoption, it is thus unclear whether their views would change once they become more familiar with this phenomenon (e.g., after encountering American families with adopted Chinese children).

From a parenting perspective, before taking a return trip parents may want to teach children that people in China may have different views about international adoption. Children need to be prepared so that they can handle comments such as "You are so lucky!" Moreover, adoptive families may need to make extra efforts to educate the people they interact with in China in order to promote a better understanding of international adoption. We feel that it is especially important for Chinese people to understand that adoptive parents often feel that, through adoption, they are the lucky ones.

35 Searching for Origins

Parent and Child Perspectives on Return Trips to China

Iris Chin Ponte, Ph.D., Leslie Kim Wang, Ph.D. candidate, and Serena Fan

INTERVIEWER: *Do you think all children should go back to China to visit their orphanage?*

CHILD: (Long pause). *They need to be brave. I think that only kids that are ready should go to see their orphanage and their finding place. And I think that kids that are not ready should not. There are ready kids and not ready kids.*

If you are considering making a return trip to China with your adopted child, you are part of a fast-growing trend. Interest in homeland trips is increasing as the cohort of children adopted from China grows older. Many organizations in China and the United States now arrange for the these visits; in the past ten years, for example, the Our Chinese Daughters Foundation (a nonprofit organization that supports families with adopted Chinese children) has alone arranged more than a thousand return visits for families from the United States, the United Kingdom, Canada, and Australia (www.ocdf.org). While many adoptive parents believe such a trip is crucial for their children's mental and emotional development, the subjective experiences of individuals who have made these journeys have not yet been systematically investigated.

In order to gain an understanding of how return visits affect the children and parents who make them, we gathered in-depth interview data from five families that returned to China between 2005 and 2007. The children in our study were between the ages of eight and eleven at the time of travel. While you may or may not visit the social welfare institute where your child lived, we focus here on families that chose to visit their children's home provinces, orphanages, and abandonment locations.

In interviews conducted in three phases—before, during and after travel—children and parents separately reflected on their experiences in China. We listen to their perspectives to explore the following themes:

- Why do parents and children feel that it is important to take a return trip to China?
- What was the lived experience like?
- Upon return, which questions did parents and children find were resolved by the trip, and what new questions (if any) have emerged?

Our study uses a three-phased research design to analyze the growing phenomenon of China return trips within the context of broader issues of adoptee belonging and the search for personal history. Until now, studies of transnational adoption and homeland voyages have tended to prioritize the views of adult adoptees and adoptive parents, leading to a dearth of children's perspectives. Our research attempts to fill this gap by giving equal weight to the voices and experiences of both young adoptees *and* their parents.

In this chapter, we will look first at what parents and adult adoptees in these other studies can tell us about return trips and the search for identity. Then we'll discuss our findings from the interviews.

Reviewing the Research to Date

Domestic Adoption and the Search for Biological History

In recent decades it has become common practice for adults who had been adopted domestically in Western countries to access birth records, locate birthparents, and learn more about the circumstances of their adoptions. Since the late 1970s, influential adoptee and author/psychologist Betty Jean Lifton has given voice and legitimacy to this "search" movement, arguing that the search for personal history is necessary for many adoptees to gain a stable sense of identity and self-worth. Adoptees' lack of biological knowledge, she writes, leads many individuals to experience intense feelings of abandonment and alienation that can be alleviated (though perhaps only partially) by connecting to the past and reuniting with the birth family (1988, 1994).

Until now little scholarly research has been conducted on the characteristics of those who search. In response to this gap in knowledge, Howe and Feast (2000) conducted a landmark study of 472 adopted adults in the United Kingdom, comparing the characteristics and experiences of those who search for birth relatives ("searchers") and those who do not ("non-searchers"). They found that searchers tend to be looking for answers to questions of identity, self-worth, and a sense of connectedness to others.

The study uncovered several interesting trends: Women were twice as likely to search as men; searchers were more likely than non-searchers to wonder why they were placed for adoption; searchers were less likely to feel that adoption was a positive experience; and transracial adoptees were more likely to begin their search at a younger age (p. 162). The reasons that individuals choose to search are complex and multi-faceted. The authors argue, therefore, that a distinction must be made between those who search because they are dissatisfied with their adoption experience and are looking to develop an alternative parental relationship, and those whose interests lay in answering questions in order to understand themselves and develop a stronger sense of personal identity.

Transnational Adoption and the Search for "Roots"

Influenced by the work of Lifton and other adoption experts, many adoptees today accept, and take action to satisfy, their implicit need to know more about their early lives. This represents a dramatic shift from the recent past. In her writings on China-U.S. adoption, Volkman (2003) notes that in the space of several decades, the perspective of the domestic adoption world has transformed from "the virtual denial of adoption and the biological beginnings of the adopted child to an insistent ideology that *without* embrace of those beginnings there will forever be a gaping hole, a primal wound, an incomplete self" (p. 43). The social pressure that domestic adoptees feel to reconstruct their past, she contends, now also exerts an effect on transnationally adopted children and their parents.

Previous research on return trips has tended to examine the experiences and perspectives of adolescent or adult adoptees (Howell, 2006; Kim, 2007; Yngvesson, 2003). Akin to domestic searches, return trips are often undertaken to answer lingering questions that individuals have regarding their adoptions, including why they were given up or abandoned by their birthparents. But cultural and ethnic differences add an extra layer of complexity to these trips, as transnational adoptees also seek to discover their "roots" through firsthand exploration of their birth culture.

Most studies on return trips to date have focused on the experiences of Korean adoptees. An estimated 3,000–5,000 adoptees now visit South Korea (hereafter "Korea") annually on return trips. Some enroll in language or cultural classes, while others actively search for birth family as a way of finding resolution with their unique stories of emotional and literal loss and gain (Kim, 2007). Korea plays a pivotal role in the lives of many adult adoptees:

> For many, Korea holds a central place in their imaginations about who they are, where they came from, and what they might have been otherwise. Many adoptee narratives express a yearning, sometimes laced with fear, to travel to South Korea, to explore cultural and biological

'roots,' and perhaps to locate missing pieces of the self. (Kim, 2007, p.115)

A major survey, conducted by the Evan B. Donaldson Adoption Institute in 1999 of 167 individuals adopted from Korea between 1952 and 1978, gives a more systematic picture of the relationship that adult adoptees have with their country of birth. Of the total number of respondents, 38 percent had chosen to visit Korea as adults, while only 9 percent had visited as children. In terms of finding birth relatives, 22 percent of respondents had or were currently in the process of searching, while an additional 34 percent expressed interest in searching in the future. On the other hand, 29 percent expressed no desire to learn more about their pre-adoption histories. These figures demonstrate the existing diversity of opinions and emotional needs among transnationally adopted individuals (www.adoptioninstitute.org/proed/korfindings.html).

Parents as "Searchers"

While the experience of Korean adoptees is important as a foundation for understanding return trips in general, the China experience is nonetheless distinct from precursors. While Korean adoptees are often able to use their adoption files to locate existing birth relatives, this option is closed off to Chinese adoptees. The complex political circumstances that render it impossible to legally relinquish children to state care in China also keep adoptees from discovering more about their lives prior to the day they were abandoned.

The young age of Chinese adoptees at time of travel—which corresponds to lesser influence over the decision to visit their birth country—is the other major distinction between the two cases. Unlike adolescent or adult Korean adoptees, who tend to be primary or equal decision-makers with parents regarding if and when to return, it is overwhelmingly adoptive parents who make the decision for children to return to China. Interestingly, parents who proactively plan and pursue return trips—rather than adoptees—are the primary "searchers" of clues to children's pre-adoption histories.

Parents are motivated to take children on return trips for a variety of reasons. Howell's (2006) study of Norwegian transnational adoptive families finds that, due to social pressure exerted by adoption experts and agencies, adoptive parents often perceive it to be their duty to take children back to their birth country even if they exhibit only a superficial interest in their child's "original culture." Parents feel that for their child to become a well-adjusted person and feel comfortable in two cultures, it is essential to visit their child's country of origin (p. 113).

Other research on return trips refers to the emotional and psychological bases that adoptive parents have for taking children to visit their birth countries. In her ethnography of a group of Swedish families that traveled to Chile on a "roots trip," Yngvesson (2003) argues that parents use such journeys as a way to "fill a gap in the belonging of their adopted children" (p. 10). Moreover, because most parents have already visited the country when completing their adoptions, a return trip allows them to relive their earliest experiences with their children, solidifying themselves as a family in the process:

> By recounting experiences that might provide their adoptive children with "something concrete to grasp onto" about their native land, parents thus become engaged not only in the work of completing a child who (it is assumed) might otherwise remain fragmented but in completing themselves as parents as well (p. 16).

More specific to Chinese adoptions, Volkman (2003) suggests that the overwhelming fascination that many adoptive parents feel towards China "may, in part, represent displaced longings for origins and absent birth mothers" (p. 29). Because the possibility of locating children's birth relatives is nearly impossible, some parents instead develop a sense of kinship with China as a country (p. 32). Thus, experiencing Chinese culture through return trips is one way in which adoptive families feel they can come one step closer to uncovering children's lost origins.

Some adolescent and adult adoptees, we've seen, feel the need to search for birthparents, or to return to the country of their birth; others do not. Many parents of children from China initiate return trips in order to help their children develop a secure identity, to begin to "fill the gaps" in their personal history. Let's now look at the findings from our study: What do the children have to say about returning to China?

A Brief Word about Our Methods

The five families in our study had adopted a total of nine children who were between the ages of four and eleven at the time of the trip; we interviewed parents and children who were eight and over. Interview questions focused on parents' and children's preparations, reasons for taking the trip, travel experiences, and subsequent outcomes. Parents and children completed semi-structured interviews during three phases: before, during, and after the trip. During interviews, parents were not permitted to hear children's responses and, likewise, children were not permitted to hear parents' responses.

Due to our small sample size, recruitment strategies (all the families in our study participate in a Chinese culture group for adopted children), and geographic limitations, we do not intend to generalize our findings to all adopted Chinese children and their families. Rather, these in-depth cases can help us begin to make sense of families' experiences with return trips to China. We hope that this study will inform further research and the development of support for adoptive families.

What We Learned from the Children and Parents

Child Comments Pre-Trip: Reconnecting to Their Lives as Babies

For many of the children, the interview before leaving for China raised issues they had not yet considered. Interviewed several months prior to the trip, many of the girls said, "Oh, that is so far away—I haven't really thought about it." However, with some thoughtful questioning, the children had a lot to share. When asked why they were taking the trip, all of the children commented on reconnecting to their life as a baby.

For example, one child explained, "It's going to feel good going back, because then I will get to see all of the places I've been in . . . when I was still a baby." Another child explained, "I am going to see my orphanage and the nanny that took care of me." In addition to these comments, the children also noted their excitement to travel to a new place. One child exclaimed, "I am going to go shopping and eat new foods!"

When we asked the children about their concerns, the majority of the comments addressed the issue of travel. One child noted, "I am not really looking forward to one-hundred airplanes." Another explained, "I know my moms are packing a lot of medicine in case I get sick."

One of the most interesting findings from this interview set was that the children had many expectations of what their parents would learn: All of the children noted that the trip to China would not only be a learning experience for them but also for their parents. One child thoughtfully explained, "My mom needs to learn a lot about China. Last time we were there to get my sister, she didn't know to bundle us up. We went into a store and all of these ladies were pinching me saying, 'Why are you, why is your child not wearing enough clothes?' My mom didn't know that Chinese people do that. She is going to learn a lot." Children also commented that parents were going to have to attempt to speak Chinese.

Parent Comments Pre-Trip: Seeking Belonging, Concern about Unpredictable Occurrences, Preparation

Before their departure, parents clearly explained that their major reason for taking the trip was deeply rooted in establishing a "sense of belonging" for their children and an opportunity for children to "experience their life pre-adoption." One parent clearly explained, "I just want my daughter to have a concrete sense of China—a real one—not just from books." For some families the emphasis was placed more on "experiencing China," while for others the goal was to learn "more information about the child's origins."

Like the children, parents also expressed some concerns about the trip. For parents the common phrase was "unpredictable occurrences," which referred to situations over which they would have no control such as illness, transportation problems, language issues, and challenges gaining access to orphanage files. However, the most frequent concern expressed by parents was that their children would be disappointed, indicating how much parents wanted the trip to China to be a positive experience. Despite these concerns, all of the parents were excited and looked forward to their journey.

Almost all of the parents interviewed in this study felt that preparation for the trip was important, while only one parent expressed any uncertainty. When asked how they prepared their children, the most frequent response was the use of discussions and external consultants (therapists, playgroup leaders, and teachers). Another common response was reviewing photos taken at the time of adoption with children, as well as raising issues in adoption support groups.

Child Comments During the Trip: Mixed Emotions

In China, one of the most drastic shifts in the children's responses was their feelings towards visiting China. Pre-departure, all of the children indicated that they felt positive emotions regarding their trip. However, during the trip itself, the majority of the children indicated that they were experiencing mixed feelings. The children implied that this emotional shift was due to visiting their orphanage and, in particular, their finding place.

While all of the children indicated that their visit to the orphanage was positive, they also pointed out the existence of other, sometimes conflicting, feelings. After visiting the site of her old orphanage, which had been demolished in recent years, one child explained, "When I was going to the place where I was found, it didn't look like what I had expected, so it felt kind of strange. I guess I expected it to be the same, more building to be there (instead of a demolition site). But it wasn't. I just thought there would be more left of my (old) orphanage." When asked about her orphanage experience, another child explained, "I don't know. Maybe I am angry. Like somewhere deep inside and I just don't know it. I just don't really know."

Although the orphanage experience was challenging, many of the children indicated that they would like to return again in the future. Many children indicated, however, that they were not sure about returning to their finding site for a second time. One child noted an uncomfortable feeling of being watched and in the public eye when she visited her finding place. She said, "I felt like everyone was watching me—that they would tell somebody else and they would all go there [the finding place] and then there would be even more people looking at me."

While the orphanage and finding place visits were emotionally challenging, the children also frequently spoke about how much fun the trip was as well. They enjoyed seeing cultural landmarks, shopping and having adventures with friends. One child commented, "We saw so many interesting things. We got to go to the Great Wall, go on this huge slide, go swimming and eat lots of breakfast."

Parent Comments During the Trip: More Positive Than the Children's Comments

Most of the parents explained that the trip was "more wonderful than they could have ever expected." The parents noted a feeling of connection with and renewed understanding of China. Much like the children, parents also expressed a mixture of feelings when reflecting on their experience at the orphanage and the finding place. However, the parents' comments generally tended to be much more positive than the children's. Some parents noted that they had gained a "deeper connection to their child's beginnings and a new understanding of their early childhood." Parents were also aware of their children's complex emotions when visiting the orphanage and finding place. A few parents mentioned that the children were experiencing a "depth of feelings that they were not able to express."

The parents' thoughts and impressions sometimes differed markedly from those of the children. One mom, on reflecting on their orphanage visit, said, "My daughter didn't have the experience of someone absolutely delighted to see her . . . I was so angry for her—she didn't get what she needed, what I know she needed. She needed to know that someone loved her. That is all I wanted for her and it didn't happen."

The daughter, on the other hand, viewed her orphanage visit much more positively, stating she was pleased that "I got to see the director and somebody that took care of me that had some facts about me when I was little." Moreover, rather than being totally focused on her own story, she expressed sympathy for the children still living in the facility. She elaborated, "I was feeling happy that I went there but I was also feeling a little sad because there were still babies that didn't have homes yet. So I was happy to see what it looked like but it was so sad to see the babies."

Regarding the abandonment location, this same mom focused on her daughter's birthparents and the act of abandonment, while the daughter was more affected by the closed-down, intimidating quality of the place itself. The mom said, "Going to her finding site was very difficult for both of us . . . I was sad because it was so, so difficult to think of my baby left there (or anywhere)! It made me ache for her birthparents and wonder about them, and angry that circumstances created this deep loss in her life." The daughter had different, more ambivalent feelings about the visit. She said, "It made me feel happy that we went there because I never really saw the gates of the old orphanage. But it also made me feel sad that it wasn't open . . . It felt a little creepy. The inside was all dark and spooky."

Child Comments Post-Trip: Importance of Seeing the Reality of Where They Are From

During this interview, children explained that while the trip did provide answers about their birth culture and personal history, it still left them with many questions. All of the children expressed a newfound awareness and understanding of China and what it means to be Chinese. Many of the girls were eager to share their travel experiences with friends, while they were more private about the orphanage and finding place visit. One child explained, "Sometimes I feel like it is okay, but sometimes I don't talk about my orphanage. It is private. Maybe I would tell them what it looks like, but I might not tell them what I did and how it exactly was."

Many of the children gave thoughtful and interesting responses to the question, "Do you think that all children adopted from China should visit their orphanage?" While some children felt that the visit to the orphanage was important, others cautioned about the emotional aspects of the trip. One child explained, "You have to be brave. Tell them they have to be brave," while another said, "Yes, they should go. I had a bunch of questions. We were wondering if we were born in the same crib—or in a whole different place. We got answers."

Even though children tended to feel that the visit to their finding place and orphanage was challenging, many explained how important it was for them to see the reality of where they are from. One child commented, "I wanted to see what it looked like, what it used to look like, because it [the orphanage] might not be there anymore. That way I would know how to go back, how to get there." Overall, the children expressed feeling a sense of unity and belonging with the Chinese people. Many children commented on how good it made them feel that everyone in China looked like them.

Throughout the after-China interview, while reflecting on their trip, all of the children commented on the necessity of preparation. As one child explained, "Getting ready is really important, it makes the whole thing less scary." Another child commented, "Before I even got to China I knew how to use a squat toilet. We practiced at home so the whole family was ready."

Parent Comments Post-Trip: Remove the Mystery

Many of the parents reported noticing a major adjustment in their child's behavior and emotions after the trip. Three of the families referred to this change as "closure." They felt that because their child had been able to see where she was originally from with her own eyes, this helped her to resolve issues and move forward. One parent thought that taking her daughter to visit her orphanage was crucial for her child's healthy emotional development, advising other parents, "Remove the mystery! Don't make it more glamorous than it actually is, don't make it mysterious, because it's either going to be now or then and the more real we are now, the more truthful we can be now, hopefully the less angry our kids will be later."

Most of the parents agreed that pre-departure preparation for themselves and their children was crucial. This preparation included a variety of things, such as thinking about how to use squat-toilets, handling difficult situations with curious Chinese people, negotiating social situations, traveling, handling food, and preparing luggage. One parent explained, "I think it's important to get your kid interested in the parts that are different and not make them weird-different, you know what I mean? We did talk to them a bit about poverty and homelessness. I think it's important to talk to them that they were going to see that, and that it might look different from home."

Finally, parents also stressed the importance of their children's exposure to Chinese culture. "They feel connected now, and because of that they are changed, we are changed, our family has changed. They don't need to pretend that they know [about China] because they have been there."

Every Child Is Different; Preparation Is Key

The interviews with parents and children were extremely powerful. One important point for all families to consider is that each person experiences returning to China differently. Many parents experienced joy and felt that the trip increased family intimacy. All parents also noted that they felt their children went at the "right" age (the children ranged from eight to eleven years old). "I think their developmental age, it was just the right time for them." For the children, their experiences tended to focus more on the challenging moments and difficult emotions that they felt. The parents' thoughts and feelings were often different from those of their children.

Children have different personalities, levels of maturity, and emotional needs, so parents are the best people to decide if these kinds of return trips are suitable for their families. Our study has shown that if the family does make the decision to return to China, preparation is key. Discussions about what to expect, potential challenges along the way, exposure to what the orphanage and finding place will be like, and open conversations about everyone's hopes and fears are essential for ensuring a positive experience for the entire family.

References

Evan B. Donaldson Adoption Institute. 1999. *Survey of Adult Korean Adoptees: Report on the Findings*. New York: Evan B. Donaldson Adoption Institute.

Free, V. 1999. "Shining Light Into Dark Corners." In *A Passage to the Heart: Writings from Families with Children from China.* Edited by A. Klatzkin. St. Paul, Minn.: Yeong & Yeong.

Howe, D. and J. Feast. 2000. *Adoption, Search and Reunion: The Long-Term Experience of Adopted Adults.* London: Children's Society.

Howell, S. 2006. *The Kinning of Foreigners: Transnational Adoption in a Global Perspective.* New York: Berghahn Books.

Kim, E. 2007. "Remembering Loss: The Koreanness of Overseas Adopted Koreans," 115–29. In *International Korean Adoption: A Fifty-year History of Policy and Practice.* Edited by K. Bergquist et al. New York: Haworth Press.

Lifton, B. J. 1994. *Journey of the Adopted Self: A Quest for Wholeness.* New York: Basic Books.

Prager, E. 2002. *Wuhu Diary: On Taking My Adopted Daughter Back to Her Hometown in China.* New York: Anchor Books.

Volkman, T. 2003. Embodying Chinese Culture: Transnational Adoption in North America. *Social Text 74*: 29–56.

Yngvesson, B. 2003. "Going 'Home': Adoption, Loss of Bearings, and the Mythology of Roots." *Social Text 74*: 7–28.

Acknowledgments

The idea for this book first developed soon after Debra, Iris and Leslie traveled together in China. Along with Debra's two children and another family, we shared the joys, challenges and emotional bumps inevitable on any homeland trip. A few months later, when Iris suggested that we work together on a book about return trips to China, Debra and Leslie readily agreed to participate. Our team, we believed, brought unique strengths to this project. Debra is an early childhood educator and an adoptive parent; Iris is a child development expert with deep research and practical experience in the China adoption community; and Leslie is a sociologist specializing in the abandonment of children in China and their subsequent care in Chinese state-run orphanages.

The perspectives we each brought led to lively discussions and, more importantly, to a shared vision for the book. We agreed that by bringing together the views and experiences of children, parents, adult adoptees and adoption professionals, and by including both personal accounts and research-based information, we could assist families to prepare for return trips and make sense of those trips once they were back at home.

We knew we would enjoy working on this project, but we had no idea how truly collaborative the process would be. Many people participated in the making of this book, and without them *From Home to Homeland* would never have happened (and the writing and editing wouldn't have been nearly as fun). Despite the collaborative nature of this book, any inaccuracies or mistakes are our own.

We owe a deep debt of gratitude to all of our contributing authors, who generously shared their personal experiences and accumulated wisdom. We feel privileged to have gotten to know each of you, even if only through e-mail.

Many families shared photographs from their trips as we hunted for the right image for the cover. Thanks to Susan Morgan, Anne Donohue, Rose Lewis, Sheena Macrae, Jane Samuel, Marion Radin, Bonnie Ward, Iris Culp, and Arabella Lyon for sending us your beautiful and moving photos. We had a very difficult decision to make in choosing just one. A special thank you to Sami Khoury, who took the photograph that appears on the cover, and to the Smith family and their daughter, Ella, whose curious expression seemed just right. Thanks also to Jo Ling Kent for coordinating the on-site photos in China; to Eulalia Andreasen, CEO of the Beijing International Committee for Chinese Orphans, for providing access and support on the ground in China; and to the Fulbright Program for funding Iris Ponte's and Leslie Wang's research in China.

To the families of *Laohu* and *Hao Pengyou*, thank you for your support of the project and especially your help in coming up with so many good ideas for a title. Final credits for our title go to the ever-creative Robin Carton.

John Hugg and Mark Sarver provided outstanding technical support, especially through a harrowing computer crash. Many thanks to John for creating our website (check it out at www.fromhometohomeland.com).

Vicki Wilt deserves much credit for editing; her changes created a tighter and more readable text. Thanks also to Michael Wilt for his editing support, and to Myra L. Hugg for her careful proofreading.

To Ann Delgehausen, kudos for creating such a striking cover and designing an elegant and cohesive interior for the book.

We are indebted to Amy Klatzkin for her interest in our project from the beginning, for sharing some of her family's story in her introduction, and for bringing us together with Brian Boyd at Yeong & Yeong. Brian, thank you for taking us on and guiding us throughout, and especially for your commitment to publishing books such as ours for the sake of helping adoptive families.

Debra would like to acknowledge a few people for their support throughout, including her parents, Joanne and Bob Jacobs, and her sisters, Cindy Jacobs and Hope Pheifer (many thanks to Hope for help on the title search, for providing child care when Debra needed to work on the book, and for listening whenever she needed an ear). Mark Sarver, Robin Carton, Meredith Smith and Joyce Tavon also supported and encouraged Debra through the process and often helped with child care so she could get an hour or two in front of the computer. Thanks also to Joyce for reading and commenting on the text, and for making great suggestions for its improvement. Finally, she would like to thank her two daughters, Rosalie Shudan and Stella Zaohong—her inspiration for this book and so much more.

Last but by no means least, we would like to express our appreciation for the Families with Children from China Orphanage Appeal, to which proceeds from this book will be donated. An all-volunteer organization, the FCC Orphanage Appeal provides foster care and sponsors "grandma's" who offer supplemental care in Chinese orphanages. The AIDS project in Anhui and Henan Provinces is another FCC Orphanage Appeal program, supporting children orphaned when a parent has died of AIDS. Other services include disaster relief, medical care and school fees for children and the orphanages that serve them. We're very grateful for the work of the dedicated volunteers who run the FCC Orphanage Appeal, and hope this book can make a difference for some of the children who remain without families.

Debra Jacobs, Ed.M.
Iris Chin Ponte, Ph.D.
Leslie Kim Wang, Ph.D. candidate

Contributors

Jane A. Brown, M.S.W., has been involved in adoption for over twenty-five years, first as a parent and later as a social worker/educator/play therapist. The creator of Adoption Playshops, Jane has eight children and a foster daughter. Five of her children joined the family through adoption from Korea and China. Originally an educator who taught young children, Jane has applied her interest in how children learn generally to how they integrate the information they receive about adoption and race. She has written extensively for adoption publications in print and online. To read additional articles by Jane, go to www.emkpress.com/janebrown.html; www.fccbc.ca/janebrown/JaneBrownResponse.htm; and www.fwcc.org/janebrowntransracial.htm.

Robin Carton and her family live in the Boston area, where she is the director of grantmaking and finances at a social justice foundation called RESIST.

Jenna Cook is seventeen years old and a senior at Phillips Exeter Academy in Exeter, New Hampshire. She enjoys playing American folk music on her acoustic guitar and Chinese folk music on her *guzheng*.

Iris Culp is mom to two girls from China. She worked for seven years in management in the travel industry and has served as a management consultant in such diverse fields as education, finance, manufacturing, and computer technology. Earlier in her career, she worked as a writer and photographer. Iris joined the Lotus Travel team in 2005, following the adoption of her second child. She coordinates a variety of programs for Lotus Travel, including the charitable matching gift program and an educational grant program.

Anne Donohue is a journalism professor at Boston University. She was a Fulbright Scholar at Renmin University in Beijing in the spring of 2008. She is the mother of two sons and a daughter, Katie, adopted from Yiyang, Hunan, in 1998.

Serena Fan currently teaches kindergarten at a bilingual school in Hong Kong and previously taught preschool in the Boston area. She holds a degree in child development and international relations from Tufts University. In 2006–2007, Serena led a Chinese culture group for ten children adopted from China. She continues to be a "Tufts big sister" to a girl who was adopted from China.

Xiaohui Fan, Ph.D., teaches at the School of International Studies, Xi'an Jiaotong University, Xi'an, Shaanxi Province, China. With an educational background in the English language, she specializes in American culture studies. Her current research interest is the experience of Chinese people in America. Professor Fan also has training in English for medical purposes and in applied linguistics.

Debra Jacobs is a child care provider, early childhood consultant, and parent coach. She co-founded the Tufts Big Sister/Big Brother program, which pairs members of the Tufts Chinese Student Association with children adopted from China, and initiated *Hao Pengyou*, a Chinese culture group/adoption support group for Chinese adoptees and their parents. Debra holds an Education Master's degree from the Harvard Graduate School of Education. She lives in Somerville, Massachusetts, with her two daughters (adopted from Hunan and Jiangxi provinces).

Jennifer* Bao Yu *"Precious Jade" Jue-Steuck is a Chinese adoptee from California. She was born in Taipei to a birthmother from Jiangsu Province, China, and is a co-founder of Chinese Adoptee Links International (www.ChineseAdopteeLinks.org). Jennifer is a freelance writer whose magazine column "Global Girls—Global Generations" highlights the voices of adopted teens around the world in *Mei Magazine* and *Adoption Today*. Jennifer is a graduate of New York University's Tisch School of the Arts and Harvard University, where she was a Bill and Melinda Gates Foundation Scholar. Visit www.Precious-Jade.com to learn more about her adoption story.

Amy Klatzkin is a marriage and family therapist intern at the University of California, San Francisco, Child Trauma Research Program, where she assesses and treats children and parents affected by trauma and loss. Amy has been active in the adoption community for fifteen years as a parent, writer, editor, and speaker. She serves on the board of FAIR (Families Adopting in Response, a volunteer organization that supports, educates, and advocates for all kinds of adoptive families), was a contributing editor to *Adoptive Families Magazine*, and has presented workshops for parent support groups and international adoption agencies in many parts of the United States and Canada. Amy edited *A Passage to the Heart: Writings from Families with Children from China* (1999); edited and wrote the introduction for *Wanting a Daughter, Needing a Son: Abandonment, Adoption, and Orphanage Care in China* by Kay Johnson (2004); and helped her daughter, Ying Ying Fry, write *Kids Like Me in China* (2001).

Mitchell Klein and his son Lee live in New York near their large extended family. They split their time between the city and the country. Mitchell is the founder of a management consulting firm specializing in operations and systems analysis for government agencies. Mitchell is president of their local Little League and Lee is an avid sports enthusiast and participant.

Rose A. Lewis is the author of two children's books, *I Love You Like Crazy Cakes* and *Every Year on Your Birthday*, and has two new books due to be published by Abrams Books in 2010 and 2011, *Orange Peel's Pocket* and *Sweet Dreams*. She is also the director of marketing and communications for Beth Israel Deaconess Hospital in Needham, Massachusetts. Lewis was a news producer for more than twenty years in Washington, D.C., and Boston, Massachusetts. She lives in Massachusetts with her daughter and their West Highland Terrier, Teddy.

Jane Liedtke, Ph.D., is the founder of Our Chinese Daughters Foundation (OCDF), and mother to Emily, adopted from Jiangmen Social Welfare Institute. OCDF is a non-profit organization with the mission of providing the highest quality Chinese culture programs, orphan support programs, and publications to adoptive families, support organizations, and educational institutions serving the wider community. Dr. Liedtke's thirty-year career as an educator and educational consultant includes extensive experience in China. She has published in the fields of industrial technology and graphic communications as well as within the China-adoption community and in Chinese culture publications. She maintains an OCDF office and home in Beijing.

Sandra E. Lundy lives with her family in Brookline, Massachusetts, and is an attorney with the Massachusetts Supreme Judicial Court. Throughout the years, Sandy has published poems, essays, and other writings in small journals. Her contribution to this volume is her most directly autobiographical writing to this point, and she hopes it is of use to returning families.

Lorena GuiFeng Lyon is eleven years old, is in the sixth grade, and wants to be a writer. She lives in Buffalo, New York, with her mother, Arabella, her sister, Coco, and her dog, Bird.

J. Meimei Ma is an older adoptive parent. Her daughter is from Yiyang, Hunan. She worked in project management and research data management in the pharmaceutical industry until 2001, when she retired after receiving her daughter's referral. Meimei and her husband are American-born Chinese who have relatives all over China. Being retired has allowed her to be active in the adoptive community in North Carolina and in fundraising for her daughter's orphanage.

Sheena Macrae lives in the U.K. with her husband and two children adopted from China. She is a full-time mother and has published articles in adoption journals in Australia, Canada, the U.K. and the U.S. She is the co-editor of *Adoption Parenting: Creating a Toolbox, Building Connections*. She also serves as an independent adoption panel member for Surrey Children's Service. Her family has taken annual trips to China since 1998.

Laurie C. Miller, M.D., is associate professor of pediatrics at Tufts University School of Medicine. She founded the International Adoption Clinic at New England Medical Center in 1988, the second such clinic in the U.S., and oversees an NIH-funded program in Russia to improve outcomes for orphanage residents. Dr. Miller serves on the board of directors of Romanian Children's Relief, the national Board of Families for Russian and Ukrainian Adoption, and the NIH Study Section for Brain Disorders in the Developing World. She has published over seventy peer-reviewed articles related to pediatrics and international adoption, as well as two books, *Handbook of International Adoption Medicine* and *Encyclopedia of Adoption* (with C. Adamec).

Susan Morgan lives in Pennsylvania with her husband and four children (two from China). She welcomes comments and questions, and can be reached at mosusan2004@yahoo.com.

Joyce Maguire Pavao, Ed.D., L.C.S.W., L.M.F.T., is the founder and CEO of Center For Family Connections in Cambridge, Massachusetts, and an adjunct faculty member at Harvard Medical School. Dr. Pavao has done extensive training and consultation, both nationally and internationally, on issues in adoption and child welfare. Herself an adopted person, she is the author of *The Family of Adoption* and the recipient of awards and honors from St. John's University's Adoption Initiative, Voice for Adoption, and the Administration for Children and Families.

Phyllis Pincus is the proud mom of identical twins, Emma and Lucy, born in August of 2001 and adopted from Hunan province at fourteen months old. She and her husband, Gary, live with their daughters in North Carolina. Phyllis was an environmental manager, but has been a happy stay-at-home-mom since the twins arrived. Emma and Lucy love soccer, horses, piano, swimming, science, and art.

Ellen E. Pinderhughes, Ph.D., is associate professor of applied child development in the Eliot-Pearson Department of Child Development, Tufts University, and a senior research fellow with the Evan B. Donaldson Adoption Institute. A developmental and clinical psychologist, she has worked as a therapist and a clinical consultant. Her research centers on the impact of family socialization processes on children who are at-risk for problem outcomes. Within the adoption arena, her work examines families who adopt or foster older children, and families who raise girls adopted from China.

Richard B. Pinderhughes, Psy.D., has been a practicing clinician in the field of adoption for more than seventeen years. Formerly with the Pre- and Post-adoption Consulting Team and the Center for Family Connections, he is currently a multicultural consultant and trainer for VISIONS, Inc., and an adjunct faculty member in the counseling department in the Graduate School of Education at the University of Massachusetts, Boston. He also has a small private practice in Braintree, Massachusetts.

Iris Ponte, Ph.D., is a postdoctoral fellow in the Eliot-Pearson Department of Child Development at Tufts University and the president of Ponte and Chau Consulting (www.ponteandchau .com). A former Fulbright Scholar, Iris has expertise in cross-cultural issues in education and child development and has conducted research in the United States, the United Kingdom, Taiwan, China, Japan, and Newfoundland. She has received scholarship and fellowship recognitions from the Children's Defense Fund, the Watson IBM Fellowship, CBS, and the American Educational Research Association, and worked in an orphanage in China that was not part of the international adoption program. She has served for eight years as leader of a Chinese Culture Group for girls adopted from China. Iris lives in Massachusetts with her husband, John.

Marion Radin and her husband, Jonathan, adopted their identical twin daughters from Guilin in 2000. Marion is vice president of the Albany, New York chapter of Families with Children from Asia. The Radins lived in Beijing from January through July 2008.

Jane Samuel lives in Kentucky with her husband and three daughters. She is a stay-at- home mother, writer, and advocate for adoption and special needs issues.

Dawn Faulkner Schmokel is the mother of two daughters born in China: Anna, from Jiangsu, and Laura Dawn, from Hunan. She has a master's degree in home economics education, and taught for seventeen years prior to adopting her daughters. She and her girls live in Hudson, Wisconsin, and may be contacted at dschmokel@comcast.net.

Tony Xing Tan, Ed.D., was born and raised in Sichuan, China. He is a Harvard-trained developmental psychologist and director of the China Adoption Research Program at the University of South Florida in Tampa. Professor Tan has studied over 2,000 adopted Chinese children's development and is currently conducting a longitudinal study on 1,200 Chinese children's post-adoption development. He hopes to use his research to inform China's international adoption policy and improve orphanage care.

Stephanie W. lives with her husband and two daughters in San Francisco. Her second daughter was adopted from China in 2009.

Leslie Kim Wang is a Ph.D. candidate in sociology at the University of California, Berkeley. Her dissertation is the first ethnographic project to examine child abandonment and collaborations between western NGOs and the Chinese state over the care of children residing in official children's welfare institutes. Bilingual in English and Mandarin, Leslie has lived in mainland China for a total of two-and-a-half years and conducted twelve months of in-depth ethnographic fieldwork in nine Chinese state-run orphanages and a range of private Chinese and western foster homes. Along with Dr. Iris Ponte, she has conducted in-depth research on adoptive families' return trips to China. Her research seeks to provide deeper insight for adoptees and their families, and to give a voice to those children who may never be adopted.

Bonnie Ward is an information technology executive who lives in New England with her two daughters and elderly mom. She enjoys traveling with her family, writing about her adventures in parenthood, and a glass of Macallan's 18 on the rocks.

Andrea Williams is a film editor. She lives in Massachusetts with her daughter.

David Youtz is Chief Executive Officer of Mother's Choice, a non-profit in Hong Kong that provides adoption services, care for children without permanent homes, support for pregnant teens, and, in 2008, launched Hong Kong's first Adoption Festival. He served as president of Families with Children from China of Greater New York from 2000 to 2007, and has held professional positions with non-profit organizations in Hong Kong, New York, and China. David lives with his wife and four children in Hong Kong.